**SAGE** was founded in 1965 by Sara Miller McCune to support the dissemination of usable knowledge by publishing innovative and high-quality research and teaching content. Today, we publish over 900 journals, including those of more than 400 learned societies, more than 800 new books per year, and a growing range of library products including archives, data, case studies, reports, and video. SAGE remains majority-owned by our founder, and after Sara's lifetime will become owned by a charitable trust that secures our continued independence.

Los Angeles | London | New Delhi | Singapore | Washington DC | Melbourne

# SOCIAL HEGEMONY
*in Contemporary India*

# SOCIAL HEGEMONY
*in Contemporary India*

Edited by
**R. Thirunavukkarasu**

Los Angeles | London | New Delhi
Singapore | Washington DC | Melbourne

Copyright © R. Thirunavukkarasu, 2021

All rights reserved. No part of this book may be reproduced or utilised in any form or by any means, electronic or mechanical, including photocopying, recording, or by any information storage or retrieval system, without permission in writing from the publisher.

*First published in 2021 by*

**SAGE Publications India Pvt Ltd**
B1/I-1 Mohan Cooperative Industrial Area
Mathura Road, New Delhi 110 044, India
www.sagepub.in

**SAGE Publications Inc**
2455 Teller Road
Thousand Oaks, California 91320, USA

**SAGE Publications Ltd**
1 Oliver's Yard, 55 City Road
London EC1Y 1SP, United Kingdom

**SAGE Publications Asia-Pacific Pte Ltd**
18 Cross Street #10-10/11/12
China Square Central
Singapore 048423

Published by Vivek Mehra for SAGE Publications India Pvt Ltd. Typeset in 10.5/13 pt Bembo by AG Infographics, Delhi.

**Library of Congress Control Number: 2020950794**

**ISBN:** 978-93-5388-633-2 (HB)

**SAGE Team:** Rajesh Dey, Satvinder Kaur and Rajinder Kaur

*To*
*The American College, Madurai, Tamil Nadu*
*and*
*Jawaharlal Nehru University, New Delhi,*
*finest institutions of higher learning*
*for their impeccable commitment*
*to liberal education and egalitarian values*

Thank you for choosing a SAGE product!
If you have any comment, observation or feedback,
I would like to personally hear from you.

Please write to me at **contactceo@sagepub.in**

**Vivek Mehra,** Managing Director and CEO, SAGE India.

### Bulk Sales

SAGE India offers special discounts
for purchase of books in bulk.
We also make available special imprints
and excerpts from our books on demand.

*For orders and enquiries, write to us at*

Marketing Department
SAGE Publications India Pvt Ltd
B1/I-1, Mohan Cooperative Industrial Area
Mathura Road, Post Bag 7
New Delhi 110044, India

*E-mail us at* **marketing@sagepub.in**

### Subscribe to our mailing list
*Write to* **marketing@sagepub.in**

This book is also available as an e-book.

# Contents

Acknowledgements ix

|  |  |  |
|---|---|---|
| | Introduction—Caste and Inequality: Mapping the New Normalcy by *R. Thirunavukkarasu* | 1 |
| Chapter 1 | Societal Complexity and Sources of Inequality: Situating India by *T. K. Oommen* | 35 |

## Section A. Social Hegemony and the Market

| Chapter 2 | Interrogating Dalit Capitalism in the Neoliberal Era: Illusion or Reality by *Amiya Kumar Das* | 57 |
|---|---|---|
| Chapter 3 | 'Migrant', 'Home' and Politics: Bihari Labour in the Metropolis by *Tanweer Fazal* | 83 |

## Section B. Social Hegemony and Politics

| Chapter 4 | Illiberal State and the Myth of a Civil Society by *R. Thirunavukkarasu* | 107 |
|---|---|---|
| Chapter 5 | Deconstructing the Practice of Manual Scavenging: Critical Insights by *Shaileshkumar Darokar* | 135 |

## Section C. Social Hegemony, Media and Culture

| Chapter 6 | Understanding the Ideological Nature of Caste Violence in Tamil Nadu: Particularism and Universalism by *Karthick Ram Manoharan* | 173 |
|---|---|---|

| Chapter 7 | Deconstructing the Language of Hegemony by *Archana Singh* | 192 |
| Chapter 8 | Revitalizing Caste Hierarchies through State, Law and Order, and Judiciary by *C. Jerome Samraj* | 207 |
| Chapter 9 | Identity, Representation and Reservation: Dravidian Politics towards Muslims by *P. Ramajayam* | 234 |
| Chapter 10 | Caste, Ideology and Hegemony in Indian Media: A Critical Inquiry by *Manoj Kumar Jena* | 268 |

*About the Editor and Contributors*     285
*Index*     288

# Acknowledgements

The idea of this volume emerged little before I joined the University of Hyderabad during the summer of 2014. I was associated with the Institute of Human Rights Education for a period of three years. Extensive travel in Tamil Nadu and later across the country and discussions with government school teachers and children from many states gave me an opportunity to assess the changing social, economic and political conditions of people who are not at all visible in our everyday glittering world of liberalization. I thank Henri Tiphagne, Executive Director of the Institute, for his encouragement. After joining the University of Hyderabad, this idea was further consolidated during my discussions with colleagues and students. When I was warmly asked by my colleague and UGC-SAP coordinator Professor Purendra Prasad to organize a seminar, I thought of expanding this idea further. Therefore, the first credit goes to him for facilitating the seminar by providing not only the required financial assistance but also enormous moral support. Discussions with my teachers Professor T. K. Oommen and Professor Avijit Pathak sharpened some of the ideas before I could finalize the larger theme of the seminar. I thank them for their profound insights and constant encouragement.

Sixteen scholars were invited to make their presentation during the two-day event. However, some could not send their papers. Compiling all these papers was not a simple job as it involved several rounds of persuasive mails and text messages before these were finally consolidated. I thank them all for their scholarly inputs. I also thank all my colleagues at the Department of Sociology for their support and encouragement, especially Dr Janardhan, whose profound theoretical insights have helped me comprehend some of the complexities of the neoliberal economic order. Some of my ideas were refined during the discussions with my students in the class. I thank them for their insightful questions. This process received momentum when Abhijit Baroi from SAGE Publications gave me the necessary impetus. But if it was not for his constant encouragement, I am sure this project may not have fructified. I am grateful to him, later Rajesh Dey, and his team for the timely and enthusiastic support for this volume. My family members' support always remains a great energizing factor. To simply say 'thank you' obviously seems far less than adequate.

# Introduction
Caste and Inequality: Mapping the New Normalcy

### R. Thirunavukkarasu

A little more than half a century ago, Selig Harrison characterized the late 1950s and early 1960s as the era of the most dangerous time for India, as the nascent post-colonial country struggled to wade through some of its most tumultuous moments. His assessment, naive though, latches its faith on the robust linguistic assertion across the country, which he foresaw would precipitate the country moving towards a despotic political condition. Harrison actually believed that the political leadership at that time was too impatient, incapable of leading the country to embrace liberal political values and may be keen on obliterating conflicts rather than slogging to manufacture consensus.[1] While looking back at the last half a century of India's political history, one would certainly endorse Lloyd Rudolph's crisp rebuttal of Harrison's work as he postulated that 'the perspective of the past places the prospects for liberty in India in a more hopeful light; is it not possible that Indians have the capacity of being guided to their own improvement by conviction and persuasion rather than compulsion?'[2]

---

[1] Selig Harrison, *India: The Most Dangerous Decades* (Princeton, NJ: Princeton University Press, 1960).

[2] Lloyd Rudolph, 'Review, India: The Most Dangerous Decades', *Far Eastern Survey* 29, no. 12 (1960): 191.

As a leading scholar on Indian politics and society, what Rudolph surmised was vindicated by the events in the country since the 1960s. The country remains the largest democracy in the world with elections regularly conducted by a statutory body; the judiciary resolutely remains independent and the media largely enjoys its freedom. All these virtues would be construed to declare that the country is indeed an envious political success story among many post-colonial countries especially in South Asia. But what is quite intriguing is the larger unanswered question: Could all these 'achievements' in the political realm embolden us to declare that we have ensured liberty and justice to all our citizens? This question looks uncomplicated but evades a meaningful and precise answer.

In spite of many 'achievements' in the political realm, a few celebrated virtues of the modern world—equality, liberty and justice—remain elusive to the overwhelming population of the country. Having realized the wretched nature of the colonial rule and the alarmingly deplorable condition in which the country was, the founding fathers of our nascent democracy were determined to draft the Constitution to not only be the supreme guiding principle for the newly dawned democracy but also the beacon of justice, equality, freedom and liberty. India, a wounded civilization and a highly hierarchical society where discrimination remains the most valuable cultural virtue, was expected to necessarily embrace justice, freedom, liberty and equality as social values. Hence, our Constitution unambiguously stated its commitment towards realizing these virtues as the country progresses.

That is the reason why the Preamble categorically states and assures to all its citizens justice—social, economic and political. The letter and spirit of this statement is that what all have been denied so far would be assured to every citizen of this country. While the Constitution (Article 14) insists on equality before law, it also categorically declares that unequally placed members of our country should not be treated equally. This is not self-contradictory; it rather clearly exemplifies the trajectory in which the country was expected to move on. We were not clueless; it is clear that we did have a document to lean on. And that document lays down unerringly the parameters which the State must adhere to—uncompromising commitment to justice, liberty and freedom. Thus, the independent Indian State declares that it would follow and protect the constitutional provisions. Ensuring all these values, however, requires not necessarily the paraphernalia of the State but an evolved consensus in the sociocultural realm. This may look quite simple but remains the most formidable challenge for the country since independence.

In other words, justice, freedom and liberty must have been part of a culturally sanctioned and socially approved virtue that must be the non-negotiable, irreducible and axiomatic premise upon which a 'nation' ought to have evolved. Somehow our conventional wisdom tends to vivisect justice from the process of inventing a nation; it also believes that the principle of egalitarianism need not be part of the 'nation'. If an attempt is made to delineate the nation as embodiment of justice and equality, many political demagogues would resort to naive rhetoric which are not only cliché but also anti-historical in their essence.

India being a welfare State, it is mandatory on its part to promise and deliver basic entitlements guaranteed in the Constitution such as education, health and a dignified life. In the process, it is obligatory on the part of the State to provide a level playing field for all its citizens since the sociocultural and economic inequalities in India require no further elaboration. Acute poverty, culturally sanctioned inaccessibility to literacy, socially regulated economic activities, ruthlessly graded hierarchy and strictly closed stratification are all monumental challenges to the nascent post-colonial State. What remains as the only hope and anchorage for the vast majority of marginalized citizens in India has been the constitutional entitlements; but the larger questions remain very profound: Why could not India as a nation achieve all that have been guaranteed in the Constitution. Why a level playing field was not or could not be established by the State in spite of its powerful tentacles? Why does providing equal opportunity to all its citizens looks quite a formidable task? Thus, analysing the 'political' after a point may not yield objective results to realize the reasons for the preponderance of abject injustice and unjust social order. It is therefore necessary to reiterate the need to problematize the sociocultural domain and the concept of nation which emerges as the quintessential manifestation of this domain.

## UNJUST SOCIAL ORDER AS NATION: GENEALOGY OF CONTEMPORARY HEGEMONY

For a long time, sociological assessments were unwelcomed while studying the concept of a nation; a conventional historical analysis of merely 'describing' how a nation produces nationalism acquires disproportionate recognition in social science literature. In fact, abundance of scholarly literature on this subject is available; yet a nation as embodiment of equality and justice has scarcely been found. Innumerable attempts have been made to establish objective criteria for nationhood or to explain why certain groups have become 'nations' while several others are not; ethnicity, language, common history, cultural traits and territory are some of the defining elements in the pursuit of explaining a nation and subsequently nationalism. While concurring with the fact that all these aspects are indispensable in comprehending and defining a nation, it is equally true that the inadequacy looms large. The nation is based on a primordial essence. Nations are believed to be authentic cultural traditions which can be explained by history and the power of enduring traditions. Nations are also inventions; they are conceived, constructed and even fabricated by social actors. The actual questions are: Why was not culture problematized? What is the role of the social structure in determining the nature of a nation? Therefore, let us embark upon analysing the sociocultural realm while discussing nation.

For Marx and Engels, a 'nation' is the direct result of the process by which the feudal mode of production was replaced by the capitalist mode. 'Modern nations' could exist only with the emergence of a capitalist political economy. One of the hugely significant features of this transition is the fragmented feudal society steadily getting united under the tutelage of an embryonic modern state. This transition directly leads to the destruction of local peculiarities and indicates a process of standardization of populations, which was an essential condition for the formation of markets and hence necessary to the capitalist system.[3] The capitalist mode of production requires two broad social conditions: (a) an intensification of division of labour and (b) a growing

---

[3] Ephraim Nimni, 'Great Historical Failure: Marxist Theories of Nationalism', *Capital & Class* 9, (1985): 58–83.

interdependence of the different units of production. Marx and Engels argued that modern European languages, particularly its Western part, organized themselves to consolidate recognizable cultural and political units, which would ensure the interdependence of the various units of production to constitute a recognizable market. The modern State patronizes this transition more concretely. These distinct and recognizable cultural–political units, delimited by the territorial area of the influence of the emerging absolutist states, were for Marx and Engels the 'modern nations'. In other words, a nation requires certain preconditions; it is not sui generis.

It is quite obvious that both Marx and Engels were simply overwhelmed by the national formation of Western Europe, especially the historical moments of the French Revolution. Among the early writings on nation, Marxist tradition stands out as a significant contribution. Joseph Stalin describes a nation as primarily a community; this community is neither racial nor tribal, but it historically constitutes a community of people. Similarly it is not a casual or ephemeral conglomeration but a stable community of people. However, not all stable communities constitute a nation, where Stalin privileges the role of the spoken language. A common language is one of the characteristic features of a nation. Yet a common language is necessary but not a sufficient feature for a nation to emerge. Therefore, Stalin insists on a common territory, which is another vital feature of a nation. In addition to these characters, he identifies three more features as important elements in defining a nation: a common economic life, economic cohesion and a common psychological make-up. As he precisely delineates,

> A nation is a historically constituted, stable community of people, formed on the basis of a common language, territory, economic life and psychological make-up manifested in a common culture. It is only when all these characteristics are present together that we can have a nation.[4]

This elaboration goes little further towards comprehending a nation as embodiment of equality and justice; yet a clearer explanation of

---

[4] Bruce Franklin, ed., *The Essential Stalin: Major Theoretical Writings 1905–1952* (London: Croom Helm, 1973), 57–61.

the term 'common culture' is certainly awaited. Here, the perspective offered by Ernest Gellner is worth mentioning. Social role/statue and shared cultural communication were not essential to preserve cultural order and effective interaction among people. When there is a break in the culturally sanctioned notions of status/role, a newfangled form of communication structure emerges; when that new status/role gets cultural approval, a nascent form of nationality dawns, as asserted by Gellner.[5] He almost suggests that the erosion of rigid social structures paves the way for the social foundations for the emergence of a nation. Gellner strongly asserts that a nation is indeed a new political community. He also strongly insists that the indigenous intelligentsia, who has hitherto experienced a highly hurdled social mobility, mobilizes opinion in favour of redemption, especially in urban environments; the new urban centres are the newly etched cultural and political landscape, where particularly native proletariats, newly educated masses, encounter discriminations. These new community members seek to establish their own nation states if at that time they have no feasible prospect of being fairly treated or assimilated. Here, Gellner highlights an inherent ambiguity. The new nation state will be modern; however, its champions visibly wish to replicate their 'glorious past—old nation' into a modern structure. This is what he says: 'Nationalism is not the awakening of nations to self-consciousness; it invents nations where they do not exist—but it does need some pre-existing differentiating marks to work on, even if these are purely negative'.[6]

The Indian subcontinent began to slowly capitulate to a new wave of social, cultural, economic and political upheavals from the time the British traders-turned-rulers brought in formidable changes in every aspect of Indian life. This change, which was in unambiguous terms, could well be described as the beginning of modernity in the subcontinent. A new world view, quite antithetical to the hitherto existing native perception of self and community, evolved. The birth of a modern mind would be the most significant corollary of colonialism in India. A word of caution and perhaps a caveat is needed right here:

---

[5] Ernest Gellner, *Thought and Change* (London: Weidenfeld and Nicolson, 1964), 155–157.
[6] Ibid., 168.

Modern mind does not certainly presuppose colonialism for its genesis nor that the end of colonialism in any way ensured the completion of this process at least in India. Colonial rule precipitated the birth of a modern mind and with its own peculiarities the subcontinent reshaped it according to its convenience.

This hierarchical character of the non-modern Indian social structure should have arguably been transformed into a liberal–democratic social fabric; in other words, a modern society must have emerged wherein individualism remains the nucleus and equality becomes non-negotiable ethos of its everyday life. On the contrary, as it was delineated above, the hierarchical character of the Indian society reconfigured during the British regime to be more rigid in its character. David Washbrook in his unerring observation notes that the simultaneity of peasantization of economy and Brahminization of culture was the hallmark of the colonial regime. Peasantization of economy was the primary focus and greed of the British for its exorbitant revenue; the same also constituted the nurturing environment for the growth of social relational Brahmanism.[7] In other words, in concert with the Brahminization of the caste ideology, taking place during the colonial regime, it had created a context in which a vast majority of subaltern masses culturally as well as socially became the Shudras or unclean humans, denigrated to subhuman location in the changing social order; this caste society in the later 19th and early 20th centuries became the tradition and cultural epithet of the modern India. The instruments of 'capitalist' modernization and Indian 'tradition' had combined perfectly to produce for the property holding castes, particularly to the Brahmins of the colonial India, the much needed supremacy and dominance.[8]

It is highly naive to argue that caste never existed before the colonial era; but what we have today as a social system and an instrument of organizing the social order caste is indeed a product of colonialism.

---

[7] David Washbrook, 'Land and Labour in Late 18th Century South India: The Golden Age of Paraiah', in *Dalit Movements and the Meanings of Labour in India*, ed. Peter Robb (Delhi: Oxford University Press, 1993), 68–86.

[8] Stephan A. Barnett, 'Approaches to Changes in Caste Ideology in South India', in *Essays on South India*, ed. Burton Stein (New Delhi: Vikas Publishing House, 1976), 149–155.

The British regime with its administrative initiatives and legal instruments reshaped the caste system into a modern phenomenon. In addition to the efforts of the colonial regime, Orientalist scholars and Christian missionaries had rendered adequate conceptual insights to shape the caste system to assume the character of a modern phenomenon. In other words, caste became a single term capable of expressing, organizing and above all systematizing India's diverse forms of social identity, community and organization during the British regime.[9] Quite similar to the changes which altered the character of the pre-colonial social structure, the new pedagogical enterprise introduced by the British to a great extent replicated a highly hierarchical social structure in the modern era also. There is a grand consensus among almost all scholars of Indian nationalism that the biggest and highest beneficiaries of the modern education were the upper castes in almost all parts of the subcontinent.

Anil Seal has noted this fact persuasively. He describes how in Bengal education was overwhelmingly dominated by Brahmins, Kayasthas and Baidyas; similarly in Bombay Presidency and Madras Presidency, Brahmins alone held near total monopoly over education. There did not emerge any new class; the same yesterday's scholars of Persian now became hyper enthusiasts for English.[10]

Thomas Macaulay—the chief architect and the principal protagonist of the modern education system in the subcontinent—stated his actual intention while proposing his education policy: to create 'a class who may be interpreters between us and the millions whom we govern'; it was intended to be applicable in administrative arena also. Colonial regime's well-established obsession to maximize revenue to a great extent converged with the interests of not only caste elites but also the newly emerged literary groups in terms of secular interests.[11] In

---

[9] Nicholas Dirks, *Castes of Mind: Colonialism and the Making of Modern India* (New Delhi: Permanent Black, 2003), 3–19.

[10] Anil Seal, *The Emergence of Indian Nationalism* (Cambridge: Cambridge University Press, 1968), 38–97; see also Judith Brown, *Modern India: The Origins of an Asian Democracy* (Delhi: Oxford University Press, 1984).

[11] This point was noted in detail by Brown, *Modern India* (Chapter II); Ashok Rudra, 'Emergence of the Intelligentsia as a Ruling Class in India', *Economic & Political Weekly* 24, no. 3 (1989): 142–150.

the newly established state administrative set-up, the products of the new education system jelled and crystallized well. By the end of the 19th century, what the modern education had created was no different from the pre-colonial monopoly of literary knowledge by ritually high-ranking castes of course suitably altered by the collaborators. In fact, the colonial rulers were at one point under intense pressure not to vernacularize education from beneficiaries of modern English education.[12] Contrary to the popular wisdom that 'modern-English' education would annihilate irrational, ascriptive identities and would help the subcontinent masses to emerge as locale of equality turned out to be a charade, the new education system was utilized to remodel miniscule elite into 'imitation Englishmen' with the same notions of ascriptive and hierarchical character.[13]

The most striking feature in spite of its inter-regional variations is that those who are atop in the hierarchy across India remain the Brahmins. M. N. Srinivas has summed it up quite categorically:

> Caste is undoubtedly an all-India phenomenon in the sense that there are everywhere hereditary, endogamous groups which form a hierarchy ... everywhere there are Brahmins, untouchables and peasants, artisan, trading and service castes. Relations between castes are invariably expressed in terms of pollution and purity. Certain Hindu theological ideas such as *samskara, karma and dharma* are woven into the caste system ... as the ordering of different varnas is clearly intended to support the theory of brahminical supremacy.[14]

Therefore, it would be correct and appropriate to arrive at a conclusive statement that caste system, particularly the ideological manifestation, had pervaded the entire subcontinent in varying degrees. It is equally appropriate to declare that a near organic and symbiotic relationship between religious order and its symbolism, mythologies especially

---

[12] S. R. Mehrotra, *The Emergence of Indian National Congress* (New Delhi: Vikas Publications, 1971), 248.

[13] Angus Maddison, *Class Struggle and Economic Growth: India and Pakistan since Moghuls* (London: George Allen and Unwin, 1971), 43.

[14] M. N. Srinivas, *Social Change in Modern India* (Hyderabad: Orient Longman, 1966), 3.

temples as vital power centres cum institutions, had indeed sustained the caste system to remain active and alive. This effectively means that the dynamic functions of the ascriptive hierarchy, where one caste—Brahmins—remains atop with other upper castes collaborating with them, had created what is called a social cohesion.[15]

Expectedly, the much adored social cohesion was deemed to be the essential ingredient for any ruler to establish his/her political/power supremacy. The subcontinent displays an interesting picture of cultural/social structure, which remains reasonably independent when the political establishment retains its autonomy. Yet the sanctions and mutual patronage between the sociocultural structure and political establishment had been highlighted as one of the salient features of the subcontinent's history.[16] Several political uncertainties—the inherent character of the oriental despotic context—to a great extent maintained cautious distance from the basic tenants of the caste system. However, recently published nuanced studies point out that the political agency did play a vital role, subsuming the power of caste elites.[17] However, several studies undertaken by several scholars in different disciplinary realms have unambiguously proved the nature and character of the political establishment in a highly hierarchical social order like that of the Indian society. The kingly system of the political structure in the pre-colonial era had several limitations and restrictions for the kings in terms of specific ways.[18]

While recognizing variations from the dominant caste ideology at the micro level in many parts of the subcontinent, one can strongly afford to believe that, by and large, the caste system as an ideology and a single-most powerful organizing principle had knitted the Indian sociocultural rubric. Hence, if it is the caste system that unites and

---

[15] David Shulman, *Reconsidering Hinduism*, in *Hinduism Reconsidered*, eds. G. D. Sontheimer and Herman Kulke (New Delhi: Manohar, 1985), 7–10.

[16] Eric Stokes, *The Peasants and the Raj: Studies in Agrarian Society and Peasant Rebellion in Colonial India* (Delhi: Vikas Publishers, 1978), 19–23.

[17] Dirks, *Castes of Mind*, 1–5, 126–129. See also Arjun Appadurai, *Worship and Conflict under Colonial Rule* (Cambridge: Cambridge University Press, 1981).

[18] Romila Thapar, *A History of Indian*, vol. I (Middlesex: Penguin Books, 1966), 19.

offers a pan-Indian picture, there are several anti-caste movements in different forms and content that had emerged from various parts of the subcontinent at different times. Starting from Buddhism and Jainism, both at the pan-Indian and local levels, there were several anti-caste movements. Therefore, while accepting the caste system as a pan-Indian phenomenon, it is absolutely necessary to recognize the powerful anti-caste, anti-hierarchical character of many parts.

It has become abundantly comprehensible that the colonial regime had crafted new modes of cultural interaction and economic activities by effectively freezing the flexibilities available within caste hierarchy in the pre-colonial era. A near perfect enmeshing of British greed for revenue and caste supremacy had resulted in a milieu, which has ironically been characterized as modern. In the process of India becoming 'modern', caste had effectively become an instrument of governance and singular identity. The depiction of M. N. Srinivas is quite self-evident of the changing character[19]:

> ...the brahmin writers on law propounded a model caste system which placed them on the top and gave them the privilege of declaring the duties of the other castes; the institution which prevailed till 1864, of attaching brahmin pundits to the British established law courts, the presence in every town of a body of western educated lawyers who tried to apply Brahmanical law to all Hindus. The translation of a vast mass of sacred literature from Sanskrit into English, the rise everywhere of 'caste sabhas' which tried to introduce reforms by Sanskritizing the way of life of their respective castes and the *growth of a vigorous anti-brahmin movement which attempted to displace brahmins from the position of power and influence...*

What is more important to assess here would be the relentless struggle for justice and equality against caste oppression by the subjugated masses. The modus operandi had perhaps been unique and acquired its own peculiar style and structure. Nevertheless, the striking feature is the anti-caste or anti-upper caste character intrinsically embedded in all

---

[19] M. N. Srinivas, *Social Change in Modern India and Other Essays* (Bombay: Asia Publishing House, 1970), 5–6 (italics mine).

these movements. In general, three major dimensions have emerged as social facts during the last seven decades of the colonial regime in India: an agitational politics and mass mobilization against the caste system or/and Brahminical social order; attempts made sporadically to escape and flee from the Brahminism-based caste hierarchy; and virulent struggle against caste-based land relations.

Therefore, the caste elites' hegemony was no longer considered as an untenable proposition for a nation to evolve; it rather became the foundation for the new India. The near perfect union of interest between the greedy British imperialism and caste/class hegemony of the native elites during the colonial era remains quite alive and active in the post-colonial period too. Political freedom obtained from the British in 1947 did not decolonize the Indian society.

The popular wisdom may embolden us to postulate that nationalism as a dynamic force would help us collectively decolonize the society at large; the reality however is that in the Indian case, nationalism to a large extent perpetuated sociocultural and economic inequality.[20] Whatever success India has achieved in the 20th century in terms of mitigating the ill effects of inequality, the incredible role of progressive elements within the anti-imperialist struggle should be recognized; however, the largely known nationalist initiatives mostly failed to obliterate political structures created by imperial rulers. In many strong agrarian zones both the Mughals and the British rulers patronized landlords, property owners. In fact, India's nationalist development-oriented regime indeed accentuated wealth accumulation of the privileged people since 1947.[21]

The anti-British struggle which many historians have with euphoria declared as a turning point in the history of the subcontinent and the dawn of independent India as the unique display of people's resolve was effectively a successful attempt to hold on to power and authority.

---

[20] For more details, see G. Aloysius, *Nationalism without a Nation in India* (Delhi: Oxford University Press, 1997).

[21] David Ludden, 'Empire Meets Globalisation: Explaining Historical Patterns of Inequality in South Asia', *Economic & Political Weekly* 47, no. 30 (2012): 217.

The cultural sanction and social approval became the nucleus of the celebrated nationalism itself. Therefore, unjust and unequal social order and the hegemonic influence of the upper echelon of this social order will not be reduced seriously without dismantling the infrastructure and knowledge production of imperial rule. By inheriting the same legacy, it is absolutely unlikely to bring in justice and egalitarian principles as crux of our sociocultural world. Thus, the celebration of cultural nationalism unambiguously reminds us the impending danger of more unjust and hegemonic sociocultural order which even the oft-repeated powerful force—market—would not be able to deter or challenge.

To comprehend the intensity of the unjust social order, Antonio Gramsci's concept of hegemony would be of immense help to us. For Gramsci,

> [Hegemony is] an order in which a certain way of life and thought is dominant, in which one concept of reality is diffused throughout society in all its institutional manifestation, informing with its spirit, all taste, morality, custom, religious and political principles, and all social relations, particularly in their intellectual and moral connotation.[22]

This crisp assessment captures the essence and spirit of the concept of hegemony. When nationalism in India sought to invent a nation which celebrates unjust social order and firmly establishes the dominance of caste/class elites, this framework of Gramsci squarely questions the idea of people's will.

Nationalism in India being a hegemonic ideology firmed up unjust social order and almost established the nation as the embodiment of unequal sociocultural structure. But the issue to be highlighted is that a nation indeed requires certain fundamental changes in social and relational orientation, and he squarely latched his faith that the dawn of this new orientation must lead to the genesis of new consciousness among the members of the new community. Moreover, the old social order cannot be refurnished and offered as a nation; instead, if a community

---

[22] Joseph Woolcock, 'Politics, Ideology and Hegemony in Gramsci's Theory', *Social and Economic Studies* 34, no. 3 (1985): 199–210.

is to be designated as 'national', some fundamental structural changes should be initiated and institutionalized. Similarly, one also has to be cautious about the likely consequences of conflating citizenship with membership of a national community.

Well before the arrival of advance theorizations on issues like citizenship, Ambedkar had unambiguously declared why it is necessary to unravel the organic relationship among citizenship, nationality and social justice. In other words, it is not being rather 'becoming a nation' as a sociocultural–political category, which occupies a vital position in Ambedkar's arguments.

> …without social union, political unity is difficult to be achieved. If achieved, it would be as precarious as a summer sapling, liable to be uprooted by the gust of a hostile wind. With mere political unity India may be a State. *But to be a state is not to be a nation and a State which is not a nation.*[23]

The unerring observation and a profound assessment by Ambedkar elucidates that any attempt to conflate a state with a nation is not only a historical fallacy but would effectively prevent all of us inventing a nation itself. This sanity in terms of conceptual understanding had actually emboldened him to probe what 'ought' to be a nation.

The crux of the argument is that a highly stratified, hierarchized social order was inherited from the British rule. The upper echelon of the social order, namely the caste elites, have appropriated not only the resources but also knowledge production which justified their hegemony. Thus, a collective force—nationalism—effortlessly consolidated the hegemony of the privileged and rendered fortified justification. Therefore, inequality is not the result of mere administrative failures and poverty is not merely the consequence of natural disasters or monsoon failure. When production especially agricultural remains largely a socially controlled enterprise, any attempt to study inequality as a policy

---

[23] Vasant Moon, ed., *Dr. Babasaheb Ambedkar Writings and Speeches*, vol. 8 (New Delhi: Dr. Ambedkar Foundation, 2014), 193–194 (italics mine).

issue would be a monumental mistake. Hunger and poverty are essentially the culturally sanctioned and socially approved Weltanschauung of a nation, because the nation did not ensure 'homogenization of power within its culture'.[24]

When the British left the subcontinent, India was depicted as the insignia of poverty, hunger, malnutrition and underdevelopment. The country was partitioned along religious lines, but a greater number of Muslims stayed back in India than those who live in Pakistan. Thus, people, especially religious minorities, have emphatically declared their secular credentials by opting to stay back in India. It is therefore pertinent to remind ourselves of this simple fact that it was Pakistan which was created along religious lines not India. This firmly declares the secular nature of not only the State but also the society at large.

Similarly, the newly emerged post-colonial country had the opportunity to experiment with three major economic models: market-friendly laissez-faire pro-capitalist model, the Gandhian model and finally the Soviet-inspired socialist model. India chose to tread along a new path of 'mixed economy'. The self-styled socialist path of development envisaged by Nehru and his adviser P. C. Mahalanobis was merely a selective replica of certain Soviet model of planning and has nothing to do with socialism per se. In fact, A. R. Desai in his no-holds-barred criticism towards Nehru–Mahalanobis strategy (thanks to Professor Sukhamoy Chakravarty) highlights the role of bourgeois state power in independent India in actually pushing through the capitalist path of development by 'initiating various measures—economic, political, and administrative resources to apportion resources to various classes, groups and organizations and also to elaborate varieties of institutions and create new ones'. He also categorically offers his assessment of the State's threefold functions—repressive, economic and ideological—to expose its class prejudice and oppressive nature.[25] The most illuminating

---

[24] Ernest Gellner, 'Definitions', in *Nations and Nationalism* (Oxford: Basic Blackwell, 1983).

[25] A. R. Desai, *India's Path of Development: A Marxist Approach* (Bombay: Popular Prakashan, 1984), 14.

and succinct analysis of Desai is his elaboration of the nature of Indian capitalist class. He says,

> ... the Indian capitalist class never sought the destruction of the politico-administrative apparatus evolved by the British. It was interested only in gaining control over it, making only minor modification to suit its own requirements and its own purposes.[26]

This clearly delineates that the actual independence was to a large extent a mere transfer of power/authority from the British Raj to the caste/class elites of the Indian society. But how do we make sense of the socialist rhetoric or planned economy initiated in the 1950s? Even before independence, Congress party had established the National Planning Committee as early as 1936 to plan for the country's development.[27] Less than a decade later, several industrialists have drafted a policy popularly known as Bombay Plan, which sought straight and active state intervention in planning, financing and managing industrial development.[28]

The intriguing point to reflect upon here is the grand consensus steadily emerging among the caste/class elites over the concept of State-sponsored planned economic model even if it was called socialist. Two centuries of British rule had virtually ruined the economy; its devastating consequences are still being chronicled. Realizing the predicaments of British rule more than anyone, caste/class elites tactically facilitated the State intervention in resurrecting the economy. In other words, the cosmetic notion of socialism actually aided bureaucracy, acquiring disproportionate power and authority in India. With caste/class elites simply monopolizing the mammoth executive structure, one could well imagine what would have emerged out of socialist policies. As Desai has elaborated the tactics of Indian bourgeois,

---

[26] Ibid., 101.

[27] V. M. Dandekar, *The Indian Economy 1947–92*, vol. I (New Delhi: SAGE Publications, 1994), 50.

[28] Robert Stern, *Changing India: Bourgeois Revolution on the Subcontinent* (Cambridge: Cambridge University Press, 1993), 210.

(i) reshuffling the rural class structure, (ii) helping rural rich in their capital formation, (iii) evolution of adequate institutional-organisational structures to help the rural rich vis-a-vis the rural poor, (iv) evolve cultural media for the domination of the rich over the poor.[29]

When the Planning Commission was finally established in March 1950, it was formally declared that the vision of socialism would guide India's economy; it sought to combine socialism with the institutions of parliamentary democracy. The creation of 'casteless and classless' society was said to be the mission of the socialist planned economy. Alleviating abject poverty and to reboot the stagnant economy, massive industrialization process and mechanization of agriculture were all envisaged in the socialist developmental model. The Green Revolution was the flagship programme of the government in the 1950s; massive dams and big industries were divinized as modern temples of India. What are the significant consequences of these policies half a century later? No doubt, as A. R. Desai has firmly summed it up, the Indian bourgeoisie has achieved success in its agrarian strategy aimed at fostering and safeguarding its basic interests.[30]

It is however worth mentioning that the socialist policies adopted by the ruling parties and the grand consensus had successfully evolved and had certain merits. India's initial attempt to go along with basic tenants of socialism even if it is nascent in its policy outreach constituted at its crux anti-imperialist development strategy, which did not promote the export of products that directly or indirectly take land away from producing good grains.[31] Let us set aside for a while the mind-boggling deliberations on the socialist economic model; the fundamental point is that socialism as a policy is unlikely to succeed unless socialism as a cultural practice is strongly encrypted in the social fabric. If the socialist culture is not favourably facilitating, the socialist economy may not yield expected dividends. What India's tryst

---

[29] Desai, *India's Path of* Development, 158.
[30] Ibid., 161.
[31] Prabhat Patnaik, 'The Nehru–Mahalanobis Strategy', *Social Scientist* 43, no. 3/4 (2015): 9.

with the nascent socialist policy has offered was a more invigorated hegemony of caste/class elites.

## THE CRISIS OF 1990 AND REDEFINING HEGEMONY

Little more than four decades later since independence, India began to face major crises not only in economic domain but also in social and political realms. On 7 August 1990, the then Prime Minister V. P. Singh declared the implementation of the Mandal Commission's recommendations, reserving 27 per cent seats in jobs and academic institutions for Other Backward Castes (OBCs). While major parts of the southern India remained quite peaceful, the northern states witnessed violent protests; some youngsters even went to the extent of immolating themselves as a mark of protest against OBC reservation. The political upheaval resulted in the collapse of V. P. Singh government. Similarly, Bharatiya Janata Party leader L. K. Advani launched a long march to Ayodhya to construct Ram Temple at the site where Babri Masjid stood. By late 1980, the external debt crisis surfaced, which brought India close to default in meeting its international payments obligations. The balance of payments situation was almost alarmingly unmanageable.

This was no doubt an important moment in post-colonial Indian history. For several historical and socio-economic reasons, the assertion of backward castes in many parts of the northern states finally became a reality. Reaction to OBC reservation announcement displayed fear, anger and restlessness among the dominant castes that what they believed as indisputable entitlement was first time legally challenged and threatened. Soon OBC reservation became a historical reality that no political party could afford to repeal and with a few caveat, the Supreme Court approved reservation for OBC little later. This piece of legal document ensured the entry of OBCs into central government jobs, including the decorated civil services in a big way. By June 1991, Narasimha Rao-led Congress government initiated drastic steps towards liberalizing the Indian economy. The intention behind this move was to ensure a wider scope for the operation of free market by dismantling the formidable structure of licences, controls and regulations which were the essential features of the hitherto celebrated socialist economic policies. The pro-market liberalization policies highlighted not only the limitations of the socialist pattern of development in India but also the impossibility of that model yielding massive success. It also implies perhaps more explicitly that the globalization of the economy is an inevitable reality; Indian caste/class elites were thrilled, as the coronation of market forces became a reality. Since economic policies, accordingly constitutional provisions, remain outside the purview of courts, such policies cannot be challenged legally in any court. When OBCs managed to enter with legal sanctions into higher educational institutions and in central government jobs in a major way, the State decided to withdraw some of its solemn obligations and permitted market forces to assume their role. Liberalizing the Indian economy, some experts do argue, was not a deliberate attempt but an inevitable step and a compulsion.

When international financial organizations and global community seemingly lose their faith in India's economic condition, they would likely refuse to lend monetary support; if so, slowly and steadily, people would also refuse to repose their faith in their government. This led to the government taking drastic steps by opening up the market and agreeing to the terms and conditions of International Monetary Fund (IMF) and World Bank.[32] The emergence of the service sector as a huge economic opportunity provider majorly altered India's face, both domestically and in international forums. Suddenly, India emerged as the favourite poster child for the success of globalization. The country is seen as one of the most preferred destinations for economic growth and prosperity. Top corporate executives, policy analysts and lawmakers made a bee line to New Delhi. India was described as a 'roaring capitalist success'.[33]

First time, concerns regarding equality, social justice, gender and domestic violence, and environmental issues slid down to seemingly insignificant issues in public realm. The euphoria that market forces

---

[32] Amit Bhaduri and Deepak Nayyar, *The Intelligent Person's Guide to Liberalization* (New Delhi: Penguin, 1996), 48.
[33] Gurcharan Das, 'The India Model', *Foreign Affairs* 85, no. 4 (2004): 2–16.

by their very logic would bring in a level playing field in a hierarchical society was consistently resonating in the corridors of power. It was widely believed that India is progressively stepping into a capitalist economic order. Economic liberalization has come to be perceived as the greatest panacea for all our economic crises. India's urban centres have witnessed rapid and visibly most stunning growth from 1991. These urban areas began to attract glitter and glamour; country's foreign direct investment soared considerably. Within two decades, a new middle class—quite formidable in terms of numbers and influence—emerged. This class began to represent the ideological hegemony of India's caste/class elites explicitly and the interests of the State vigorously. The crisp analysis of Pankaj Mishra says it all:

> ... business-centric view of India suppresses more facts than it reveals. Recent accounts of the alleged rise of India barely mention the fact that the country's $728 per capita gross domestic product is just slightly higher than that of sub-Saharan Africa and that, as the 2005 United Nations human development report puts it, even if it sustains high growth rates, India will not catch up with high income countries; nor is India very fast on the report's human development index where it ranks 127 just two rungs above Myanmar and more than 70 below Cuba and Mexico. Despite recent reduction in poverty levels, nearly 380 million people live on less than a dollar a day.[34]

This effectively captures the character of liberalized India. For the first four decades since 1950, the country was rejoicing over the promises of the socialist pattern of the economic order; with massive industrialization, mechanization of agriculture, blooming Green Revolution and cooperative experiments resulting in steep rise in milk production, it was promised that the country would soon be prosperous. The essential messages were that abject poverty, hunger and massive unemployment would be drastically minimized; an inclusive social order could emerge soon; and all sections of the Indian society could access resources without major discrimination.

---

[34] Pankaj Mishra, 'The Myth of New India', *The New York Times*, 26 July 2006.

By late 1990 and early 1991, with the balance of payments crisis becoming too severe to manage, many advocates of neoliberal economic policies began to belittle the first four decades of socialist economic policies as 'Hindu rate of growth'.[35] Contrary to the popular opinion, strong advocates of the market economy have categorically claimed that India's growth rate and progress during 1950–1970 was not as bad as many tend to believe; in fact, India's growth rate was slightly ahead of China during those two decades.[36] Therefore, the Nehruvian notion of socialism in spite of its inadequacies promised to alleviate poverty and hunger and ensure inclusive social order. The stronger State intervention into developmental activities without diluting the constitutional spirit of establishing an inclusive social order must not be looked down upon, as the growth rate in the initial four decades was not flamboyant but very stable. However, when economists analyse the progress of the country, the foundational dimension perhaps unwittingly remains bypassed.

> At the time of its independence in 1947, India had: a literacy rate of 18 per cent; an investment rate of around 9 per cent of its GDP; life expectancy at birth of 32 years; an annual population growth rate of 1.25 per cent; and an average annual growth rate of GDP of around 3 per cent. In 2005/6, India had: a literacy rate of around 60 per cent; an investment rate of around 30 per cent of its GDP; life expectancy at birth of 63 years; an annual population growth rate of 1.5 per cent; and an annual growth rate of GDP of around 8.4 per cent.[37]

---

[35] Baldev Raj Nayar, 'When Did the Hindu Rate of Growth End?' *Economic & Political Weekly* 41, no. 19 (2006): 1885–1890; for more details, see Arvind Virmani, 'India's Economic Growth: From Socialist Rate of Growth to Bharatiya Rate of Growth' (working paper no. 122, Indian Council for Research on International Economic Relations, New Delhi, February 2004); Baldev Raj Nayar, *India's Mixed Economy: The Role of Ideology and Interest in Its Development* (Bombay: Popular Prakashan, 1989); Dani Rodrik and Arvind Subramanian, 'From the Hindu Growth to Productivity Surge: The Mystery of the Indian Growth Transition' (IMF working paper no. WP/04/77, IMF, Washington, DC, May 2004).

[36] Subramanian Swamy, *Economic Growth in China and India 1952–70* (Chicago, IL: University of Chicago Press, 1973).

[37] Kaushik Basu and Annemie Maertens, 'The Pattern and Causes of Economic Growth in India', *Oxford Review of Economic Policy* 23, no. 2 (2007): 144.

There has been no doubt a steady progress; but by the late 1980s, all that were perceived positively had been depicted as the major reasons for the stagnation in development. This intriguing dimension requires a more sociological analysis than what data-based conventional wisdom offers.

It is not inappropriate to conclude that the socialist model latched its faith, limited though in bringing incipient stage of inclusive social order. However, what is truly intriguing is the way bureaucracy acquires a disproportionate role in regulating and controlling both social and economic affairs. The omnipotent nature of the Indian bureaucracy was the natural and the most preferred choice of caste/class elites; with massive funding from the State, many higher education institutions including the illustrious technological institutes flourished. All of them simply embodied the 'progressive' nature of post-colonial India.

Exorbitant funding from the State for industrial development in many pockets of the country rapidly increased employment opportunities for thousands of Indians. A new class of managerial jobs in both private and public sector companies was swiftly appropriated by caste/class elites; since educational qualifications and essential skills were considered vital, it was fairly expected that those positions would be occupied by the caste/class elites.[38] In spite of being a robust License Raj, entrepreneurial opportunities did spring up in many parts of the country. Most of those opportunities were largely manned by people from traditional business families. Those people had the privilege of having hands-on experience in the everyday running of the company. Many, if not all, industrial firms in India have been largely administered and run by their own family members. The conventional opinion that industrialization along with modernization would radically alter and modify the traditional social structure seemingly reminds an unproven or a hypothetical proposition.[39] In fact,

---

[38] S. C. Jain, *Indian Manager: His Sociological Origin and Career* (Bombay: Somaiya Publications, 1971); see also Suren Navlakha, *Elite and Social Change* (New Delhi: SAGE Publications, 1989).

[39] M. N. Panini, 'Corporate Culture in India', *Economic & Political Weekly* 23, no. 35 (1988): M86–M94.

the traditional understanding of patron–client relations, ties of kin network and caste affinity emerged as more powerful.[40]

In other words, the so-called socialist model of planning for development was intended for the welfare of a large section of the downtrodden masses; it is naive to attribute ill intention to the leaders who devised this strategy. However, it is equally pertinent to underscore why the agriculture sector, wherein a whooping majority of Indians has been associated with received proportionally, is less importance. Little more than 80 per cent of the masses lean on agriculture and agri-related activities for their livelihood; they received cosmetic attention, but not a substantial one as happened in the heavy industrial sector. Mechanization of agricultural activities may often be cited as a radical step towards realizing inclusive growth in rural areas. Mechanization and massive economic subsidies for fertilizers were necessary but not sufficient to bring in credible changes in rural areas. What was more compelling was land reforms–land to the tiller; it remained merely a hollow slogan in many pockets of the country.

When the Congress party leadership in almost all regions was largely controlled by landed caste groups, it was unfair to expect them work against their class interests. The land reforms were carried out successfully only in Kerala and West Bengal, particularly in protecting tenants and making them owners of land. This was no doubt possible due to intense gross-roots political movements.[41] This leads us to conclude that if the socialist pattern of development had to succeed, it was mandatory to create a conducive atmosphere in the sociocultural realm. Socialist policies certainly cannot yield expected dividends unless the socialist culture is well established. That is to say, homogenization of power within culture remains the nucleus of a social order where egalitarian economic policies would bring in credible changes in the society.

---

[40] Mark Holmstrom, *Industry and Inequality: The Social Anthropology of Indian Labour* (Bombay: Orient Longman, 1985).

[41] Atul Kohli, 'Parliamentary Communism and Agrarian Reform: The Evidence from India's Bengal', *Asian Survey* 27, no. 7 (1983): 783–809; see also T. K. Oommen, *From Mobilization to Institutionalization: The Dynamics of Agrarian Movement in 20th Century Kerala* (Bombay: Popular Prakashan, 1985).

## ECONOMIC LIBERALIZATION AND SOCIAL CONSERVATISM: HEGEMONY REINVIGORATED

Thousands of pages were already devoted explaining what led to opening up the market in India and how liberalization of the Indian economy radically changed the course of its economic progress, especially the image of the country itself. Till the late 1980s, India was projected as the typical poster child of Third-World poverty and a despotic, stagnated society/economy. Any optimism of India's growth/development was summarily dismissed not only by foreign scholars but also by Indian scholars. Any hint of citing progressive symptoms in India's development received menacing sarcasm. June 1991 turned out to be a watershed moment in post-colonial India, as the economy braced for a new paradigm. Manmohan Singh as the finance minister rolled out a new strategy, which was popularly known as New Economic Policy (NEP), which effectively ended India's well-known License/Permit Raj.[42]

Let us set aside for a moment what development economists and corporate captains have lavishly eulogized on economic liberalization; also let us not bogged down by mind-boggling details on GDP growth rate and per capita income spike after liberalization. But how India's image changed abruptly after liberalization is something worth reflecting. India's 'spectacular' success was repeatedly projected as a model for others to emulate; the sudden euphoria and even adulation on India's economic progress at both domestic level and global forums were truly stunning. The newly found euphoria declared that by liberalizing its economy, India was inaugurated into a new wave of globalization. One of the bestselling authors Thomas Friedman declares that India's entry into new globalization is a spectacular success story.[43]

---

[42] However, there have been strong arguments that the country was preparing itself to embrace NEP for a long time; the budget presented by C. Subramaniam during the Emergency was the first major step towards adopting the NEP and, similarly, by the late 1980s, the brief stint of Chandrashekhar government also laid down a stronger foundation for liberalized economic policies; see Vinod Vyasulu, *Crisis and Response: An Assessment of Economic Reforms* (Delhi: Madhyam Books, 1996), 19–20.

[43] Thomas Friedman, *The World Is Flat: A Brief History of Twenty First Century* (New York, NY: Farrar Straus Giroux, 2005).

The developed countries—the First World—believed in the supremacy of the market-oriented economic order, which quickly established a promising bonhomie with India; policymakers, corporate executives and elected members from Western countries welcomed India into the globalized, pro-capitalist (neocapitalist) economic order. What kind of capitalism is it? Can market-driven economic policies effortlessly turn the country into a capitalist society? What all is required, sociologically speaking, for a society to be a 'capitalist society'? Moreover, can India ever become a capitalist society, with India's sociocultural complexities and hierarchical social order retaining their supremacy? These questions may look pretty simple but require profound analysis.

Contemporary neoliberalism as a political/economic policy postulates that human well-being can best be advanced by unfettered market freedom and unflinching State support to trade, heightened individual liberty and legal sanction to even limitless private property. The State does retain its sovereignty but remains subservient to the tutelage of the market. Today, the manufactured consensus in favour of the neoliberal or capitalist economic order is considered as the new normalcy. Some of its basic tenants have been steadily injected into our common sense that neoliberal, market-friendly capitalism is the only way forward for the entire humanity. In the case of India, it was repeatedly told that market can neutralize if not annihilate the tyranny of caste. It was glorified that this policy would bring in gender parity, as women would also be absorbed into a new economic order as equals; since market demands only 'skills and talents', advocates of the neoliberal economic policy firmly declared that gender equity was just a matter of days once we liberalize our economy. Millions of new employment opportunities would be created and millions would be lifted from their chronic, abject poverty, as declared the cheer leaders of the corporate world.

Globally too, the euphoria has been quite strongly orchestrated in favour of neoliberal policies in spite of their dismal performance. As David Harvey has rightly pointed out,

> Aggregate growth rates stood at 3.5 per cent or so in the 1960s and even during the troubled 1970s fell to only 2.4 per cent. The subsequent

global growth rates of 1.4 percent and 1.1 percent for the 1980s and 1990s, and a rate that barely touches one percent since 2000, indicate that neo-liberalism has broadly failed to stimulate worldwide growth.[44]

In fact, neoliberalism has not proven effective at revitalizing global capital accumulation, but it has succeeded in restoring class power. Notwithstanding such deplorable performance, we all are told to believe that the so-called triumph of capitalism is unquestionable and total.

The complex nature of the contemporary global capital rests upon, as Kalyan Sanyal in his thought-provoking analysis sums up, two major propositions: (a) the global capitalist economy consists of interlinked complex with two distinct spheres—one defined by the circuits of capital proper, that is, the accumulation economy which dominates the advanced capitalist countries and (b) there are other types—the need economy which exists outside the circuits of capital proper and is the dominant form in the post-colonial economies.[45] Contemporary global capitalism continues to dispossess and disempower people/society who choose to remain outside its circuit; however, the ideological foundation of contemporary capitalism would ensure that such dispossessed communities are not becoming antithetical to its policies and, instead, would eventually become part of the need economy. Today's capitalism in post-colonial societies does not produce 'wage laborers'; it simply creates space for them to be 'excluded'.[46]

Classical Marxian framework insists on convoluted trajectory of 'transition' from the feudal society to the capitalist society and to the socialist social order. The class contradiction if accelerated would not only precipitate the transition but also bring in the same. Contemporary

---

[44] David Harvey, 'Neoliberalism as Creative Destruction', *The Annals of the American Academy of Political and Social Science* 610 (March 2007): 33.

[45] Kalyan Sanyal, 'Introduction: Rethinking Capitalist Development', in *Rethinking Capitalist Development: Primitive Accumulation, Governmentality and Post-Colonial Capitalism* (New Delhi: Routledge, 2007).

[46] Kalyan Sanyal, 'Difference as Hegemony: Capital and the Need Economy', in *Rethinking Capitalist Development: Primitive Accumulation, Governmentality and Post-Colonial Capitalism* (New Delhi: Routledge, 2007).

capitalism with its complexities facilitated especially post-colonial societies to live with this dualism. Post-colonial countries like India are contented to put up with these two spheres. Accumulative capital effortlessly metamorphosized itself into 'crony capitalism' and the need economy is not antithetical to it; both do coexist simultaneously. In other words, we are not only into globalization but also into these two worlds.

For example, the Government of India usually declares poverty in terms of access to 2,400 calories per person per day in rural areas and 2,100 per person per day in urban areas. If we take these norms as yardsticks, the proportion of rural population falling below 2,400 calories in 2004–2005 was 87 per cent, up from 74.5 per cent in 1993–1994; and the proportion of urban population falling below 2,100 calories was 64 per cent in 2004–2005, up from 56 per cent in 1993–1994.[47] The point to be noted here is the changing nature of contemporary neoliberal, market-driven capitalism, especially in countries like India. Capitalism arguably must dismantle old social structure and usher in conducive sociocultural–economic order in which capitalism could flourish. However, today's capitalism in India is nothing but a crony capitalism desperate to retain the status quo; it pushed millions of subaltern masses into a state where they are absolutely disempowered and dispossessed as part of the need economy. One of first steps towards empowerment has been education. With heightened pace with which education sector has been privatized, it is indeed alarming; millions of people from subaltern sections simply could not afford to access education as the State silently and deliberately withdrew from its financial obligation in supporting the educational sector. The future looks bleak and that future is here and alive.

With the exponential growth of crony capitalism in India, the public sphere or civil society would continue to be influenced and even coerced. That is to say, small manufacturers, peasants and artisanal communities may have to endure the tyranny of crony capitalism. The plight of people in the unorganized sector and landless labourers is all

---

[47] Prabhat Patnaik, 'Globalization and Social Progress', *Social Scientist* 39, no. 1/2 (2011): 49.

likely to be quite excruciating. This disempowerment may not result in reinvigorated class consciousness, nor does it lead to a 'class-in-itself' to 'class-for-itself' moment. This condition is indeed part of the capitalist system itself today. If so, how does it affect the highly hierarchical caste-based social system? The consequences would be truly complex, monumental and truly detrimental to subaltern masses.

A whopping majority of the subaltern masses will have to lose their means of production; however, the cunning rationality of our crony capitalism would ensure that they are absorbed into its tyrannical structure; their employment is essentially to exploit them. The compulsion of electoral politics may safeguard their political existence and may prevent them from being depicted as 'dangerous elements' in the eyes of the 'general public'. But it is a complex situation; subaltern masses will have to negotiate with both crony capitalism and the comprador bourgeois State[48]. With sizeable majority still living in rural areas in India, the rural may undergo radical transformation; however, it may not vanish as it has been foreseen.[49] This argument is effectively premised upon the hypothesis that caste and village are organically enmeshed; hence, weakening of village would effectively neutralize the intensity of caste itself. Claims such as villages are shrinking as a sociological category and approximately 24 per cent of villagers are engaged in non-agricultural activities require thorough scrutiny.[50]

Villages are not shrinking as a sociological category; the geographical and administrative understanding of villages of course underwent tremendous changes in the last three decades. The idea however of a village is something sociologists must necessarily pay attention to. With the changing nature of a village, let us not assume that caste would also simply wither away. Since some of the early social anthropologists attached divine status to village–caste relation; it does not have to be a sacred truth. Many studies have strongly disputed such claims and asserted

---

[48] Partha Chatterjee, 'Democracy and Economic Transformation in India', *Economic & Political Weekly* 43, no. 16 (2008): 62.

[49] Dipankar Gupta, 'Whither the Indian Village: Culture and Agriculture in Rural India', *Economic & Political Weekly* 40, no. 8 (2005): 751–758.

[50] Ibid., 752.

the role of politics in reshaping castes' everyday dynamics. Castes can and do live outside villages also.

Similarly, people engaging in non-agricultural activities may not guarantee the effects and intensity of castes' weakening. Wages for both agriculture and non-agriculture activities do not look quite impressive; in fact, the wage gap between them for regular workers in rural areas has been narrowing. The overall income inequality demonstrates a continuous increase over the period, with a sharp increase during the post-liberalization period.[51]

But the supremacy of the new/perpetually expanding urban will have monstrous supremacy. The crucial point is the robust emergence of 'tradition' in the era of ascending crony capitalism. Tradition is virtually reinvented to legitimize the perpetual and consistent disempowerment of subaltern masses. In other words, cultural and traditional sanction for caste goes uninterrupted. The perfect union of interest between crony capitalist greed and casteist hegemony is refurnished to be suitable and acceptable to the contemporary times. Caste-based discrimination in 'new India' is not only stunning, but its intensity is rather alarming. From neighbourhood to higher educational institutions, intensity of caste discrimination and gender violence is truly appalling.

In fact, official documents recently began to highlight the level of systemic discrimination and marginalization of not only Dalits and tribes but also Muslims. Prime Minister's High Level Committee headed by Justice Rajinder Sachar to look into social, economic and educational status of the Muslim community (popularly called Sachar Committee) clearly spelt out the deplorable condition in which majority of Muslims live in India. The systematic marginalization starting from housing, healthcare, education, employment opportunities and financial assistance for entrepreneurial ventures has been well documented.[52]

---

[51] Sandip Sarkar and Balwant Singh Mehta, 'Income Inequality in India: Pre- and Post-Reform Periods', *Economic & Political Weekly* 45, no. 37 (2010): 54.

[52] http://www.minorityaffairs.gov.in/sites/default/files/sachar_comm.pdf (accessed on 23 August 2020).

Thus, creating more inequality and making that process as a culture have become the hallmark of India's crony capitalism. The oft-quoted term 'private sector' was ruthless when asked to implement reservation policy. The usual and perhaps most contemptuous response has always been that reservation would ruin merit in economic activities. 'Reservation and merit are antithetical concepts beyond a shadow of doubt,' categorically says a leading industrialist, Rahul Bajaj, in an article.[53] The impression given by captains of industries is that their recruitment policies are absolutely meritorious and highly professional; the fact is that as much as 72–85 per cent of workers are recruited through 'informal channels'.[54] Actually, an informal channel unambiguously proves the powerful role of caste and kin network in employment opportunities. An interesting study by Surinder Jodhka and Katherine Newman on interview data analyses the attitudes of employer/hiring managers in India's private sector towards the caste and community attributes of their potential employees. It clearly says the major role of ascriptive qualities in selecting candidates.[55]

The highly prejudiced opinion that people belonging to marginalized communities, especially Dalits and tribes, are not meritorious and cannot provide efficient service has been meticulously fabricated. Such prejudices are not aberrations in India's crony capitalism; it is rather the culture. That is the reason when a person from a marginalized community performs exceedingly well in studies or in his/her profession, it becomes news and people get a 'cultural shock'.

In other words, taking pride in being a member of a dominant caste or religion is no longer an unwarranted residue of eclipses of the feudal era; discrimination, humiliation and social exclusion of Dalits, tribes and Muslims are now infused in our common sense, and one would find

---

[53] Sukhadeo Thorat, Aryama, and Prashant Negi, eds., *Reservation and Private Sector: Quest for Equal Opportunity and Growth* (Jaipur: Rawat Publications, 2005), 250.

[54] Ibid.; see the essay by T. S. Popala and S. Madheswaram in the same volume.

[55] Surinder Jodhka and Katherine Newman, 'In the Name of Globalisation: Meritocracy, Productivity and the Hidden Language of Caste', *Economic & Political Weekly* 42, no. 41 (2007): 4125–4132.

them in private enterprises even in the most dynamic modern sectors of the Indian economy.[56] Business conglomerates that became disproportionately powerful from 1991 simply turned the responsibility on to the State when they were asked to adhere to the reservation policy in private sectors. In fact, two of the major Indian business conglomerates simply dismissed the role of caste in the labour market in India; they rather reverted back to their favourite jargon—meritocracy and efficiency. The summary of one of their reports says,

> ...competitiveness of enterprise and economy is not negotiable and must be achieved and maintained through knowledge and competence in the rapidly developing Indian economy. To accelerate growth and competitiveness of the Indian economy, institutions must have autonomy and flexibility in order to create and expand job opportunities for all section of society. Inclusiveness would ultimately be achieved through universal access to quality education which presumably is a responsibility of the State.[57]

The State's fast withdrawal from spending on education, especially on school education, is quite obvious, and education has become one of the most lucrative private enterprises today in India.

What we see today is a paradox. On the one hand, the privileged castes are publicly on a denouncing mode that caste is no longer an issue to reckon with; on the other hand, their desperation to establish or maintain caste hegemony is truly stunning. Thus, one would come across caste elites' repeated assertion that caste is the major hurdle for India's growth; caste-based reservation is quite detrimental to the country's progress. This may surprise especially the outsiders; they would wonder where caste is. When Andre Beteille declares that 'caste is

---

[56] Sukhadeo Thorat and Paul Attewell, 'The Legacy of Social Exclusion: A Correspondence Study of Job Discrimination in India', *Economic & Political Weekly* 41, no. 42 (2007): 4144.

[57] Surinder Jodhka, 'Caste and the Corporate Sector', *Indian Journal of Industrial Relations* 44, no. 2 (2008): 191; see also Sukhadeo Thorat and Nidhi Sadana, 'Caste and Ownership of Private Enterprises', *Economic & Political Weekly* 44, no. 23 (6–12 June 2009): 13–16.

longer an important agent of social placement or control,'[58] one would be thoroughly perplexed. This country has been witnessing several attempts by the caste elites to invent the so-called castelessness since independence; whereas the less-privileged subaltern masses have been forced to rely on caste identities as the only way to negotiate with the State for resources. This effortlessly enabled the caste elites to declare the subaltern masses as 'casteist' people and as people unwilling to contribute to the progress of the country.[59]

Most interestingly, the caste elites turned their culturally sanctioned and socially approved capital into different nomenclature; in other words, terms such as 'merit' and 'efficiency' are basically camouflaged words to reassert the hegemony of caste elites. Therefore, merit and efficiency are not to be treated as mere words; they are the responses of caste elites to the subaltern assertion. To put it simply, the resources that caste elites have accumulated over a period of several centuries are now metamorphosized into modern capital; the modern nation state is very pleased with this modern capital; modern institutions especially educational institutions are legally sanctioned to adhere to it.[60]

This synchronized interest between caste elites and crony capitalists establishes nefarious hegemony to be challenged by subaltern masses. Marginalized communities—Scheduled Castes and Scheduled Tribes—have their representatives: Nearly 80 lawmakers in the Parliament and roughly 500 legislative members to various states are elected, and scores of people are recruited through highly competitive exams to various levels of bureaucracy. This representational democracy is necessary but not sufficient to be designated as liberal democracy, since the spirit of substantive democracy is conspicuously missing. It would be absent precisely for reasons which are delineated above—the incredible bonhomie between the cultural hegemony of caste elites and greedy

---

[58] Andre Beteille, 'Caste in Contemporary India', in *Caste Today*, ed. C. J. Fuller (Delhi: Oxford University Press, 1996).

[59] Satish Deshpande, 'Caste and Castelessness: Towards a Biography of the General Category', *Economic & Political Weekly* 48, no. 15 (2013): 32–39.

[60] Ajantha Subramanian, 'Making Merit: The Indian Institutes of Technology and the Social Life of Caste', *Comparative Studies in Society and History* 57, no. 2 (2015): 291–322.

character of crony capitalism remains the most powerful stumbling block on our way to achieve substantial democracy. Market-driven liberalized economic policies may have created little more economic opportunities; as a result, a good number of women and subaltern masses may have obtained employment opportunities. This may have elevated their economic status. But the crux of the argument remains: Are we moving closer to an egalitarian society where homogenization of power within culture is assured? Are we ensuring inclusive India where humiliation of people based on their ascriptive identities is not declared as a tradition/culture? How far have we evolved to ensure justice to all?

In the process of finding out a plausible way forward, a set of scholars highlighted different dimensions of the contemporary nature of inequality in India. While Professor Oommen lays down a broader conceptual framework to be undertaken in analysing inequality, he highlights our constitutional provisions and the need for State intervention when required to mitigate the ill effects of inequality. Similarly, he also cautions us regarding the perils of majoritarianism assuming the status of nationalism which he asserts would destabilize the foundations of democracy itself in our country.

The relationship between caste and capital is truly intriguing; there are a few who firmly believe in the progressive potentials of the market; this resulted in the emergence of the Dalit Indian Chamber of Commerce and Industry with a motto to give jobs. The assumption is that capital per se is value neutral; hence, it could facilitate the upward mobility of Dalits and other marginalized sections. This point, contentious though, has inspired a few important works. Amiya Kumar Das has analysed the significance and implications of this proposition with his study. Similarly, a village as a sociological category is perceived to be the nucleus of caste structure; therefore, massive urbanization is often presented as a viable alternative to mitigate the ill effects of caste. This too remains a contentious point. Tanweer Fazal and Shaileshkumar Darokar have in their studies focused on different contexts, highlighting the changing nature of urbanity and the question of labour. At the realm of cultural reproduction, caste hegemony could be deciphered with its inherent subtleties. Archana Singh and Manoj Kumar Jena have attempted to unravel Dalit women autobiography and the glittering world of media, respectively, to comprehend the nuances of caste hegemony in contemporary India.

The twentieth-century Tamil society offered several interesting challenges; from being the epicentre of anti-caste agitation to reshape itself as an anti-Brahmin movement, the Tamil society has come a long way. Different dimensions of caste politics and atrocities against marginalized communities are elaborated from different perspectives. C. Jerome Samraj has focused on the State's mischievous and quite belligerent attempts to simply project caste assertion of subaltern masses as mere law and order problem, whereas Karthick Ram Manoharan has underscored the oscillating ideological foundation of caste conflicts in some parts of Tamil Nadu. R. Thirunavukkarasu has attempted to analyse the character of the state in probing violence against Dalits; police firing on Dalits and the subsequent judicial enquiry report that virtually absolves police certainly reflect the illiberal character of the State itself. When communal riots, especially against Muslims, remain recurrent phenomena in many parts of northern India, southern India particularly Tamil Nadu to a large extent remains not only peaceful but resolutely displays its anti-Hindutva politics. Dravidian movement and its offshoot—the two major Dravidian political parties—successfully knitted a fascinating cultural fabric in which the Tamil language as value is utilized for all Tamil-speaking people, including religious minorities particularly Muslims, to become one political voice. This incredible arrangement has been yielding high political/electoral dividends since the late 1960s in Tamil Nadu. P. Ramajayam in his analysis has sought to furnish details on the changing nature of Muslim politics in the state and how it tries to reconcile Tamil identity with liberalization providing huge business and trading opportunities for many non-Brahmin/dominant castes. In this modest attempt, the volume puts forward a thematic coherence as well as seeks to unsettle some of the taken-for-granted political positions as everyday normalcy.

# Chapter 1

# Societal Complexity and Sources of Inequality
Situating India

T. K. Oommen

## SOME CONCEPTUAL CLARIFICATIONS

The phenomenon of inequality can be analysed only with reference to the units of analysis and the contexts in which it exists. If equality is elusive in India, the unit of analysis, namely India, is enigmatic. Therefore, we need to decipher the nature of societal complexity and the sources of inequality in India. Here, we are severely handicapped because of the persisting tendency to borrow indiscriminately Western concepts and theories, ignoring Indian specificities. As Bauman observes,

> ... with hardly any exception, all the concepts and analytical tools currently employed by social scientists are geared to a view of the human world in which the most voluminous totality is a 'society', a notion equivalent for all practical purposes, to the concept of the 'nation state'.[1]

---

[1] Zygmunt Bauman, *Culture as Praxis* (London: Routledge and Kegan Paul, 1973), 78.

The fact that the institution of nation state, a product of the Treaty of Westphalia concluded in 1648 in Germany based on the principle 'for each nation its own state', is utterly inadmissible in the Indian case because the nation state assumes co-terminality between political and cultural boundaries. When many nations coexist in one polity, the possibility of 'internal colonialism'[2] and consequent inequality between the constituting units is perennially present. In India, the inequality between provincial states constituted on the bases of language, tribe and even religion (although often denied) provides a context of inequality. This empirical possibility is absent in a polity which is culturally homogeneous. Therefore, it is better to designate India as a national state[3] which admits cultural heterogeneity within a polity.

The second conceptual liability in understanding the specificity of the Indian social reality arises out of our endorsing the Enlightenment Idea, which celebrated its triumph in inventing the universal men/women who by definition transcend all primordial ties—religion, language, tribe, nationality, etc. The Enlightenment Project had its inception one and a half centuries after the Treaty of Westphalia. When anti-Jewish riots broke out in 1789 in Alsace in France, the Court of Claremont-Tonnerre declared: 'The jews should be denied everything as a nation, but granted everything as individuals.' Because if the Jews have allegiance to one another, this would endanger their terminal loyalty for France as citizens. If the Jews were recognized as a nation, a religious minority or a group, they may eventually demand collective rights. The Enlightenment Idea endorsed the University of Human, that is, individuals, but completely denied the specificities of human groups—religious, racial, linguistic, tribal, caste, etc. That is, the idea of a nation state upholds individual freedom, even sovereignty, but denies group identities. Such a conceptualization of 'society' in which there are no intermediary structures between citizens and the sovereign state is against the grains of India. In his analysis of democracy in America,

---

[2] Michael Hechter, *Internal Colonialism: The Celtic Fringe in British National Development 1536–1966* (London: Routledge and Kegan Paul, 1975).

[3] T. K. Oommen, 'Political Federalism, Community Identity and Cultural Pluralism', in *Federal Power Sharing: Accommodating Indian Diversity*, ed. Akhtar Majeed (New Delhi: Manak Publishing, 2009), 22–43.

Tocqueville[4] noted the strategic importance of intermediary structures between the citizens and the state for the sustenance of democracy, unlike in France.

The third conceptual disjunction in understanding inequality arises in the context of the structural adjustment programme, popularly referred to as globalization, which descended on India by the mid-20th century. Thus, the understanding was that the market operates within the confines of the polity, regulated by the State. But the global market operates in a 'borderless world', wherein inequality within the polity is only part of the issue. Not only that material inequality between the employers of the corporate world and the State sector within the polity is often reported and discussed but inequality on a world scale is brought into play, creating deprivations and discriminations between citizens of some State located within the State territory and outside of it—the much envied Non-resident Indians (NRIs) should also be brought into the frame of the inequality discourse.

The three issues concerning the unit of analysis for the discourse of inequality in the Indian situations thus are (a) the inapplicability of the notion of the nation state which assumes the co-terminality between political and cultural boundaries; (b) the untenable assumption that the universality of individuals independent of primordial ties functions within the polity; and (c) the tension between political citizens who are loyal to the State and economic entrepreneurs who are wedded to the global market. The turns and twists brought about by these factors profoundly condition the contexts and contents of inequality in the Indian polity today.

In addition to these, the complexity of the social structure also impinges on the discourse of inequality. All societies are based on gender, class or rural–urban variations, although their relative significance differs. Thus, in both ancient China and modern Japan, age was/is an important factor, contributing to inequality as compared with other societies. Thanks to the persistence of patriarchy, men dominate women in all societies although the velocity of this dominance is less in urban–industrial

---

[4] A. de Tocqueville, *Democracy in America*, 2 vols. (New York, NY: Knopf, 1956). Original 1835 and 1840.

societies in general and Scandinavian countries in particular. Salience of class is much more intense in capitalist democracies as compared with 'socialist' countries. The advent of the structural adjustment programme irreversibly increased material inequality between citizens and different blocks of them, within and across polities.

The ratio between the incomes of the richest and poorest countries has widened over the years. It was only 3:1 in 1820 but rose to 35:1 in 1950 and a staggering 72:1 in 1992. In 2000, the richest 1 per cent of the world's population received as much income as the poorest 57 per cent. Around 25 per cent received 75 per cent of world's income. And nobody can deny that with the emergence of the global market, the disparity between the rich and the poor in the world has been incessantly on the increase. Democracy does not provide the required economic succour to the poor, as the sharpest increase of economic inequality is experienced by capitalist democracies. The much-heralded 'basic needs' of the poor have also been virtually decimated from the lexicon of development. While in 1950 almost 790 million people were found to be food insecure, in 2000 their number stood at 2,000 million according to the statistics provided by the Food and Agriculture Organization (FAO). The geography of hunger is more telling; its epicentres are Sub-Saharan Africa and South Asia. The G7 countries with 11.8 per cent of world's population had 64 per cent of the world's GDP in 1997. In contrast, the G77 countries with 76 per cent of world population had only 16.9 per cent of the world's GDP. The latest report from Oxfam discloses that world's richest 62 persons (53 men and 9 women) own as much wealth as the 3.6 billion, the poorest half of the world's total population. (Mercifully there is none from India in the 62 richest.) I hope you are convinced that economic (i.e., class) inequality is a world phenomenon and is not specific to India.[5]

Gender inequality is also a world phenomenon and it often manifests in violence—physical, structural and symbolic—against women.[6]

---

[5] T. K. Oommen, *Development Discourse: Issues and Concerns* (New Delhi: Regency Publications, 2004).

[6] T. K. Oommen, *Understanding Security: A New Perspective* (Delhi: Macmillan India, 2006).

The present concern is specifically about inequality, and I cannot do any better than quoting the *Human Development Report*.

> In most societies women fare less well than men. As children they have less access to education and sometimes to food and health care. As adults they receive less education and training, work longer hours for lower incomes and have few property rights or none.[7]

The burden of my argument is that class and gender inequalities are world phenomena, affecting all societies, including India. Therefore, we need to look elsewhere to understand the specificity of the sources of group inequality in India. Herein lies the critical importance of conceptualizing India as a national state as against the proclivity of defining India as a nation state. A national state consists of several states renouncing 'nations' which opted to coexist in one sovereign state, although each of these nations may have their own provincial states.[8] Derivatively, the Indian society is a heterogeneous 'society' consisting of numerous cultural and a few racial groups. Indian population is drawn from all the three giant races—Caucasian, Mongoloid and Negroid—but there is no pronounced economic inequality between them, although discrimination of the people of Northeast India having specific phenotypical features manifests in 'social' inequality, which has surfaced in urban India.

However, heterogeneity of the Indian society is mainly anchored to culture—religion and language. A total of 82 per cent of Indians are enumerated as Hindus; the remaining 18 per cent make a staggering count, nearly 200 million, larger than the total population of most countries in the world. And inequality between religious communities of India is mainly social, although religious communities such as Jains and Sikhs are economically ahead of other religious communities. Inequality of religious communities is not based on the majority

---

[7] United Nations Development Programme, *Human Development Report 1994* (New Delhi: Oxford University Press, 1994), 3.

[8] T. K. Oommen, 'New Nationalism and Collective Rights: The Case of South-Asia', in *Ethnicity, Nationalism and Minority Rights*, eds. Stephen May, Tariq Madood, and Judith Squires (Cambridge: Cambridge University Press, 2004), 121–143.

(Hindus)–minority dichotomy but anchored to the sources of their origin and the perceived threat they pose to the Hindu *samaj* (society). Thus, the religious minorities of Indian origin such as Sikhs, Buddhists and Jains are treated as part of the Hindu samaj[9] not only by the organized section of the Hindu civil society, the Rashtriya Swayamsevak Sangh (RSS), but also by the Indian State as evident from their inclusion in the Hindu Code Bill as well as in the policy of reservation. The religious minorities who came to India to escape persecution in their homelands–Jews, Zoroastrians and Baha'is—are tiny groups and are not objects of unequal treatment in the society. But the Indian State has recognized only Zoroastrians, known as Parsis, as a minority, denying the other two groups of their entitlements.

The largest two religious minority groups—Muslims and Christians—are objects of social discrimination and inequality in a variety of contexts, rendering the Indian society 'plural' in the sense in which Furnivall[10] had invoked the term. In a plural society, the inhabitants are privileging the former and marginalizing the latter. Thus, the Hindutva ideologue Golwalkar wanted to treat 'Muslims and others (read Christians), if not actually anti-national at least outside the body of the nation'.[11] This formulation is at least partly endorsed by the state legal system in India as noted above. Indeed, this amounts to differential and unequal treatment to religious minorities of Indian and non-Indian origin.

While almost all countries in the world endorse one language as their national/official language, given India's linguistic diversity, 22 languages are recognized as official from among numerous mother tongues spoken in India. And yet Article 353 of the Indian Constitution privileges Hindi 'as a medium of expression for all the elements of the composite culture of India', thereby making Hindi virtually the national language. This is in contrast to the position taken by the Official Language Commission (1956), which wrote: 'The variety of

---

[9] V. D. Savarkar, *Hindutva* (New Delhi: Bharat Sahitya Prakashan, 1949).

[10] J. S. Furnivall, *Colonial Policy and Practice: A Comparative Study of Burma and Netherlands India* (Cambridge: Cambridge University Press, 1948).

[11] M. S. Golwarkar, *We or Our Nationhood Defined* (Nagpur: Bharat Prakash, 1939), 56.

India linguistic media is not a national Skelton to be ashamed of and to be sometimes hidden away.' Instead of following this sane advice, the Indian State and Hindu samaj seem to be following a policy of culturocide, that is, systematic destruction of small and weak cultural communities. This is particularly the true of Adivasis.[12] The point I want to underline here is that given the stupendous cultural heterogeneity of India based on religion and language, the policy of the Indian State and proclivity of the majority groups—Aryan Hindus and Hindi speakers—are transforming India into a plural society, juxtaposing not only religious communities but also linguistic groups.

Just like Muslims and Christians are conceived and treated as cultural outsiders for the whole of India, particular linguistic groups are treated as outsiders within provincial states. The emergence of 'senas' (army) and the phenomenon which privileges the 'sons of the soil' attest to this. Inequality which manifests in these contexts is anchored to groups and not to individual citizens.

If plurality produces unequal groups based on the insider–outsider dichotomy, inequality is institutionalized through hierarchy among those who are accepted as insiders. The three sources of inequality, namely stratification, heterogeneity and plurality, are found in other societies in different combinations and intensity hierarchy is the distinctive feature of South Asia, particularly India and Nepal, thanks to the hegemony of Hinduism in these two societies. The present concern is with India and I shall confine my analysis to the Indian situation.

In the case of a nation state, the co-terminality between polity and society is assumed, even if not a fact. But the Hindu understanding of the state–society relationship, wherein the samaj has precedence over the state, is crucial. The core of the Hindu samaj is dominated by high-caste male, occasional concessions are made to high-caste female and lip service for the incorporation of low castes, notwithstanding. In the current Indian context, the tension between the party in power and the organized part of the Hindu civil society, that is, RSS and its affiliate, points to the struggle for hegemony.

---

[12] T. K. Oommen 'Insiders and Outsiders in India: Primordial Collectivism and Cultural Pluralism in Nation-Building', *International Sociology* I, no. I (1986): 53–74.

But this struggle existed since the formation of the Indian Republic as evidenced by the expansionist view of Hinduism incorporating not only Buddhists, Jains and Sikhs but also the Adivasis if they do not explicitly claim their affiliation with one of the alien or non-Indic religions. Thus, viewed 'home coming' was initiated by the Indian State in 1951 through an administrative fiat, implemented by the Indian Census authorities. This expansive understanding of Hinduism undermined the cultural identity of religious minorities of Indian origin. On the other hand, the non-Indic religious minorities are denied equality not only by the Hindu samaj but also by the Indian State, by characterizing them as cultural outsiders.

The intersectionality between plurality and hierarchy is particularly excruciating for those who are placed at the lowest ladder of caste hierarchy because if and when they exercise the constitutionally guaranteed freedom of conscience and convert to Islam or Christianity, they retain the traditional disadvantages but lose special protections available to fellow citizens of the same social background. Media frequently reports the obstacles that Dalits and Muslims encounter in hiring houses even in metropolitan cities, admission to cooperative housing societies and the like. The obstacles they encounter in following their preferred dietary practices or dress codes are too well known. But the point to be underlined is that these are not inequalities based on their location in class structure but religious and caste contexts, that is, social inequality.

The state–society disjunction gives birth to legal pluralism. In a nation state, the state legal system (SLS) prevails, but in a national state like India, there are at least two other legal systems—religious legal system (RLS) and folk legal system (FLS; caste and tribal). While SLS is endorsed with state legitimacy, both RLS and FLS lack legitimacy. And the tendency is either to create a homogenous civil legal system (e.g., uniform civil code) or to establish hegemony of the legal system of the majority- (e.g., Hindu Code Bill). Both these adversely impact the texture of cultural pluralism. The way out is to scissor away the undemocratic elements in RLS and FLS so that the principles of equality and justice are firmly entrenched in the society. As of now, the effort is to establish the hegemony of a majoritarian legal system entrenched in caste—Hindu norms denying equality to religious minorities perceived as cultural outsiders, to those caste blocks occupying the lower levels of caste hierarchy as well as to Adivasis. Sociologists and social anthropologists have provided legitimacy to these state measures by justifying processes such as Sanskritization[13] and Hindu mode of absorbing the Adivasis.[14]

The consequences of the above-noted legal infirmities differentially impinge on both religious minorities and Scheduled Castes (SCs) and Scheduled Tribes (STs), favouring or denying them legal equality. Thus, while the policy of reservation was applicable to both SCs and STs right from the beginning, the change in religious identity adversely affects only the SCs. All STs irrespective of their religious faiths are entitled to have all benefits of reservation. Second, the SCs of Hindu, Buddhist and Sikh religions are entitled to all benefits of reservation, but the SC converts to Islam and Christianity are denied most of the benefits. In fact, they instantly become OBCs in the reckoning of State and get only limited benefits as those of Hindu OBCs. Third, the constitutional right to freely profess, practise and propagate one's religion vide Article 25 (1) is largely denied to religions of alien origin but endorsed in the case of religions of Indian origin, because all of them are conceptualized as Hindus by both the Hindu Code Bill and RSS ideologues. It is thus clear that the source of group inequality is deeply entrenched in the Indian society and transcends the class structure.

## DIMENSIONS OF CITIZENSHIP AND STRUCTURE OF SOCIETIES

It is time that I situate India in the wider context of discourse on citizenship and equality. The idea of equality was/is ineluctably linked with the notion of citizenship rights and civil rights consisting of liberty of person, freedom of speech, thought and faith, right to own property, right to conclude valid contracts and right to justice was the first to emerge. Political rights are mainly the right of franchise and the right to public office. Economic rights consist of the rights

---

[13] M. N. Srinivas, *Caste in Modern India and Other Essays* (London: Asia Publishing House, 1962).

[14] N. K. Bose, *Culture and Society in India* (Bombay: Asia Publishing House, 1967).

to a modicum of economic welfare and social security, to a full share of social heritage and to live a decent life according to the standards prevailing in the society.

Civil and political rights are individual rights and were known as 'public liberties' in France and 'rights of defence' in Germany, and there was universal endorsement of these rights. But economic rights are entitlement for the economically disadvantaged, say those who are below the poverty line and hence group rights. These rights are often viewed as charity availed of by the lazy and the undermotivated, the free riders. In this rendition, poverty is perceived as the function of individual attributes and not structural deficiencies and hence the objection to economic rights by some. There is, however, a deeper reason why the civil and political rights are universally endorsed and economic rights are suspects in the contemporary capitalist democracies. Economic rights are perceived as eroding the state exchequer, but civil and political rights are defined as cost free. This is indeed a flawed argument because the state has to make enormous institutional investments for facilitating the practice of civil and political rights, to illustrate, the installation of institutions of judiciary and the Election Commission, prerequisites for the practice of civil and political rights, and huge cost of the state exchequer.[15]

The structural distinction between individual and collective rights is that in the case of the former, the state has to pursue a policy of non-intervention, whereas in the case of the latter, the state has to intervene consciously and decisively. The state is not expected to intervene in the freedom of press, religious freedom, the right to peaceful assembly or even to interfere in the process of production and exchange of goods and services in a capitalist democratic society. In contrast, the state has to identify, based on prescribed criteria, those who are entitled for economic rights and provide them with the required assistance. Therefore, the real distinction between individually anchored civil and political rights on the one hand and collectivity-oriented economics rights on

---

[15] S. Holmes and C. S. Sunstein, *The Cost of Rights: Why Liberty Depends on Taxes* (New York, NY: W. W. Norton, 2000).

the other is non-intervention in the first set and intervention in the second set of rights by the state.

Economic entitlement of citizens is relevant to all those who have incomes below a certain level, irrespective of gender, race and caste. However, for those who are subjected to discrimination because of their social birth marks as in the case of ex-untouchables in India, economic entitlement may be necessary but not sufficient. That is why we need to make special provisions for them so that citizenship is rendered meaningful in their cases. This calls for the recognition of a new type of rights—the social rights. At the time of Marshall's conceptualization in 1965, the nation state was the central institution and citizenship was the dominant identity in West Europe.[16] Further, nation states incessantly pursued the idea of cultural homogenization; creating co-terminality between political and cultural boundaries was an important quest of nation states. However, this was only true of capitalist democracies; socialist one-party systems consciously attempted to create multinational polities. If nation states endeavoured to fuse citizenship and nationality, multinational states recognized the conceptual distinction between citizenship and nationality; the former referring to the political and economic dimensions and the latter to the social and cultural dimensions.

New empirical reality emerged with colonialism. The New World consisted of a collage of cultural communities drawn from different parts of the world coexisting under one polity creating hybrid identities (e.g., Asian American, Irish American, British Canadian and French Canadian), which gave birth to the idea of multicultural citizenship.[17] In contrast, post-colonial states of Africa and Asia consisted of several national and ethnic groups. And yet not only that most of these states did not explicitly endorse the notion of multinational state but also vigorously pursued the goal of building 'nation states'. But given their social milieu, cultural rights of many groups and communities had to be

---

[16] T. H. Marshall, *Class, Citizenship and Social Development* (New York, NY: Anchor Books, 1965).

[17] W. Kymlicka, *Multicultural Citizenship: A Liberal Theory of Minority Rights* (Oxford: Clarendon Press, 1995).

recognized. The idea of a nation state is ill-suited in their cases, and the notion of national state seems to be the correct appellation as I noted at the outset. The distinction between the two is crucial in that while national states endorse, recognize and celebrate cultural diversity, nation states are committed to create culturally homogenous polities[18,19]; given the denouement of national states, they have to provide for cultural equality to their citizens.

It is necessary to take cognizance of the need for instituting social rights in multiracial and hierarchical societies. Those who are subjected to social discrimination may also be economically deprived but the two need not operate in conjunction. For example, the Black bourgeoisie in the USA are racially discriminated, and the elite among the SCs in India are socially discriminated. Therefore, to ensure social rights to those who belong to such categories as Blacks in the USA and SCs in India (and women in all countries), the states need to create appropriate laws and implement them effectively. Let me illustrate this with special reference to India.[20]

The practice of untouchability was an abominable aspect of India's traditional society. The Indian Constitution, promulgated in 1950, had forbidden the practice of untouchability, and its practice in any form was made punishable. Additionally, a country-wide legislation—the Untouchability (Offences) Act—was passed in 1955 to provide access to SCs to all public places, including places of worship and public utilities. To augment the scope of this Act, the Protection of Civil Rights Act, 1976, was passed. As the socio-economic conditions of a section of the SCs improved, they gained courage to protest against their erstwhile masters. In turn, this resulted in those above the ritual pollution line unleashing atrocities against the SCs. To meet this development, the Scheduled Castes and Scheduled Tribes (Prevention of Atrocities) Act, 1989, was passed. All these Acts specifically address the social inequalities of SCs, which are quite distinct from their economic deprivations. The need to distinguish social rights

---

[18] Oommen, *Understanding Security*; Tilly 1990.

[19] Charles Tilly, *Coercion, Capital and European States A.D. 990–1900* (Cambridge: Basil Blackwell, 1990).

[20] T. K. Oommen, *Crisis and Contention in Indian Society* (New Delhi: SAGE Publications, 2005).

from economic rights is thus clearly evident. It may also be noted that the content of social discrimination (who are discriminated and in which context) varies between societies.

The above discussion was intended to provide the rationale which informs the conceptual expansion of the notion of citizenship, encapsulating civil, political, economic, social and cultural rights. While civil and political rights are about individual equality, economic rights are about creating conditions of equality for the economically under privileged. As against this, social and cultural rights are concerned about identities in addition to inter-group equality. These distinctions are vital for an adequate understanding of the relationship between citizenship and equality in a national state.

What are the implications of the five citizenship rights to create equality and negotiate cultural boundaries? Civil rights are essentially property rights and hence the non-propertied are outside the pale of this set of rights. However, discrimination even among the propertied in terms of inheritance laws, be it primogeniture which privileges the eldest male or which discriminates against women, either completely disinheriting them or denying equal share in the property, is being interrogated and gradually done away with. But capitalist democracies are committed as they are to the protection of individual property ownership; civil rights are not an instrument of equality for them. In contrast, socialist one-party systems through socialization of ownership in productive resources created equality in the civil context between the citizens, although this could not be sustained for long. While several post-colonial states also attempted regulation of private property rights, they too did not succeed. The contemporary societies are a spectacle of deepening economic disparities not only between them but also within them. Thus viewed, civil rights remain an instrument of protecting property rights and hence perpetuating inequality between classes.

It should be noted here that even in capitalist democracies, the perceptions regarding the content of citizenship vary immensely. As Fraser and Gorden note,[21] Americans rarely speak of economic citizenship

---

[21] N. Fraser and L. Gorden, 'Civil Citizenship against Social Citizenship? On the Ideology of Contract versus Charity', in *The Condition of Citizenship*, ed. Bart van Steenburgen (London: SAGE Publications, 1994), 90–107.

(the authors following Marshall's terminology refer to social citizenship) because it implies rights and entitlements embedded in a contract and not charity wrapped up in institutional welfare benefits. Welfare is stigmatized, but work is sacralized. Unemployment is viewed as a private predilection and not as a manifestation of social policy or economic pathology. In contrast, civil citizenship is highly valued. The hero of the civil society, created by civil rights, is the property-owning individual; the civil society is exemplified by 'possessive individualism'. In fact, as the civil society is possessed by individualism, it is very difficult to liberate the body (civil society) of the spirit (individualism).

The robbing of economic citizenship of its contractual character and viewing it as an instrument of charity has several consequences. First, the beneficiary becomes a mere recipient of charity with no entitlements, as a situation that is morally degrading. Second, the giver of charity assumes instant superiority and accumulates moral merit, the concern being the giver's entry into the other world and not the receiver's physical survival in this world. Third, since the giver and receiver are strangers, the recipient cannot demand charity but can only solicit it; and 'the cultural mythology of civil citizenship stands in a tense, often obstructing relationship to social (read economic) citizenship'. This is nowhere more true than in the USA, where the dominant understanding of civil citizenship remains strongly infected by the notions of 'contract' and 'independence' while economic provision has been constructed to connote 'charity' and 'dependence'.[22]

The consequence of this juxtaposition of economic and civil citizenship in terms of charity and contract is manifested in the widespread belief in the USA that the opportunity for economic betterment is widely available, social mobility is determined by the individual's efforts and therefore economic inequality is fair.[23] Further, the feeling that the recipients of a welfare exaggerate their needs, cheat the state and avoid work is widespread. That is, Americans are far more concerned about the duties or social obligations of the poor, particularly those

---

[22] Ibid.

[23] J. R. Klugel and E. R. Smith, *Belief about Inequality: America's View of What Is and What Ought To Be* (New York, NY: Aldine de Gruyter, 1986).

who receive welfare support, than about their rights: 'It is the moral fabric of individuals, not the social and economic structure of society that is taken to be the root of the problem.'[24]

Citizenship rights are moulded is the internal social milieu of societies. I distinguished between four broad types of societies: homogeneous, heterogeneous, hierarchical and plural.[25] Even homogenous societies are stratified along gender, age, class and kinship lines. But if a society's population is drawn from the same race, religion and language, it may be viewed as a homogeneous society. Citizenship was not a universally bestowed status in the beginning even in those societies, being the privilege only of the propertied male as noted above. However, one of the features of democratic societies, if they are homogeneous, is the possibility of universal citizenship. This is not to deny the fact that even in such societies, the poor, women and youth are not always fully fledged citizens.

But the situation changes drastically when one considers the case of heterogeneous societies, that is, multiracial, multireligious, multinational and poly-ethnic societies. In heterogeneous societies, there is a greater possibility of inter-group inequality emerging and persisting. Nevertheless, it is conceivable and possible that communities and groups that are equal may constitute a heterogeneous society. But in hierarchical societies, group-based inequalities are institutionalized. This was the case in the entire New World in the beginning in which the First Nations were marginalized and the Blacks were brought in as slaves. The worst case of institutionalized inequality prevailed in apartheid South Africa, where the settlers did not even constitute a majority. As for Asia, the worst case of institutionalized inequality was that of the caste system in South Asia. These societies were hierarchical in that lowly placed castes could not cross the social boundaries. But today in all these societies, the erstwhile underprivileged are granted a formal citizenship status irrespective of their social background.

---

[24] W. J. Wilson, 'Citizenship and the Inner-city Ghetto Poor, in *The Condition of Citizenship*, ed. Bart van Steenburgen (London: SAGE Publications, 1994).

[25] T. K. Oommen, *Pluralism, Equality and Identity: Comparative Studies* (Delhi: Oxford University Press, 2002).

It is equally important to remember here that in spite of the depressed status of the erstwhile, Indian 'untouchables', these groups were not considered as outsiders to the polity. This may partly be due to the fact that they were viewed as indispensable for maintaining the position of the privileged. To the extent that the internality of a category to the society was not questioned, the possibility of that category achieving full citizenship status was greater as democratic values spread. To put it differently, the prospect of citizenization of the poor, or the 'untouchables', is greater as they are considered as insiders, that is, nationals. On the other hand, if some groups are perceived as outsiders, the prospect of their becoming citizens is extremely limited.

This brings me to the fundamental feature of a plural society. A plural society is stratified like a homogeneous society; it is characterized by diversity like heterogeneous societies, but it may or may not be hierarchical in that inequality need not be institutionalized in them. But one or more segments of the population in plural societies are not even considered as members of that society, and such segments are treated as outsiders, which are often immigrants, but some of those who are native to the land are subjected to a process of externalization, for example, some of the religious communities, particularly Muslims and Christians in India. In so far as the notion of citizenship is linked to nationality and/or religion, there is limited possibility of these social segments securing equality.

There are two ways of getting out of this impasse. First, nationalization of outsiders: The prospect of this is bleak, partly because the insiders invariably do not welcome it and partly because outsiders do not always want it, as it results in the eclipse of their identity. Second, citizenization of outsiders: This means conferring the citizenship status on them without insisting that they should abandon their cultural identity. This allows for retention of their cultural identity and availing of citizenship entitlements, a distinctive feature of national states.

The foregoing discussion prompts me to conclude that as the complexity of a society increases, the dimension of its citizenship also increases. A stratified society needs to provide for only civil, political and economic citizenship. But heterogeneous and plural societies should also ensure cultural rights. Societies characterized by stratification, heterogeneity, hierarchy and plurality should provide for all the five citizenship rights—civil, political, economic, social and cultural. This is the road to create an egalitarian society.

## ONTOLOGICAL EQUALITY AND CONDITIONS OF EQUALITY

In this section, I want to explore the relationship between citizenship rights and equality. Social classes are unequal entities, but citizenship entitlements are expected to moderate the inequality between them. To realize this, citizens of democratic polities are promised equality by the state, irrespective of their personal attributes—gender, race, class, cultural identity, social standing and national/ethnic background. Constitutions of democratic polities often provide for this ontological equality, but most of them may not strictly adhere to the promise. Once the promise exists, it has to be translated into practice through equality of opportunity.

Equality of opportunity can attend to most of the issues in homogeneous societies, although discrimination based on gender persists in most societies in some of the contexts. For example, women do not enjoy equality in the religious contexts to this day even in the most advanced/modernized societies; they are invariably denied entry into the religious hierarchy.

Equality of opportunity cannot be easily availed of by the underprivileged even when they are materially well off. But the underprivileged are usually cumulatively dominated, that is, in terms of class, power and status. Therefore, it is absolutely necessary to create equality of conditions so that equality of opportunity is made meaningful. This is the rationale behind the policy of protective discrimination in caste-based hierarchical societies such as India. The point of theoretical interest here is that one cannot mechanically apply the concept of citizenship, if it is to be an instrument of equality, to all societies ignoring their internal social milieu and the nature of their social structures.

It is also necessary to provide a few clarifications here regarding the structure of rights. Civil and political rights are widely perceived as basic rights and are believed to be of universal applicability. With the introduction of universal adult franchise, political rights are increasingly becoming so in this limited context. But in most other contexts, political rights are yet to be universalized. Civil rights are shells without substance to the propertyless in all societies. Herein lies the relevance of the prophetic words of Dr B. R. Ambedkar, who drafted the Constitution of India. He observed: 'On 26 January 1950 (the day India became a Republic) we entered a life of contradictions. In politics we will have equality and in social and economic life we will have inequality (1994).'[26] And inequality in the social context persists in India to this day, although one cannot deny considerable improvements. As for economic inequality, it is steadily on the increase in spite of better opportunities.

Economic rights take the form of entitlements for the destitute, the underclass, those who are below the poverty line and/or those who face periodic economic stress due to disasters. Thus, the citizens are to be differentially treated in providing economic rights which are resented by some and hence these rights are not universally endorsed. In this view, individual attributes—laziness, inadequate motivation and refusal to work—are responsible for their predicament. In contrast, those who support economic rights argue that these rights are justifiable because the victims are products of structural deficiencies. Which is to say, ideological orientations determine the legitimacy/illegitimacy of economic rights.

Just like economic rights are applicable only to some sections of citizens, social rights are also relevant only for certain sections. But the criterion differs; in the case of economic rights, it is the level of income or class, and in the case of social rights, it is social disabilities. These disabilities exist for women in most societies, non-Whites in multiracial societies, tribes where they are minorities and lower castes wherever caste system exists. While low social status can, and often does, adversely impinge on income levels, there is no isomorphism between the two. Better economic condition in itself and by itself

---

[26] B. R. Ambedkar, *Dr. Babasaheb Ambedkar Writings and Speeches*, vol. 13 (Mumbai: Government of Maharashtra, 1994).

cannot cope with social stigmatization. If women are not allowed to become priests, if Blacks and tribes do not have parity in wages (in spite of parity in education and competence), if lower castes are denied temple entry and/or compelled to pursue certain occupations, we need to institute relevant social rights to make them fully fledged citizens.

Cultural homogenization designed by nation states cannot be pursued in multinational states and multicultural polities due to the turbulence of migration caused by globalization. Contemporary states have national and/or ethnic minorities; while the former are territorially anchored cultural communities, the latter are spatially dispersed cultural groups. And both demand the preservation of their cultural identities within the polity, along with equality. This calls for the recognition of cultural rights as a specific type of rights.

To ensure economic, social and cultural rights, the state needs to act positively and intervene consciously. But the nature of intervention differs in each of these cases. In the case of economic rights such as rights to shelter, health, education and the like, the state should create an adequate database in relation to the economic condition and income levels of the citizens so that the criteria of eligibility can be clearly laid down and implemented.

Finally, despite the increasing cultural complexity within national states, the tendency to pursue cultural majoritarianism persists. The identity of the cultural mainstream is often reckoned as a national identity, the manifestation of which is often found in recognizing a single official/national religion and/or language. This creates instant cultural deprivation for the religious and linguistic minorities. The contemporary democratic state has the responsibility to make decisive intervention to protect the cultural rights of all its citizens—majorities and minorities.

The obsolescent notion of unicultural nation states has passed into history, and the contemporary idea of multicultural national states has arrived, alive and kicking. This calls for the explicit recognition of cultural rights as a specific category of rights. However, a familiar objection to conceding cultural rights is that it endangers constitutional patriotism, which provides the required glue to multinational and multicultural societies to hold together. But this is a flawed argument because constitutional patriotism manifests in the context of individual rights. In contrast, cultural rights provide for 'the protection of forms of life and tradition in which identities are formed...'[27]; they are collective rights. Constitutional patriotism and cultural rights are structurally different and cannot be anchored to the same principle.

I want to conclude this chapter by noting that it is necessary to constantly recast concepts and theories for two reasons: (a) to cope with the unfolding empirical realities and (b) to address the shift in value orientations. In the course of my analysis, a third point emerged, namely the need to incorporate those societies which were outside the cognitive gaze of analytical framework developed by Western scholars so as to augment the theoretical power of our argument. I have attempted such an exercise with special reference to India, even if inadequately.

---

[27] Jürgen Habermas, 'Citizenship and National Identity: Some Reflections on the Future of Europe', *Praxis International* 12, (1992): 1–19.

# Section A

# Social Hegemony and the Market

# Chapter 2

# Interrogating Dalit Capitalism in the Neoliberal Era
Illusion or Reality

Amiya Kumar Das

## INTRODUCTION

The ushering of the new economic reforms of the 1990s which strived to pull the economy to new heights instilled enormous optimism among its citizens. It implied rolling back of the state and free play of market forces—demand and supply. These new economic reforms supposedly gave transcendence to free market competition and were perceived to thwart social identities that emanated from inequalities and injustice, thus eradicating poverty and marginalization and catalysing upward mobility. These neoliberal policies had implications across different social categories, namely caste, class, ethnicity, religion, region, gender and so on.

In this backdrop, the relationship between caste and the neoliberal policies and its repercussions on the emancipatory Dalit politics need to be analysed critically. In the Indian context, some scholars writing on the relationship between caste and market economy agree with the overall underpinnings of neoclassical and new institutional economics;

that is, markets have the capacity to marginalize the influence of social identities in shaping market outcomes. Markets have also acquired prominence because political democracy (equality through a constitutional guarantee based on the liberal principle of citizenship—one person one vote, irrespective of social location) has not met the hopes for economic prosperity.[1] Thus, this chapter tries to understand Dalit capitalism (DC), its dynamics as well its tendency towards its emancipatory politics and navigates towards the internal exploitation and marginalization of Dalits themselves.

## BLACK CAPITALISM AS A PRECURSOR TO DC

In the Marxian sense, usually capitalism is defined as a system where the production and exchange of commodity occur for profit through private ownership. Generally, the profit in the capitalist system is extracted from the surplus value of the working class labour through an exploitive social relationship.

The idea of DC is drawn from Black capitalism originated in the USA. The debate and contestation between Booker T. Washington and W. E. B. Du Bois are well known. Selfa links Black capitalism to Washington's philosophy of 'self-help'. Washington argued for building a capitalist system by ignoring political action. This position of Washington was strongly opposed by Du Bois in his work *The Souls of Black Folk* (1903). Du Bois attacked Washington by pointing out that Blacks' lives were not improving; rather, it was getting disenfranchised. Du Bois argued for full civil and political rights for Blacks and articulated that 'self-help' and 'Black capitalism' represent a way to accommodate to a system that is itself the cause of Black oppression. Black emancipation will only occur when capitalism will be overthrown.[2] Although Du Bois was influenced by Marx, it

---

[1] Aseem Prakash, 'Caste and Capitalism', *Seminar*, no. 633 (May 2012).
[2] Lance Selfa, 'Booker T. Washington and Black Capitalism' (2012). Available at: https://socialistworker.org/2012/05/11/booker-washington-and-black-capitalism (accessed on 24 April 2020).

is interesting to note that unlike Marx, Du Bois made both race and the state constitutive of capitalism.[3]

## CONTENTION FOR DC

When one hears about the term 'Dalit capitalism', one question may come to the mind immediately: How are two non-compatible paradigms such as Dalit and capitalism combined together? The idea of Dalit originated from the oppressive caste system in the Indian context; on the other hand, capitalism was originated in the Western context. One is social and cultural but has economic repercussions and the other is economic but has social and cultural dimensions. The relationship between caste and economy has been analysed from various perspectives in the domain of social sciences. Of late, the idea of DC has become the focus of discussion in the public domain with the establishment of the Dalit Indian Chamber of Commerce and Industry (DICCI) in 2005 by Milind Kamble. The chamber envisions 'developing business leadership' with a mission 'Be job givers, not job seekers'. It aims to 'fight caste with capital'. Here begins the contention. Pro-DC ideologies argue that casteism can be abolished through capitalism and the market, whereas critics argue that capitalism would reinforce the caste system and re-marginalize and deprive Dalits more than ever.

DICCI think tanks argue that fierce competition created by reforms in 1991 paved the way for competitive markets which are dependent on cheapest supplies of labour and materials irrespective of caste. Milind Kamble and Chandra Bhan Prasad, who are the great proponents of DC, argue that the market opened up new spaces of competition for Dalits. For them, Adam Smith is the enemy of Manu and capitalism as a revolutionary force, which will smash casteism. They feel that money has become bigger than caste, and capitalism is changing caste system much faster than any other human intervention. The caste

---

[3] J. Phillip Thompson, 'Taking Freedom: Capitalism, Democracy, and W.E.B. Du Bois' Two Proletariats' (2018). Available at: https://psmag.com/social-justice/taking-freedom-capitalism-democracy-and-du-bois (accessed on 29 April 2020).

system in India categorically excluded Dalits from accumulation of wealth. However, the free market economy will provide Dalits with an opportunity to fiercely assert for their share of wealth. Therefore, Dalits should look up to capitalism as a crusader against caste. Kamble interprets Ambedkar, who saw capitalism's potential in breaking caste shackles but could not practise it himself.

At this juncture of this debate, it is equally important to mention Ambedkar's idea on caste and class and Marx's position on class at the background. For Marx, labour was a 'living class' fighting for their indifferent history and political subjectivity through politics, while for Ambedkar, Dalits were an enclosed class. Ambedkar engaged with labour universalism in his famous essay in the *Indian Antiquary* (1917), 'Castes in India: Their Mechanism, Genesis, and Development', where he described caste as an 'enclosed class'. Moreover, this Dalit labour cannot be a class 'in' itself and 'for' itself because of the intrinsic idea of stigma attached to this form of labour, which is hence an impediment for labour universalization and an antagonistic force to the capitalist force.[4] On the other hand, Ashwini Deshpande and Smriti Sharma argue that entrepreneurship as a tool for social mobility for Dalits is far from the reality. Certain traditional business castes and communities have better networks than Dalits to have a flourishing business in the so-called free market. They put forward through their study that even in the era of market-led growth and development, caste continues to virtually shape all aspects of production.[5] In the similar line, Munshi[6] affirms that community and kinship networks have always played a very crucial role in the businesses. In order to succeed, a Dalit entrepreneur not only has to be a good businessman but invariably also a social and political entrepreneur, which becomes a double challenge. DICCI has

---

[4] Anupama Rao, 'Stigma and Labour: Remembering Dalit Marxism', *Seminar*, no. 633 (May 2012).

[5] A. Deshpande and S. Sharma, 'Entrepreneurship or Survival? Caste and Gender of Small Business in India', *Economic & Political Weekly* 48, no. 28 (2013): 38–49.

[6] Kaivan Munshi, 'The Birth of a Business Community: Tracing Occupational Migration in a Developing Economy' (2007). Available at: www.econ.brown.edu/fac/Kaivan_Munshi/diamond10.pdf (accessed on 25 July 2016).

been criticized for providing a space in the capitalist system which is based on exploitation of economically underprivileged sections of the society, including Dalits. Anand Teltumbde[7] articulates that the ideas of DC and globalization strengthen the present exploitative order which sucks the underprivileged and marginalized. Arguing for DC means giving direct consent to the neoliberal policies and supporting the state-initiated move towards privatization.

Both the campaigns and criticisms seem to suggest that the emergence of DC needs to be examined from the standpoint of political economy as well as the principle of social justice governing anti-caste movements. DC is not a redefinition of capitalism to ensure the principles of liberty, equality and fraternity which Ambedkar argued that the Indian society needs to be more democratic. The foundation of DICCI lays in the argument that capital, in the form of asset or labour, has been monopolized within a few castes. Without the emergence of entrepreneurs and market players among Dalits, this crucial public place, composition of which is not mandated by the state, will not be represented. DICCI has in principle saddled itself into that transformative role of establishing Dalit participation over yet another public space. More importantly so when political democracy is so invested in caste. Beyond this, the role of capitalism—with or without Dalit capitalists—in countering caste needs to be objectively understood. Advocates of market and recent sociological studies of caste suggest that market forces have greatly weakened the caste structure, and caste has transmuted into something more secular to allow modern practices. Does DICCI envisage influencing such problems beyond the neoliberal arguments of job and wealth creation is an important question to consider?

Thus, the chapter seeks to understand DC, the relationship between caste and neoliberal market policies and what it entails for Dalit emancipatory politics. It would analyse the claims how money is dismantling casteism while examining critics' notion of stark oppressions perpetrated by DC. A good democracy needs representations of all communities in

---

[7] Anand Teltumbde, 'Dalit Capitalism and Pseudo Dalitism', *Economic & Political Weekly* 46, no. 10 (2011).

all the spheres including the market. It will be interesting to see how DC would deal with the internal contradictions of exploitation and marginalization among Dalits themselves.

## DALIT MOBILITY OR MARGINALIZATION

In the Indian context, it is worthwhile to understand the nature of caste if we need to have a brief understanding of Dalits as entrepreneurs or labours in a neoliberal regime. Balmurli Natrajan reviews literatures on caste-based division and mentions that the 'caste system' has been based on a tripartite foundation of hereditary occupational specialization, ritualized hierarchy and mutual separation. All these divisions are further reinforced by, and kept in place by, political forces such as dominant caste groups, violence, patriarchy and state. In the sphere of social and cultural practices, the caste system is reinforced in the village. Natrajan demonstrates the paradoxical nature of the caste system; he argues that despite the relative decline of the caste system, the caste-based identities are invoked in public, and persist and flourish in the Indian society in both electoral politics and everyday life regarding access to land, credit, capital, employment, housing, knowledge, prestige and power.[8]

It is seen that prior to the neoliberal policies, especially from the 1980s, there was a certain shift in the economic situation of some of the Dalits. These came in the forms of improved pay, fair working conditions, migration from villages and moving out of agricultural/ bonded labour, which could be attributed to a changing economy. Economic growth also prompted the government to introduce a host of welfare measures for Dalits, for example, housing projects for the poor, sanitation, electrification, roads, community buildings, micro-credit schemes for women and state-supported projects for the construction of statues of Dalit icons. Education and affirmative action facilitated their access to government colleges and universities, and a section of minority Dalits also gained salaried state employment and henceforth a strong and influential middle class began to grow.[9]

---

[8] Balmurli Natrajan, 'From Jati to Samaj', *Seminar*, no. 633 (May 2012).
[9] Clarinda Still, *Dalits in Neo-Liberal India: Mobility or Marginalisation* (New Delhi: Routledge, 2014).

But this picture of gradual upliftment and upward mobility came under much debate and scrutiny. Commentators noticed that with the introduction of the neoliberal policies, the state had begun to roll back its welfare measures and it would be futile if they still continued to fight for a share of the state resources. This was a serious concern, and as the private sector grew, Dalits would not be in a position to obtain the lucrative opportunities of the growing economy because of lack of necessary capital (financial, educational, social and political) to survive in a free market economy. Moreover, the sordid argument that came forward was that due to the lack of affirmative action policies providing them equal opportunities, Dalits would be marginalized all over again.[10]

In that economic scenario, when capitalism was gaining momentum, it obviously implied opening up of new economic structures and opportunities that were previously denied to Dalits. Hence, there was an inclination towards grabbing the opportunity among them before it was seized by the dominant castes. This was also seen as liberation of Dalits from being mere labourers to being entrepreneurs and so much so as capitalists as well. This ongoing process of social change was widely discussed and analysed in academia, media and other knowledge production centres.[11]

The establishment of DICCI by Milind Kamble backed the above discourse on many fronts, including being job givers instead of job seekers and fighting 'caste' with capital. To a certain point, we can agree with this argument only to the extent of accepting that capital does not take into consideration any social identity, nor does it favour any particular community. But beyond that, it would undermine the very lack of the basic infrastructural capital of Dalits which is prerequisite to sustain in a free market economy. The following discussion tries to establish how lack of economic, political and social capital within the neoliberal regime has been marginalizing and preventing inclusion into the business economy of this particular section of people.

---

[10] Ibid., 11.

[11] Vishal Thakare, 'Dalit Capitalism: Is It the Way to Emancipation' (2016). Available at: https://roundtableindia.co.in/index.php?option=com_content&view=article&id=8519:dalit-capitalism-is-it-a-way-for-emancipation&catid=119:feature&Itemid=132 (accessed on 23 August 2020).

In this context, Thorat and Sadana[12] maintain that neoliberal India opened up avenues to be controlled and exploited, which was as a fact detached from the traditional caste occupational structure, which was possible through micro-entrepreneurship and ownership of small private enterprises. And keeping in mind the agenda of inclusive development, the government did extend policies to encourage Dalit ownership of private enterprises such as supply of capital to Dalits, preferential allocation of sites for business, training in entrepreneurship skill and incentives for market development. Shedding scepticism on this effort of the government, Vidyarthee[13] counters that in spite of government policies, there are certain local-level forces at work that categorically segregate Dalits entering the business economy, and these policies need to be re-examined and reformulated by understanding these phenomena in order to improve the economic incorporation of Dalits into the business economy. Despite the efforts made by the state to bring in inclusive development, as single economic growth alone was not feasible, it did receive a setback because of certain social dynamics. Some scholars argue that the upper castes do not allow Dalits to progress as they feel the reservation policies are already in action, ensuring their upliftment in terms of public sector jobs.

Sumeet Mhaskar sheds light on the economic engagement of various caste groups' ex-mill workers in Mumbai. His findings are rich in terms of reflecting the occupational options available to them. In terms of the caste-based occupations, Brahmins continue to do religious and preaching work. Lack of job security and hiring and firing jobs make these preachers much sought after among their clients. Sometimes even when individuals do not have the required skill to go for traditional caste occupation, caste networks help its people to set up related business. The Nhavi (barber) caste is also engaged in their traditional caste occupation and is in much demand. They have adapted accordingly to the taste of the 'middle class' and with sophisticated products, they have been providing services of high-end salons. However, it also depends

---

[12] S. Thorat and Nidhi Sadana, 'Caste and Ownership of Private Enterprises', *Economic & Political Weekly* 44, no. 23 (2009): 13–16.

[13] K. K. Vidyarthee, 'Trajectories of Dalits' Incorporation into the Indian Neoliberal Business Economy', in *Dalits in Neoliberal India: Mobility or Marginalisation?* ed. Clarinda Still (New Delhi: Routledge, 2014).

whether their traditional caste occupation is in demand or not. As for instance, the availability of plastic ropes and *chatais* (mats) has resulted in a decline of demand for rope and basket makers for the Mang Dalits, who have been historically doing so. In analysing non-caste occupations, one can see the relation between caste and occupations. Dalits are absent from occupations that require skilled labour like repairing stove, bicycles, bags, wielding, etc. While some businesses are open to them, small businesses continue to exclude them categorically. In an era of neoliberal regime, self-employment is encouraged and hence in this case falling back upon one's own traditional caste occupation is best if not the safest option. Interestingly, the service sector that requires continuous supply of labour force does not discriminate on the basis of caste. But again, these jobs include low wages, erratic and long working hours and lack of job security. Mhaskar concludes that small businesses rely on political patronage and caste-based networks, and the service sector economy has not led to the dissolution of the caste as a social institution and Dalits remain on the margins in terms of self-employed occupations.[14]

Dalit entrepreneurs invariably experienced an adverse reaction by the state officials whenever they tried to access the state's resources. In their view, state resources can only be accessed through social networks. They understand social networks as a critical social resource which could enable them to cultivate a relationship with state officials in order to get favourable treatment to enhance their business ventures.[15] This hints at the importance of social networks that are crucial in order to procure government resources, funding and business deals.

A positivist approach is taken by Aiyar[16]; he emphasizes that DICCI is consisting of more than 3,000 millionaire Dalit members. Among these, the richest is Rajesh Saraiya, who runs the Steel Mont Pvt. Ltd,

---

[14] Sumeet Mhaskar, 'Locating Caste in a Globalised India City: A Study of Dalit Ex-millworkers' Occupational Choices in Post-Industrial Mumbai', in *Dalits in Neoliberal India: Mobility or Marginalisation?* ed. Clarinda Still (New Delhi: Routledge, 2014), 123–129.

[15] Prakash, 'Caste and Capitalism'.

[16] Aiyar, S. A., 'Waiting for a Hundred Dalit Billionaires'. (2013). Available at: https://timesofindia.indiatimes.com/blogs/Swaminomics/waiting-for-a-hundred-dalit-billionaires/ (accessed on 20 April 2016).

based in Ukraine, and has business in eight countries. He has a turnover of more than ₹2,000 crore. He is considered as the first Dalit billionaire. Aiyar quotes Kamble, who opines that earlier business was dominated by few dominant castes which did not let others come in or compete. In the post-independence periods, the Licence/Permit Raj of Nehru and Indira Gandhi protected a few from competition.

As argued by the proponents of the free market, one wonders that if the market is a level playing field, then why could not Black capitalism flourish in the hub of world capitalism? African-Americans are more segregated and marginalized now than ever. 'If capitalism is so democratic and benign, why is it that it's biggest crisis since the Great Depression—the financial crisis in 2008—had a particularly devastating effect on the African-American population?'[17] Further, Mannathukaren presents the inherent contradiction and flaw of DC. He questions the objectives of DC by asking how it can find equal space for Dalits as capitalism itself is based on a highly exploitative system. It is a pity that those who had been exploited by the capitalists will now enter the same system to exploit their brethren.

Closer home, Milind Khandekar's *Dalit Millionaires*[18] is an inspiring book for the burgeoning Dalit entrepreneurs, which tells the success stories of 15 individuals who fought and overcame obstacles only to set up multi-crore business enterprises. These entrepreneurs are from every sector of the economy. Kalpana Saroj transformed Mumbai's Kamani Tubes Limited into a profit-making company. Ashok Khade, Hari Kishan Pippal, Devkinandan Son, Savitaben Parmar and Devjibhai Makwana's success stories debunk the theory of Dalits progressing with reservations and government support. But such stories, even if highly appreciated, do little to the emancipatory nature of Dalit politics as well as for the Dalit masses. In Khandekar's book, a basic question was put to these successful entrepreneurs: Was caste an impediment to their success? An affirmative answer was in

---

[17] Nissim Mannathukkaren, 'The Chimera of Dalit Capitalism' (2013). Available at: https://www.thehindu.com/opinion/op-ed/The-chimera-of-Dalit-capitalism/article12011003.ece (accessed on 20 April 2016).

[18] Milind Khandekar, *Dalit Millionaires* (New Delhi: Penguin, 2013).

common. Although they acknowledged that liberalization has opened up new avenues for them and that outsourcing and foreign investments have allowed them to break the shackles of their traditional caste occupations, a subtle discrimination was common to all, be it in terms of availing government loans or in terms of procuring raw materials from a higher caste.[19]

Prakash[20] proposes that India is changing its nature from a nation state into a market state. He articulates that the relationship of caste and capitalism does not take merit and efficiency into its account. He looks at the market in terms of social relationships, which are generally influenced by social customs, norms and age-old conventions. It may not operate in the realm of modern contracts, merit and efficiency. Through an empirical study of several successful Dalit entrepreneurs, he finds that there is still discrimination of Dalits in the market system, which is usually caused by social networks that are controlled by upper-caste business people. He further mentions that Dalits enter into the markets thinking that it will break the stigma of humiliation. Some of the major hurdles for Dalit business persons he enlists in findings are the unfavourable local state and market, which are embedded with social networks in terms of religion, region, caste and familial connections, etc.

Guru,[21] in his analysis of DC, brings in Debord's framework of the ideology of spectacle as false consciousness, which forges a fake association between a person or a social collectivity. He analyses Dalit efforts to move from the ordinary and explode into the extraordinary as millionaires from the concept of spectacular in the context of DC. He finds Guy Debord's theory of the spectacle a useful starting point for looking at DC as both deceived gaze and false consciousness. He writes, 'Debord's framework, the spectacle is an ideology, which, as false consciousness, necessarily forges a fake association between

---

[19] Swamy Kalva, 'Tracing Ambedkar in Dalit Capitalism', *Economic & Political Weekly* 51, no. 47 (2016).

[20] Prakash Aseem, 'Dalit Capital and Markets: A Case of Unfavourable Inclusion', *Journal of Social Inclusion Studies* 4, no. 1 (2018): 51–61.

[21] Gopal Guru, 'Rise of the "Dalit Millionaire": A Low Intensity Spectacle', *Economic & Political Weekly* 47, no. 50 (2012): 41–49.

a person or a social collectivity, and the spectacle'.[22] A similar social reality was perceived in a study by Surinder Jodhka[23] on the self-employed Dalits in the cities of Saharanpur and Panipat. In the study 'Dalits in Business', he tries to seek the ways in which the new Dalits in business negotiate in the urban labour market. The main reasons for Dalits to join business were that it is (a) a source of livelihood and (b) a source of dignity which helped them come out of their caste-based occupations. The most important source of economic support came from their family and extended kin. The two most crucial problems faced by them were primarily in procuring finance for their enterprise and secondly in finding a structure/shop to set up their venture. Here, caste played second fiddle for Dalits. Due to paucity of ideal locations for their business, they were forced to open kiosks in places that were not suitable for their ventures, which would often have a negative impact on their daily business. This discouragement sometimes resulted in setting up ventures like grocery shops in Dalit-dominated areas themselves. Jodhka's study reveals that there are still certain areas where Dalits find no problem in operating their business, for instance, the Chamars of Saharanpur and Karnal who are involved in leather business. Although a majority of their respondents have a non-Dalit clientele, not every client knew their caste identity. This brings us to one pertinent question: Does caste matter in business? The reply of the respondents was affirmative that caste played an important role in their everyday lives.

The biggest obstacle is the inclusion of Dalits into the business economy. The upper castes do not like Dalit players in their business and perceive them as 'odd players', as this sector has not been their social universe since ages. Moreover, the identification of their shops or enterprises in terms of their caste identity, and not in terms of the goods or the services they provide, also tends to have a negative impact on their business. This also adds to their humiliation and

---

[22] Ibid., 41.

[23] Surinder S. Jodhka, 'Dalits in Business: Self-employed Scheduled Castes in Northwest India' (working paper, vol. 4, no. 2, Indian Institute of Dalit Studies, New Delhi, 2010).

is a dent on their social status as well.²⁴ The method of negotiation of these respondents was interesting. Almost 94 per cent of these entrepreneurs claimed to have an association with Dalit mobilization in their region or country. Those who have had little success in their ventures have had an inclination towards electoral politics. Denied social and cultural space, electoral politics and reservation of quota seats for the Scheduled Castes (SCs) increased their probability of political success, which provided them a shield in an insecure environment and a boost to their business as well.²⁵

This subtle discrimination needs to be analysed with a broad spectacle. It seems to skew opportunities provided by the neoliberal regime and entrenches social discrimination. Social differentiation, which is derived from the notion of caste, needs to be questioned and analysed at all levels of knowledge-producing areas.

## CAPITALISM AND THE FUTURE OF DALITS

Thakare raises some pertinent questions: Does the rise of Dalit millionaires imply that they are economically better off and do not rely on the upper castes for employment? Does it mean that the entire community would benefit from this class of 'Dalit millionaires'? Does accumulation of wealth by Dalit capitalists ensure that they would be devoid of any stigma and discrimination? Or does it dilute the aggression of the emancipatory Dalit politics?²⁶

Chandra Bhan Prasad, chief mentor of DICCI, believed that the liberal markets can aid in breaking the traditional caste-bound occupations of Dalits and hence lead to their social and political emancipation. The proponents of this campaign reanalysed Ambedkar's emancipatory politics in relation to the contemporary changes in the market. Prasad also maintains that the reservation has given them a launch pad. Now it is their duty to take off from that launch pad. Thus, these views of such Dalit leaders hint at a new Dalit assertion, which is supportive

---

²⁴ Ibid., 14–19.
²⁵ Ibid., 22–23.
²⁶ Thakare, 'Dalit Capitalism', 1–2.

of the idea of neoliberal policies of liberalization and globalization being capable of bringing positive developments for their community.[27] Chandra Bhan Prasad opines that democracy is the only form of government that distributes capital among its citizens. Hence, democracy and capitalism are inseparable, as the ownership of corporations is mostly social and the poor can be a part of those corporations. According to Prasad, it was the rise of capitalism in democratic nations that led to the loosening of the concentration of wealth in the hands of a few. Capital does not take cognizance of social identities and hence has the inherent capability of overseeing social markers based on birth per se and only on sheer hard work. This characteristic was seen by these leaders having immense potential of destroying the caste system and its practices. Thus, economic emancipation and material markers would enable Dalits to a path of emancipation from their long history of subjugation, oppression and humiliation.[28]

The other viewpoint on DC does not believe in the emancipatory potential of capitalism. Political analysts like Anand Teltumbde reiterate the view that Ambedkar was against this profit-making business and capitalism. He[29] argues that caste is enmeshed into the modern secular institutions, and citing stray examples of Dalit millionaires would be a cruel joke on their community. The mere assumption of solidarity of interests between Dalit entrepreneurs and Dalit masses is fallacious, and capitalism might just favour the former while the rest would be left with nothing.[30]

Economic census data from 1990 to 2005 show that the 'enterprises owned by members of SC's and ST's tend to be smaller and employ labour from outside the family especially belonging to the informal or the unorganised sector'. In 2005, the SCs accounting for 16.8 per cent of total population across India owned 9.8 per cent of all enterprises

---

[27] N. G. Jayal, 'Affirmative Action in India: Before and after the Neo-liberal Turn', *Cultural Dynamics* 27, no. 1 (2015): 128–129.

[28] Kalva, 'Tracing Ambedkar, 80.

[29] Teltumbde, 'Dalit Capitalism and Pseudo Dalitism'.

[30] Jayal, 'Affirmative Action', 128–129.

and employed only 8.1 per cent of non-farm workers.[31] These statistics speak volumes about the poor performance of Dalits in a free market economy owing to deficiencies in the structural factors that are essential in order to survive in a competitive market.

Teltumbde[32] explains how caste plays the role of an important source of capital in the Indian context. Capital was initiated during the colonial times, but it did not have to contend much with the feudal forces. The caste system and its logic of capital accumulation helped capitalism grow by dividing the proletariats (low castes) from the bourgeoisie (upper castes). After the post-independence era, these upper castes could put to use its capital and make much use of the reform policies introduced in independent India, including the land reforms which eventually led to the Green Revolution. This accumulated wealth then found its way into the capitalist industries. Tiruppur, a world leader in the knitted garment industry, belongs to the Gounders, a typical middle farming caste of Tamil Nadu.

In the book *Annihilation of Caste*, Ambedkar emphasizes on three elements which become the power of a man. These are physical heredity, social inheritance in terms of socialization and education, and his/her own efforts. What is striking here is that individual efforts and discipline come last and physical hereditary and cultural and social capital come first. In a country like India, the very assumption of capital being indifferent to social identities is falsified. The process of capital formation by means of imparting education and knowledge of technology and access to such areas providing such facilities is highly skewed and highly influenced by factors such as caste, gender and ethnicity. As a result, it affects the skills and behavioural patterns of the socially excluded communities and hence they are at the end of the ladder, engaging in jobs with low productivity, survival activities, etc.[33]

---

[31] Lakshmi Iyer, Tarun Khanna, and Ashutosh Varshney, 'Caste and Entrepreneurship in India' (working paper no. 12-028, Harvard Business School, Boston, 2011), 4–6.

[32] Teltumbde, 'Dalit Capitalism and Pseudo Dalitism'.

[33] Thakare, 'Dalit Capitalism', 2–3.

The new Dalit assertion is radically different in ideals as compared to the revolutionary Dalit Panthers or the mainstream Bahujan Samaj Party. A clear understanding of this new assertion is yet to be fully understood, but what we can conclude from their assertions is that they are explicit about their economic ideology being the sole method for Dalit emancipation. They firmly believe that there is a dire need to look away from the provisions provided by the government for their development and to focus on individual efforts rather than collective mobilization in order to break the shackles of the caste system and casteism.[34] Favouring capitalism and overlooking the injustice and inequalities this particular form of economic organization has historically inflicted on the masses might have serious repercussions for the Dalits. The idea of capital being a crusader of caste seriously undermines Ambedkar's view of emancipation for his people.

## CASTE, CAPITAL AND AMBEDKAR

B. R. Ambedkar occupies the highest echelon within the Dalit community. In terms of the recent bifurcation between the Dalit assertion for political emancipation on the one hand and economic emancipation on the other, the latter seems to have misunderstood and misinterpreted Ambedkar's views on capitalism. The proponents, tangent to the idea of capital and globalization, have even painted Ambedkar as a monetarist, and thus his image is distorted to the extent of being a campaigner for neoliberalism. Anand Teltumbde tries to reverse this confusion and reminds the advocates of DC that Ambedkar, while addressing railway workers in Manmad in 1938, declared the two enemies of untouchables. One is Brahmanism and the other is capitalism. His party believed in the principle of a peaceful transition to socialism and discouraged capitalism. He even termed capitalism the 'dictatorship of the private employer'. This leader of Dalits was an avid believer in the power of democracy, to be precise social democracy, and opined that 'capitalism favours the rich and not the poor while socialism appeals to the poor and not to the rich'.[35]

---

[34] Jayal, 'Affirmative Action', 128–129.
[35] Teltumbde, 'Dalit Capitalism and Pseudo Dalitism'.

In the context of these two contending debates, Anupama Rao provides an explanation of Ambedkar's relation to Marxism. The critique of labour exploitation leads to a more complex representation of the 'difference' of caste. Ambedkar struggled to delineate the subtle yet complex relation between caste and class. Marxism takes into consideration labour universality antagonistic to the capitalist class. In that sense, the caste system in the feudal economic organization saw the lower caste as a form of class providing labour to the upper castes. Yet Ambedkar sought to explain that this class of 'lower castes' cannot be a class 'in itself and for itself'. These lower castes groups cannot be equated with Marx's account of labour universality, which is antagonistic to the universalizing force of capital. A social history endowed by the civic disability of caste and untouchability produced a stigmatized identity for Dalits, which would serve them negatively. He argues that this stigma cannot become the ground for political mobilization for Dalits, because stigma is a form of embodiment that cannot be abstracted or universalized. Thus, caste, which entails stigma, cannot be equivalent to the value-producing labour (class) in Marx's account. B. R. Ambedkar argues that without a regime of rights, Dalits would be fated for marginalization and hyper-exploited.[36]

Many scholars assert that capital came to India during the 1970s; however, it was only after the post-1990s reforms that capital in India grew at an unprecedented rate. These reforms also led to the witnessing of the shift in ideology; that is, the socialist ideology intrinsic to the Nehruvian idea of planned development lost its charm and the 'markets and the middle class' came to receive a focal point. Rolling back the state meant retrenchment of employment opportunities in the public sector, which also meant decline of jobs in the reserved categories.[37] David Harvey, in his book *A Brief History of Neoliberalism*, elucidates the brutal nature of neoliberalism. He writes, 'Neoliberalism tends to strip away the protective coverings that liberalism allowed and occasionally nurtured'.[38] Thus, the marginalized

---

[36] Rao, 'Stigma and Labour'.
[37] Jodhka, 'Dalits in Business'.
[38] David Harvey, *A Brief History of Neoliberalism* (New York, NY: Oxford University Press, 2007), 168.

community was bound to join and compete in the private sector for a livelihood. The private sector does not understand the logic for affirmative action within itself, and thus these historically marginalized sections of masses were thrown into the informal sector without any skills to compete and shield themselves.

The various studies that are being discussed above imply that the neoliberal policies did give an impetus to Dalit entrepreneurship, but these could not provide an enormous deliverance in terms of being 'job givers' instead of 'job seekers'. The few success stories of Dalit millionaires need not overshadow the tyranny of hundreds of Dalits squabbling for jobs with low productivity and status. At the end of this chapter, a significant question needs to be raised on how the social differentiation is still attached to Dalits, which obviously emanates from the caste system, and needs a different discourse altogether.

The market does not only consist of the formal economic organizations and the state. It is also shaped by the social institutions and social values that are born from the age-old ideology of the caste system, which then leads to the formulation of new rules, norms and behavioural patterns that are against the assumed rationalities of the market and capital, at least in the context of India. There are neither blockades to prevent Dalit engagement with capital nor an environment for complete inclusion of Dalits as economic players.[39]

To bring in Du Bois's position on Black capitalism, Haynes[40] presents a different view of W. E. B. Du Bois. He points out that Du Bois recognized the importance of economic cooperation for Black Americans, which was one of the most important projects of his life. Haynes writes that Du Bois's research is an outcome of his concern for the oppressed. The wretched condition of the poor led him to pursue the proposition that economic self-sufficiency through cooperation is an important avenue for economic and social progress for Blacks as well

---

[39] Prakash, 'Caste and Capitalism', 5–6.

[40] Curtis Haynes Jr., 'From Philanthropic Black Capitalism to Socialism: Cooperativism in Du Bois's Economic Thought', *Socialism and Democracy* 32, no. 3 (2018): 125–145.

as for all Americans. But Wendland[41] opines that Du Bois understood the domination of Whites in the context of capitalism. He dreamt of an economic democracy which is based on collectivism, free of colonialism, and dignified labour value.

In a moving story of his own and reflections on the caste system in India, Suraj Yengde[42] argues that capitalism has been developed in India for selfish reasons, and it is furthered by religion. By linking DC to Black capitalism, Yengde mentions the affinity of Ambedkar with Du Bois. He brings in Du Bois's criticisms to Washington's Black capitalism, where Du Bois argued that capitalism could not transcend race and supplied labour to White capitalists. In his monograph, in a chapter titled 'Dalit Captialism', he strongly argues against DC saying that capitalism in India and elsewhere is based on unethical practices. In India, it is bania capitalism, which thrives on malpractice and cheating. He quotes Kancha Ilaiah and condemns the Indian market as a 'Hindu market'. He questions DC on its nature and raises a serious question that what type of alternative structure it has. Like Du Bois argued that Black capitalism is all about shifting the Negro problems to Negro shoulder, DC will also work in that same way. Yengde alleges that DC is a shrewd strategy to keep Dalits marginalized, and it is imitating the dominant caste capitalism. The romantic idea of DC is sailed through the popular culture and media dominated by upper caste capitalists. Both Ambedkar and Du Bois believed in the liberation of toiling masses, but capitalism in India is deep-rooted with caste, as Yengde laments.

The way these caste ideologies are played out in the civil society as well as in the market needs critical engagement. The campaigners for DC also need to comprehend that the mere increase of consumerism among their community and sub-castes does not necessarily imply emancipation. It could possibly be a growth of the middle class without

---

[41] Joel Wendland-Liu, 'W.E.B. Du Bois Exposed Capitalist and colonialist Roots of White Supremacy' (2020). Available at: https://peoplesworld.org/article/w-e-b-du-bois-exposed-capitalist-and-colonialist-roots-of-white-supremacy/ (accessed on 28 April 2020).

[42] Suraj Yengde, *Caste Matters* (New Delhi: Penguin, 2019).

much transformation in their social status. If we see from a panoramic view, capitalism might just have succeeded in dividing Dalits along class lines: the millionaires being the upper class, the middle class born out of consumerism and the lower class consisting of those still engaged in their traditional menial jobs. The consequence would be a divide within the community along economic interests as well, which would have a directly proportional impact on radical Dalit activism.

To elaborate further, in a country like India, the service sector would always need a steady supply of labour force to be engaged in the informal sector without any basic rights and privileges. It is of grave concern that the overlapping of caste and class on the socially excluded marginalized section of the lower Dalit class might be the apt source of supply of such labour. Moreover, these neoliberal policies have exacerbated consumerism and urbanization, and the culture of malls and smart cities just received an impetus. These constructs give birth to a demand for an 'underclass', which would provide them with menial services in terms of scavenging and waste management including sewage.

Mhaskar[43] mentions that the change in the nature of cleaning work as well as the nomenclature from *safai kam* to housekeeping has led high-caste Hindus to shed their hesitations to do these jobs. But alternatively, when it comes to dealing with the actual dirt, the traditional castes engaged in these occupations would be sought after. This deliberate oppression and exclusion of these castes to cater to the upper class and the elites alike would amount to serious democratic pitfalls.

These opinions on labour were explained extensively by David Harvey.[44] At the crux of the liberal and neoliberal theory lies the necessity to construct markets for land, labour and money, and capitalism cannot function without these fictions. The individuals enter the market as individuals with certain social capital and relations, as physical beings with identifiable characteristics such as gender, with various skills (human capital) and tastes (cultural capital). But for the capitalists, the

---

[43] Mhaskar, 'Locating Caste in a Globalised India City'.
[44] Harvey, *A Brief History of Neoliberalism*.

labour enters the market as a mere mode of production, as an entity that holds 'labour value'. It fails to acknowledge the complex realities that entail a person perforating into the labour market. The capitalist class wants the following characteristics to be inherent within this particular means of production: physical strength, skills, docility, flexibilities and appropriate for certain tasks. Workers are preferred to be hired on a contractual basis under the neoliberal scheme in order to maximize flexibility.[45]

In the light of the above critical nature of neoliberalism that is devoid of the ideology of the emancipation of individuals, let alone marginalized communities, the projection of the idea of capital being a means for the upliftment of Dalits might fall short of its visions and assumptions in relation to its emancipatory politics. Teltumbde[46] opines that Dalit capitalists' advocating the policies of globalization and seeking favours of the ruling class is not only dishonesty but defies Dalit interests. Moreover, this particular labour force without protectionist schemes and skills to survive in the informal or rather private sector might be vulnerable as they might serve as the ideal source of means of production (labour) for the capitalists. The latter could rip them off easily because of their poor bargaining strength and such labour force easily brings down the cost of production. Even if Dalits become big capitalists or big bourgeoisie, they alone cannot shoulder the emancipatory project of Dalits, as true emancipation lies in social transformation and embracing social democracy. At this juncture, let us deflect to the inherent question again. Does 'class consciousness' necessarily replace 'caste consciousness'? Various studies of scholars like Surinder Jodhka, Aseem Prakash and Anand Teltumbde establish the fact that caste is an important variable in the business sector. Jodhka[47] reveals how the association of Dalit business enterprises with their caste identity leads to their humiliation and also has an adverse effect on their business. These caveats need to be addressed before the idea of capital in fighting caste spearheads the Dalit movement. A critical thought needs to

---

[45] Ibid., 167–168.
[46] Teltumbde, 'Dalit Capitalism and Pseudo Dalitism'.
[47] Jodhka, 'Dalits in Business'.

emerge that by creating a concept of the market, simultaneously, it is also outsourcing its own conception of labour: flexible, unskilled and poor bargaining strength.

## CONCLUSION

The term 'Dalit' emerged in the context of anti-oppression. The concept of Dalit denotes resisting any form of oppression. Capitalism is based on the principle of exploitation and oppression. That is why both the juxtaposition of DC are unfeasible and cannot work together.[48] DC is not a redefinition of capitalism to ensure the principles of liberty, equality and fraternity, which, Ambedkar argued the Indian society needs to be more democratic. The foundation of DICCI was laid in the argument that capital, in the forms of asset or labour, has been monopolized by a few castes. Without the emergence of entrepreneurs and market players among Dalits, this crucial public place, the composition of which is not mandated by the state, will not be represented. DICCI has in principle saddled itself into that transformative role of establishing Dalit participation over yet another public space. This is more importantly so, when political democracy is so invested in caste. Beyond this, the role of capitalism—with or without Dalit capitalists countering caste—needs to be objectively studied. Advocates of market and recent sociological studies of caste suggest that market forces have greatly weakened caste structure, and caste has transmuted into something more secular to allow modern practices. Does DICCI envisage influencing such problems beyond the neoliberal arguments of job and wealth creation? This is an important question to consider.

DC is based on the inherent idea that capital and entrepreneurship can help Dalits break the shackles of caste. But research shows otherwise. As discussed above, studies of scholars like Jodhka[49] and Mhaskar[50] reveal that these first-generation Dalit entrepreneurs mostly own petty shops with single proprietorship, employing labour from the informal sector, without formal credit and mostly based on support provided

---

[48] Yengde, *Caste Matters*.
[49] Jodhka, 'Dalits in Business'.
[50] Mhaskar, 'Locating Caste in a Globalised India City'.

by their family and extended kin. Large businesses in sectors like food, health and education are dominated by the upper castes. On the other hand, sectors like leather industry and sanitation work are occupied by the masses of the lower castes.

Aseem Prakash[51] analyses the problems that Dalit entrepreneurs experience from his empirical study in some of the bigger states of North-Central India. Dalit entrepreneurs face problems and huge challenges with respect to credit, which is not instantly available in their caste networks. It is a huge task for them to get credit from the formal sources as well. In the realm of market, they face problems from the consumers and hostile competitors. In terms of employing workers, upper-caste workers hesitate to join their corporation. Dalit entrepreneurs also face the problems from the non-Dalit firms not supporting them in the business or creating hurdles for them. Referring to Jyotirao Phule's position on the upper-caste dominance of government institutions, he analyses that market outcomes are embedded in the existing social structure. Shah and Lerche[52] propose the idea of 'conjugated oppression', which are central to the spread of contemporary capitalism. According to them, the co-constitution of class relations and social oppression, which constituents caste, tribe, gender, region, etc.—affects Dalits and Adivasis the most in India. They systematically argue that the social relations of oppression of Dalits and Adivasis continue to be pervasive and have become systemic to capitalism. This oppression is seen as an inseparable aspect of the constitution of exploitative capitalist class relations by the authors. Heyer,[53] through an extensive fieldwork, argues that caste institutions have operated to subordinate Dalits. Their mode of operation has changed, but the outcome has remained very much as before. Capitalists are using caste institutions to control labour

---

[51] Aseem Prakash, 'Dalit Entrepreneurs in Middle India', in *Comparative Political Economy of Development Africa and South Asia*, eds. Barbara Harriss-White and Judith Heyer (New York, NY: Routledge, 2010).

[52] Alpa Shah and Jens Lerche, 'Conjugated Oppression under Contemporary Capitalism: Class Relations, Social Oppression and Agrarian Change in India', *Journal of Peasant Studies* 45, no. 5–6 (2018): 927–949.

[53] Judith Heyer, 'The Marginalisation of Dalits in a Modernising Economy', in *Comparative Political Economy of Development Africa and South Asia*, eds. Barbara Harriss-White and Judith Heyer (New York, NY: Routledge, 2010).

in India. She further argues that capitalists will build on strong caste institutions where they are able to use caste institutions to increase their control over labour. Then it is important to reflect and ask questions, as advocated by the proponents of DC; capitalism will demolish caste. Heyer's thesis proves that instead of dismantling the caste, capitalism is reinforcing it for its profit and sustenance. There are many researchers who have proved that capitalism is not helping Dalits; instead, it is reinforcing the disparity.

Chandra Bhan Prasad[54] appeals to the Dalit communities who are in jobs to open their own bank to sponsor and invest in the business of Dalit entrepreneurs. If Dalits could invest only 1 per cent of their income, they will be able to fund the DC project, which is having the capacity to produce Dalit billionaires. Prasad while appealing to the community members by following the footsteps of American Blacks who have built their own economy. But it is not true. In the American context, Baradaran[55] contends that without the help of the state, it is difficult for the Black Americans to fix the problem on their own. She articulates that the movement in support of Black economic self-sufficiency will falter without government help.

Jürgen Habermas,[56] in one of his most popular propositions on public sphere, questions the notion of civil society; he underscores it as an exclusive sphere. But he maintains that public sphere is a space where anybody can participate and enter into a dialogue to exercise one's democratic views and rights. Taking a cue from the Habermassian concept of public sphere, DC could also transform itself into a democratic space. Already, the idea of economic democracy has entered into the discourse of capitalism; there are other kinds of views on alternative

---

[54] Chandra Bhan Prasad, 'Fellow Dalits, Open Your Own Bank: If No One Else, Dalit Middle Class Can Fund Dalit Capitalism to Produce Dalit Billionaires'. Available at: https://timesofindia.indiatimes.com/blogs/toi-editorials/fellow-dalits-open-your-own-bank-if-no-one-else-dalit-middle-class-can-fund-dalit-capitalism-to-produce-dalit-billionaires/ (accessed on 27 April 2020).

[55] Mehrsa Baradaran, *The Color of Money: Black Banks and the Racial Wealth Gap* (Cambridge: Belknap Press, 2017).

[56] Jürgen Habermas, *The Structural Transformation of the Public Sphere: An Inquiry into a Category of Bourgeois Society* (Cambridge: MIT Press, 1991).

capitalism. Why cannot DC reconfigure itself to be an alternative capitalism which would dismantle the caste and class structure?

In the Habermassian sense, public sphere entails public which is open to all and not exclusive. It is a realm where public opinion could be formed and all citizens have the right to share a space in the public sphere. Public opinions are formed in the domains of health, education, common good, etc. Habermas advocates that public is related to the idea of common as against the private.

Like modernity is not singular and differs in the context, space and time, capitalism is also different in different parts of the world. This is a unique opportunity to bring in economic democracy in the pretext of DC, if at all the members of DICCI want to bring in any positive change. As it has been observed that the state is not able to ensure participation of Dalits in the market, DC is having the capability to create an alternative model of capitalism, which will be similar to cooperative capitalism where the distinction and difference between the owner and workers will be minimal. Like all ideologies and movements keep reinventing themselves, why cannot DC reinvent itself?

Omvedt[57] argues for a true alternative which is very essential. She suggests for the alternative of a more democratic capitalism to lay the foundation for the movement forward. Omvedt proposes that

> There is a role for both the state and the market (remembering that both are oppressive) and there is a role for 'sunrise industries'—which forecast the new society—including what we know as information technology and the development of alternative energy and raw material sources. All of this may not seem to be much within the framework of capitalist hegemony, but it is the responsibility of those who like to think of themselves as revolutionaries to develop them, direct them, link them up, work them to the point where they may indeed 'come into conflict with the existing relations of production' and so herald an era of revolutionary change.[58]

---

[57] Gail Omvedt, 'Capitalism and Globalisation, Dalits and Adivasis', *Economic & Political Weekly* 40, no. 47 (2005): 4881–4885.
[58] Ibid., 4884–4885.

In the similar line, it is the need of the hour to reinvent and work for a different kind of DC, which will not be based on blind growth but would rather work more towards breaking the caste barriers and emancipate the Dalits from their sociocultural stigmatized identity.

Alternatively, maybe a good democracy needs representations of all communities in all the spheres including the market. In the Habermassian sense of democratic representation in the public sphere, Dalits also need to be part of the capitalist competition. If it goes right, then it will be interesting to see how the sociopolitical movement of Dalits can be synchronized with this economic movement. Thus, it will be remarkable to see how DC would deal with the internal contradictions of exploitation and marginalization among Dalits themselves.

## BIBLIOGRAPHY

Teltumbde, Anand. 'FDI in Retail and Dalit Entrepreneurs'. *Economic & Political Weekly* 48, no. 3 (2013).

# Chapter 3

# 'Migrant', 'Home' and Politics
Bihari Labour in the Metropolis*

Tanweer Fazal

## INTRODUCTION

This chapter emerges from my own subject location, the anxiety of being a migrant, of being poised between the duality of the 'house' and the 'home'. With this as the subtext, I seek to examine the subjectivities of migrant 'blue-collar' workers, the most visible and vulnerable among Biharis outside the state. The chapter was originally conceived in the backdrop of the assembly elections in Bihar. It is proposed that the questions of citizenship, migrants' ideas about politics and the imbrication of these ideas with their comprehension of 'home' and 'non-home' bear imprints of electoral mobilization. The chapter seeks to understand how these pressing concerns are structured by the existential conditions of a fractured identity: of being a worker, a migrant and also a migrant worker. It is also an attempt to understand the everyday strategies of survival—negotiations, persistence and routine resistance—by primarily blue-collar workers originating from the state of Bihar.

---

*This chapter was earlier published in the journal *Indian Anthropologist*'s special issue on 'Everyday State and Politics', vol. 46, no. 2 (2016, July–December): 93–110.

By attempting to recover the politics of the migrant, the chapter expresses its disquiet over the primarily culturological construction of 'home' in sociological and anthropological literature on migration. Social science literature on migration is rich. Typically, the economists and demographers have concentrated principally on variables such as demand for labour, wage differentials, extent of migration, age and sex selective nature of migration patterns, urbanization and patterns of regional inequality, and impact of remittances on native economy to provide a rationale for migration.[1] The historians also seem to borrow some of these tools from the former and trace the trajectory of migration and the shifts in preferences and factors that have prompted sections of populations to migrate.[2] Sociology focused on the structures and networks of migration, where caste, ethnic or religious affiliations appeared significant. It examined the impact of rural migration on urban life and noticed the emergence of ethnic enclaves in the cities.[3] Migration is not necessarily linked to urbanization, and there is sufficient sociological interest in seasonal and cyclical migration to Green Revolution areas of Punjab and patterns

---

[1] Amitabh Kundu and Shalini Gupta, 'Migration, Urbanisation and Regional Inequality', *Economic & Political Weekly* 31, no. 52 (1996): 3391–3393, 3395–3398; Ben Rogaly, 'Workers on the Move: Seasonal Migration and Changing Social Relations in Rural India', *Gender and Development* 6, no. 1 (1998): 21–29; Mahendra K. Premi, 'Aspects of Female Migration in India', *Economic & Political Weekly* 15, no. 15 (1980): 714–720.

[2] Anand A. Yang, 'Peasants on the Move: A Study of Internal Migration in India', *The Journal of Interdisciplinary History* 10, no. 1 (1979): 37–58; Arjan de Haan, 'Migration and Livelihoods in Historical Perspective: A Case Study of Bihar, India', *Journal of Development Studies* 38, no. 5 (2002): 115–142.

[3] A. K. Gupta, D. R. Arora, and B. K. Agarwal, 'Sociological Analysis of Migration of Agricultural Labourers from Eastern to North-Western Region of India', *Indian Journal of Industrial Relations* 23, no. 4 (April 1988): 429–445; David Mosse, Sanjeev Gupta, and Vidya Shah, 'On the Margins in the City: Adivasi Seasonal Labour Migration in Western India', *Economic & Political Weekly* 40, no. 28 (9–15 July 2005): 3025–3038; Lionel Caplan, 'Class and Urban Migration In South India: Christian Elites in Madras City', *Sociological Bulletin* 25, no. 2 (1976): 207–224; M. S. A. Rao, 'The Migrant to the City', *Yojana* 18 (1974): 7–13; M. S. A. Rao, ed., *Studies in Migration: Internal and International Migration in India* (Delhi: Manohar, 1986).

of exploitation.⁴ The anthropological engagement with the question of migration typically focuses on migrant culture, the processes of assimilation or adaptation, the hermeneutic meaning of what it is to be a migrant, the sense of loss and belongingness that migrants are assumed to develop in the alien world and the variegated experience of migration.⁵ In most such literature, therefore, the 'home' and the 'house' are the two loci that stand in contrast: one being the migrants' most natural abode, which he or she fondly remembers and hopes to return to, and the other being his/her adopted place, but one to which he/she remains an alien, whose 'otherness' confronts him on a daily basis.

Typically, in much of the social science literature on migration, the politics of the migrant finds little attention. In this chapter, an attempt is made to recover the migrant, particularly the migrant labour, as a political being, one who is denied equal rights and wages, security, social status and recognition in migrant places but longs to realize it at home. Thus, social exclusion, problems of assimilation, denial of citizenship entitlements, exploitation and everyday violence become critical ingredients of analysis. Home, the chapter argues, is not just a nostalgic or a subliminal presence, manifesting itself occasionally in the form of Bhojpuri and Maithili songs, folk tales and cuisines, or through a worker's frequent visit to 'home' to reaffirm kinship ties. The home is a domain of politics too, where the worker, denied his/her full citizenship in migrant locations, seeks to exercise in the more familial world of home. However, a worker's involvement with home and politics varies and is structured by his/her social location, longevity of stay in the 'host' society, intergenerational mobility, etc. The 'house'

---

⁴ K. Gopal Iyer, ed. *Distressed Migrant Labour in India: Key Human Rights Issues* (Delhi: Kanishka, 2004); Manjit Singh, 'Preference for Migrant Agricultural Labour in Punjab', *Economic & Political Weekly* 47, no. 29 (21 July 2012): 27–28.;

⁵ See for instance the works of Radhika Chopra, 'Maps of Experience: Narratives of Migration in an Indian Village', *Economic & Political Weekly* 30, no. 49 (1995): 3156–3162; Sudha Gupta, 'Role of Primordial Ties in causing Migration of Factory Workers', *Indian Anthropologist* 23, no. 1 (1993): 49–63; W. L. Rowe, 'Caste, Kinship and Association in Urban India', in *Urban Anthropology*, ed. A. Southall (New York, NY: Oxford University Press, 1973).

and the 'home', in the lives of these migrant workers, do not exist in opposition to each other but in continuity.

The subject of enquiry in this chapter is the migrant labour originating from the state of Bihar. Bihari migrants have both flocked to metropolises such as Kolkata, Bombay and Delhi and inundated agricultural fields and industrial sites of Punjab and Haryana. One can even find them in the cashew, rubber and coir units of Kerala, in the shops of Manipur or in the plantations of Assam. Unlike the labour migrants from other states, the Bihari worker is marked and stigmatized. However, frequent violence by chauvinist groups—the Maharashtra Navnirman Sena (MNS) and Shiv Sena in Maharashtra, the Khalistani militants in Punjab or United Liberation Front of Assam (ULFA) and various other tribal insurgents of Northeast India—has rarely deterred them.

## THE MIGRATION STORY: BEYOND THE TYRANNY OF STATISTICS

That the working class migration is both sex selective and seasonal in nature has been widely acknowledged. For proof, one needs to look no further than the packed compartments of Bihar-bound trains. In the last assembly elections in Bihar, for many analysts, the role of migrants emerged as a subject of heated discussion. The explanation for women voters outnumbering men in Bihar rested on the premise of male-centric labour migration. Yet, paradoxically, we were also informed that the Bihari migrant, overwhelmingly male, came back to vote in droves.

But this is only a part of the story, and one hastens to add, a highly erroneous one. For one, Bihar is not the only state that sends out migrants to big cities and industrial locations. The 2001 Census data on interstate migration lists Bihar along with other poorer states such as Jharkhand, Orissa, Rajasthan, Madhya Pradesh and Uttar Pradesh (UP) as the states whose net out-migration outscores the number of people who adopted them as their homes. However, lest we believe in the thesis that economic distress could be a major push factor for population mobility, we must bear in mind that Census unmistakably also lists Tamil Nadu and Kerala as two of the relatively prosperous states that have continuously propelled their people and workforce out.

Equally, in states and cities that attract mobile populations, Biharis do not necessarily constitute the largest bloc among recent migrants. In Maharashtra, which received the largest number of migrants in the period 1991–2000, people from Bihar were far fewer in number than those from UP, Karnataka, Madhya Pradesh and Gujarat. Among those heading towards Delhi, the share of Bihari migrants was less than half of those from UP. A more or less similar pattern could be discerned for the state of Punjab where the word 'Bihari' has almost become a euphemism for the Hindi-speaking working population.[6]

Second, a large number of migrants, whether in Haryana and Punjab or in big cities such as Delhi, Kolkata and Mumbai, have been living there for decades and have grown roots. Migration of farm labour from Bihar to regions outside the state is centuries old, although the preferred destinations have continually changed: In the late 18th and early 19th centuries, the choice ranged from the fields of Rangpur and Mymensingh districts in eastern Bengal to distant Burma. Typical to the labour migrants, the migration was seasonal and short-lived—rarely more than four–six months—and primarily male. With the growth of industry in the late 19th century, the destination of Bihari migrants began to change. They now began to head to Calcutta and 24 Parganas, the two industrial hubs in the Bengal Province. By the 1920s, however, another perceptible variation in the pattern of migration surfaced, this time prompted by a gradual decline in the demand for unskilled labour in urban and rural Bengal.[7]

Post-independence too, out-migration from the state remained consistent; both the 1951 and 1961 enumerations listed around 4 per cent of the Bihar population as living outside the state. The 1960s saw

---

[6] Census of India 2001, 'Migration Tables', 24. Available at: http://censusindia.gov.in/Data_Products/Data_Highlights/Data_Highlights_link/data_highlights_D1D2D3.pdf (accessed on 1 October 2016).

[7] Arjan de Haan, 'Migration and Livelihoods in Historical Perspective: A Case Study of Bihar, India', *Journal of Development Studies* 38, no. 5 (2002): 126–127.

the destination for farm labourers and other unskilled workers from Bihar changing once again. They were now heading towards Punjab, Haryana and western UP, the pull factor being the wage differential in areas of the Green Revolution. The migration was typically rural to rural: from the villages of Bihar to the agricultural fields of the states that were in the throes of capitalist agricultural transformation. The surplus so generated also fuelled the out-migration of Punjabi workforce to countries overseas, and Bihari labour was enlisted to meet this labour shortage. In a way, the immigrants kept the fields tilled and harvested, and later the industries of Punjab running.

The choice of Delhi for large-scale population movement from Bihar seems to come rather late in the day. Up till 2001, as one survey suggests, Bihar's share in the migrant population of Delhi was 14 per cent. Delhi and its emerging industrial-cum-residential suburbs such as Gurgaon, Ghaziabad and Noida are sites of new waves of migration. If the place of birth is taken as a criterion, migrants comprised nearly 40 per cent of Delhi's population in the year 2001.[8] Next to Maharashtra, in recent times, Delhi has emerged as the most preferred destination for migrants seeking employment outside their states. The total count of in-migrants in Delhi in the decade 1991–2000 was 2.2 million, whereas the number of those who left the city totalled a meagre 0.45 million by comparison. The 1.7 million net migrants in the capital during this period were nearly 35 per cent higher than the previous decade. Biharis comprised around 20 per cent of those migrating into Delhi during this period; they still did not constitute the biggest bloc, as migrants from UP headed to the city in a much larger proportion (40%, see Table 3.1). This was followed by other states such as Haryana (8.04%), Uttarakhand (5.22%), Rajasthan (4.15%) and West Bengal (3.96%) (see Table 3.1). Migrants from all these states cited work/employment as the most important reasons for leaving their 'homes'. Among the Bihar male migrants, we notice that employment and work seem to be even much greater a motivation than those from other states. This sort of migration was highly sex selective, as rarely did women from Bihar move to the national capital in search for employment or for that matter education (see Table 3.2).

---

[8] Census of India 2001, 'Migration Tables'.

**Table 3.1a** *Percentage of Migration and Reasons of Migration (%) to Delhi (All States; 1991–2000)*

|  | States of Origin (%) | |
| --- | --- | --- |
|  | 2001 Census | 2013 Perception Survey |
| Uttar Pradesh | 41.00 | 46.50 |
| Bihar | 19.51 | 30.70 |
| Haryana | 8.04 | 4.10 |
| Rajasthan | 4.15 | 2.90 |
| West Bengal | 3.96 | 2.90 |

*Source:* Census of India 2001, 'Migration Tables'. Available at: http://censusindia.gov.in/Data_Products/Data_Highlights/Data_Highlights_link/data_highlights_D1D2D3.pdf (accessed on 1 October 2016); Institute for Human Development, *Delhi Human Development Report 2013* (Delhi: Institute for Human Development and Academic Foundation, 2013).

**Table 3.1b** *Reasons for Migration*

| Reasons for Migration | 2001 | 2013 |
| --- | --- | --- |
| Work/employment | 37.54 | 28.00 |
| Business | 0.54 | 0.71 |
| Education | 2.67 | 1.41 |
| Marriage | 13.80 | 18.40 |
| Moved after birth | 2.35 | 2.53 |
| Moved with households | 36.78 | 34.20 |
| Other | 6.28 | 13.60 |

*Source:* Census of India 2001, 'Migration Tables'; Institute for Human Development, *Delhi Human Development Report 2013*.

By the year 2013, however, a phenomenal 31 per cent of the migrants in the city had their origins in Bihar. The shift towards metropolitan cities demanded an orientation different from that required for farm work—new skills and willingness to confront the pressures of a

**Table 3.2** Reasons for Migration to Delhi among Bihari Migrants in the Period 1991–2000 and 2001–2010

| Reasons for Migration | 1999–2000 | | | 2001–2010 | | |
|---|---|---|---|---|---|---|
| | Persons | Male | Female | Persons | Male | Female |
| Work/employment | 50.8 | 71.5 | 4.3 | 36.7 | 58.7 | 3.72 |
| Business | 0.3 | 0.4 | 0.1 | 0.37 | 0.5 | 0.20 |
| Education | 3.3 | 4.4 | 1.0 | 2.2 | 3.2 | 0.81 |
| Marriage | 6.9 | 0.1 | 22.3 | 11.1 | 0.3 | 27.40 |
| Moved after birth | 1.9 | 1.5 | 3.0 | 2.3 | 2.2 | 2.40 |
| Moved with households | 30.5 | 15.8 | 63.7 | 36.7 | 21.6 | 58.70 |
| Other | 6.2 | 6.5 | 5.7 | 10.7 | 13.4 | 6.60 |

*Source:* Computed from Census of India 2001, 'Migration Tables', 29–30; Census of India 2011, 'Migration Tables', Table D3.

big city—and the workers seemed prepared to brave it. An overwhelming majority, nearly 86 per cent, in a city like Delhi are employed in the service sector as transport workers, construction labourers, repair mechanics, security guards and delivery persons—predominantly informal, most arduous and least rewarding.[9]

A third point that warrants attention is that a considerable proportion of Bihari migrants today is composed of a relatively well-heeled middle class: the skilled and white-collar workers. Although the desire for overseas locations has remained feeble among the Bihari elite, a substantial section of the middle-class professionals took to interstate mobility to exploit opportunities. The escape by this section of the population from Bihar is relatively recent, spurred essentially by student migration to institutions of higher learning outside the state. Arvind N. Das attributed this to the 'push factor'—a fallout of the 'academic mafia' that had presided over the demise of higher education in the state.[10] Such was the skewed spread of educational infrastructure in the country that till very recently, central institutions—whether IITs, IIMs, central universities or various science research establishments, considered to be at the apex of institutional hierarchy—had bypassed Bihar. The middle classes whose aspirations for income mobility are tied inextricably to educational attainments were left with little option but to send their wards outside the state.

Little studied, but perhaps a potential area of research in this context, is the impact of the politics of social justice—first the Karpoori formula and a decade later the Mandal Commission—on the state of academic institutions. The ascent of the backward castes was accompanied by a substantial decline in the pre-eminent position that the landowning castes enjoyed in the universities and colleges of Bihar. This struggle for hegemony had its manifestation in campus violence, extended periods of shutdowns, strikes and a general crumbling of academic institutions, enough to prompt the flight of affluent castes and classes.

---

[9] Institute for Human Development, *Delhi Human Development Report 2013* (Delhi: Institute for Human Development and Academic Foundation, 2013), 65.
[10] Arvind N. Das, 1998. 'India in the Image of Bihar', *Economic & Political Weekly* 33, no. 49 (1998): 3103–3104.

As observed in migration patterns elsewhere, in Bihar too it is not just poverty that pushes people to move out, but prosperity can also be a compelling reason. Long-distance migration requires material wherewithal as well as established networks. It is, therefore, no surprise that the propensity to migrate in recent years is most discernible among classes located at two extremes of the agrarian structure: the landlords and agricultural labour. A study on migration from rural Bihar, therefore, noted major alteration in the process of out-migration with latest trends suggesting a palpable decline among middle peasantry and a rising tendency among the landed, with 60 per cent of such households reporting trends of out-migration and among the land starved, every second household of whom had a migrating member to supplement family income.[11]

In a primarily rural economy, land remains a critical, although a grossly overlooked, subject. The decades of the 1970s and 1980s saw substantial changes in the political landscape of the state. In post-independence Bihar, the anti-zamindari sentiments aroused by the Kisan Sabha-led peasant movement forced a reluctant state to initiate reforms in the agrarian structure. However, deliberate and inordinate interruptions in the promulgation and implementation of Bihar Abolition of Zamindari Act (1949) defeated its very purpose, thereby allowing the persistence of a semi-feudal structure. The piecemeal social change that zamindari abolition in Bihar produced impacted only the interstitial strata of agrarian caste–class structure. The abolition of large estates propelled certain agrarian castes, such as a section of the Yadavs and Kurmis, to the ranks of the middle and rich peasantry. It precipitated the rise of a politics centred on demands for representation and social justice which successfully mobilized the lowest castes—the quintessential fieldworkers—alongside. In subsequent years, new political alliances produced fresh categorizations, wherein relatively affluent Dalits were separated from the poorest ones, thus paving the way for the emergence of a new social and political identity, the Mahadalits. Earlier, a similar exercise of sub-categorization led to the rise of another new

---

[11] Anup Karan, 'Changing Pattern of Migration from Rural Bihar', in *Migrant Labour and Human Rights in India*, ed. K. Gopal Iyer (Delhi: Kanishka Publishers, 2003), 102–139.

identity, the extremely backward castes, as different from the backward castes. A more or less identical process could be seen among the Muslims of Bihar with the emergence of the Pasmanda and Dalit Muslim movements.

The skewed employment pattern and land relations are evident from the NSSO (2009–2010) figures, which suggest that 47 per cent of the SC/ST and 21 per cent of the OBC—as compared to only 11 per cent of the upper caste—households have no land and survive solely by selling their labour. Almost inversely, nearly 40 per cent of the high caste—12 per cent of the OBC and merely 4 per cent of the SC/ST households—owned more than 1 hectare agricultural land.[12] The agrarian economy therefore remained largely stagnant with the state even failing to introduce capitalist transformation that could have enhanced wages. As a result, the lowest strata in the caste–class structure retained little hope in the state's production processes. A new surge for seasonal employment in the lands of Punjab, Haryana, Western UP and elsewhere could be observed among the landless wage workers of Bihar.

## MIGRANT WORLD: HOUSE, HOME AND THE IDEA OF POLITICS

The construction of 'home' in diaspora studies/anthropological literature on migration warrants a re-examination. Unlike the classical anthropologists' obsession with 'totalizing places' fixed in time and space, and frozen with social relations and cultural routines, those studying population movements discovered spaces which were frequently being visited and vacated by individuals and groups. Marc Auge thus argues for 'non-place' as real measures of our times when migration is the quintessential experience of the age. 'Non-places' are transit points and temporary abodes: waiting rooms, refugee camps, malls, stations and hotels. For Auge, 'non-place' which is beyond territory and society is an essential component of modern societies and atypically shapes our identity. It follows that no place is completely itself, and therefore no place is completely other; people are

---

[12] Tanweer Fazal, 'The Problem', *Seminar—Symposium on Bihar Ballot* 678 (2016): 1.

always and never 'at ease with home'.[13] As is evident, Auge's ideas of 'non-place' is framed in terms of the anxieties of identity of mobile individuals and groups. That non-places could also be power-laden settings with variegated experiences of exclusion and inclusion is not within the scope of Auge's primarily cultural conceptualization.

The anthropological discussion on home produces other paradoxes too. The 'home' is not merely a product of remembrance and a locus for belonging but also an outcome of an innate politics of exclusion that the 'migrants', essentially from low-income groups, are compelled to suffer in host societies. Rise of migration has also precipitated a concomitant burgeoning of particularisms. Hobsbawm makes interesting use of the German distinction between *heim* and *heimat*. Heim is individual's memory, fantasy and longing; 'Heim is essentially private. Home in the wider sense, Heimat, is essentially public. It is almost always a social construction rather than a real memory.'[14] Heim is impacted by heimat, which is an attempt collectively to impose home as a social fact and a cultural norm to which some claim authentic adherence and from which others must be excluded. Thus, while people generally refer to heim, the personal home which could be a village, a neighbourhood or a mufassil town, it is in situations of exile and immigration which brings them into a wider, public solidarity of heimat. No wonder then that the immigrant labour from Bihar discovers itself as a Bihari in the uncertain and trying conditions of being a vulnerable and marginalized identity outside the state.

Around the end of 2009, Ludhiana, Punjab's industrial hub, reported pitched street battles between local police and migrant workers in the city. This soon transformed into a conflagration between the workers and local Jat strongmen, with the former's homes being attacked and burnt down. The partisanship of the local press was all too obvious, as it unscrupulously exaggerated the role of the migrants, holding them responsible for taking to violence even as that by the 'natives' remained largely unreported. As part of a fact-finding team consisting of university

---

[13] Marc Auge, *Non-places: Introduction to the Anthropology of Supermodernity* (London: Verso, 1995), 78–79.

[14] Eric Hobsbawm, 'Introduction', *Social Research* 58, no. 1 (1991, Spring): 67.

teachers, we found that the brutality visited on the workers on the day of the clashes was only a minor part of the story. Ludhiana's 'migrant workers' had been subjected to a far more insidious, routine violence of relentless marginalization and violation of citizenship. Indeed, the category 'migrant' itself was pregnant with ideas of exclusion.

Most anthropological accounts of migration are replete with the migrants' retention of cultural patterns which they bring with them from the home society. The urge to do so however may not be universal among migrants across classes. For instance, the workers living in Punjab made notable moves towards assimilating with the host culture. Many of them spoke fluent Punjabi and sent their children to Punjabi-medium schools. In the discursive domain, however, including the police and the press, they continued to be abusively referred to as 'Biharis' or *bhaiyyas*. The process of cultural stigmatization perversely synchronized with their political exclusion and economic marginalization. Very few workers had been provided ration cards or voter cards despite many continuous years of residence. An ethnically differentiated labour market had emerged in the industrial areas of Ludhiana (and perhaps the whole of Punjab), wherein the 'migrants' were employed at rates far lower than the market- or state-determined wages. This was compounded by the fact that almost all of them (except for those working in larger units) were unorganized.[15]

During the recent assembly elections, reports from Punjab spoke of the mobilization of workers by different political parties to vote in their native villages in Bihar.[16] Underlying these efforts to persuade the migrant Biharis (an estimated two million, according to a news item) to return to vote was the assumption that workers were bereft of their

---

[15] The minimum wages on 1 September 2009, as per the Department of Labour, Government of Punjab, were ₹3,398 per month and ₹130.71 per day. However, this was followed only as an exception. Most workers were found to be employed at a fixed *mazdoori* of ₹2,200 a month, which amounted to about ₹70 a day. Fact Finding Report of Jamia Teachers' Solidarity Association (unpublished), December 2009, available at: https://kafila.online/2009/12/23/report-on-violence-against-workers-in-ludhiana-jtsa/

[16] *The New Indian Express*, 'Elections in Bihar, Campaigning in Punjab to Woo Bihari Migrants', 4 October 2015.

politics in the state of their residence—Punjab in this case. The migrant is deemed to be disenfranchised in places of work and residence while being considered a rights-bearing, conscious citizen at 'home'. This binary however is too simplistic and one would do well to bear in mind that the migrants' association with politics is mediated by a range of variables including income group, duration of migration (seasonal or long-term) and inclusive processes in the host society.

I have drawn some conclusions based on interviews conducted with Bihari workers employed as skilled, unskilled and service sector workers in Gurgaon's Udyog Vihar. The workers had variegated duration of migration from their native villages, adopted distinct routes to eventually find employment here, and differed in terms of their skills, education and social background. They also differed from each other in terms of their earnings, duration of stay as well as nature of employment—whether contractual, daily wage or permanent with certain social security. Invariably, however, they maintained some ties with the native place, both physical and emotional. Forty-five-year-old Suresh Prasad belongs to Bishnupur village in Bihar. He was the first person in his family to have left the village sometime around 1990, first moving to Chandigarh, and later to Delhi and Gurgaon. In the meantime, he upgraded his skills, and from a helper graduated to become a welder. He belongs to Khairwar caste, whose members were traditionally employed as domestic workers in the houses of the landlords. The family, therefore, owned a small patch of land, which was insufficient to provide livelihood.

It is difficult to categorize him in either of the two binaries: seasonal or permanent migrant. He goes to the village twice a year—during festivals and harvest time—usually for a short duration as long leave from his permanent employer (he has worked with the same firm for the last 15 years) is not easy to get. While in Chandigarh it was common to hear native workers complain that the influx of Biharis had lowered the prevailing wage rate, Delhi (including Gurgaon), Suresh found, was more welcoming. Almost all the workers came from outside, though the landlords who rented out dingy rooms to workers like Suresh were extremely exploitative. More than two-thirds of Suresh's monthly income is sent back to support his family and educate his two children.

In his early 50s, Kailash Sharma has a longer history of migration. He left his village after completing high school and trained in electricals from the local industrial training institute (ITI). The first destination was Calcutta in 1978, where his cousin secured him a job. He then moved to the Ordnance Factory, Muradnagar (UP), in 1980, and thereafter to a private company in Delhi. For the last 30 years or so, Kailash has been employed in the same engineering unit where he has risen in seniority and stature. Over the years, his family, including two children and wife, joined him, all moving into a house which he eventually bought.

In fact, all of Kailash's brothers took technical training, found employment and ultimately settled in industrial towns—Jamshedpur, Bokaro and Gurgaon. They left the village early in life and along with it the hereditary occupation, carpentry. Although their father also worked in a public sector unit (PSU), he had continued as a carpenter and, unlike the sons, returned to the village on retirement. Leaving the village altogether has certainly helped the family secure significant intergenerational mobility. Kailash's children, the son and the daughter, completed their master's degree in business administration and have found white-collar employment in MNCs.

For Kailash, 'home' is laden with complexity. Village Thuve in Chhapra district of Bihar, where his family still owns a small piece of land, is his connect with his past, his lineage, his paternal kin. In his own words, his visits to the village are limited to '*achhe* and *bure din*', that is, on occasions of marriage and death. Since Kailash has fully relocated to Gurgaon, he is not among those who regularly send remittances back home, neither is he involved in village politics, the contestations over power and entitlements. In 1994, when Kailash applied for a ration card in Gurgaon, he was required to get his name deleted from the village voter list and get the ration card terminated. However, when he had to marry his children, he looked for their spouses from among his castemen who came from the same region.

Virendra Prasad, the third worker interviewed, began as a welder and has remained so. In 1987–1988, he went in search of a job to Phagwara in Punjab because others from his village had found employment there. The work assigned to him in the factory at Phagwara was perilous, compelling him to move to Delhi where again a fellow villager was instrumental in helping him find work. Before his elder son found employment in a speaker-manufacturing factory in Gurgaon, Virendra was the only person from among his extended family to have moved out of the village. Back home, Virendra owns a small patch of land which is self-cultivated, but this hardly assures subsistence. Besides, farming itself requires regular investment. Like Suresh Prasad, Virendra also sends back most of what he earns and survives on a bare minimum. And again like him, he visits his village, Tehatti in Chhapra district, a couple of times in the year, generally coinciding with sowing and harvest.

Virendra maintains a close association with other village folk who live and work in the city. The interaction in the city, however, is qualitatively different, touching as it does on the hardship of urban life, problems with the employer and the landlord, and so on. The village in the city is sans its politics. In his words, 'We are all working people here, away from our village. We did not meet as often in the village as we do here.' In the village, though, Virendra is not able to vote. However, he has no regrets as in his absence, his kinsmen or his son cast the ballot on his behalf. In Ahir Tola, where they reside, the caste elders collectively decide whom to vote for. In the recently concluded Bihar elections, all of his caste brethren voted for former Chief Minister Lalu Prasad Yadav's RJD—a choice which he feels is an outcome of rational decision-making. During Lalu's tenure, two factories were set up in the area, one of which is still functioning. Besides, the Babu Sahebs also began to respect the Yadavs in the village. In Virendra's thinking, all talk of 'jungle raj was a mere figment of some people's imagination', as there was no difference between Lalu's rule and the regime that preceded or followed his.

Kailash Sharma's family is upwardly mobile, facilitated by a longer urban experience which has ensured a degree of disconnect from the village. Although dissociated from everyday politics of the village, Kailash keenly followed the elections and hoped that Bihar would give a decisive mandate to the NDA's 'Vikas' agenda. He claims to have been a Congress voter earlier, but during the Lok Sabha election of 2014, his entire family shifted to the BJP.

He argued,

> Modi is sincere about bringing development and enabling industrialization, but he needs time. During Nitish's rule, Bihar showed some semblance of development and tightening of the law and order machinery, but his joining hands with Lalu is a setback. Besides, Lalu is extremely casteist. We need to leave the past behind.

Then why did BJP lose the election if they had the positives on their side? This, he felt, was primarily because the BJP in Bihar is still dominated by the Babu Sahebs who reproduce old hierarchies in their style of politics.

Neither Kailash Sharma nor Virendra Prasad and Suresh Prasad are members of workers' unions. The small engineering unit in which they work has only a few permanent employees, most being contractual. For Virendra, it is not the factory but the village which is his domain of politics and the context in which to visualize an alternative world. But for Kailash Sharma, now more or less a complete city dweller, the realm is the 'nation' itself. Bihar is not isolated from the nation but critical to its construction. Therefore, a victory for the BJP in Bihar would have meant a triumph of his idea of the nation—industrially advanced and powerful. Despite being completely uprooted from the village and the state, for this section of Bihar migrant workers, home is not just the nostalgia for the old country; if they were to return to them, they must become a new country. As Kailash Sharma explained,

> Bihar seems to be stuck in a time warp, it has to get free of it. *Desh ko vikas chahiye aur Bihar mein vinash hai.* If I had not moved to Delhi with my family, my children would never have seen the world outside, wouldn't have ever achieved what they have been able to in Gurgaon.

But why does Suresh Prasad remain evasive on the question of politics? Coming from one of the lowest caste and class locations, Suresh Prasad's interaction with other members of his village is very limited: 'There is too much conflict in the village, so I don't like meeting them here as well.' He regularly visits his village but until recently did not possess a voter identity card. The question of travelling to the village just to vote does not arise as trains are crowded, tickets too expensive and the leaves very short. 'In any case, nothing seems to change whoever comes to power, so why bother,' he complains. In terms of existing power hierarchies, therefore, Suresh and his castemen remain outside the process of decision-making—politics offers scarcely any motivation or excitement. Land and labour, and the everyday indignities, have remained inconspicuously absent from the national and vernacular public sphere. Nevertheless, the poor in India do come out to vote, that too in higher proportion than the affluent—a conundrum which has no convincing explanation.

Workers in the various industrial units situated in Gurgaon's Udyog Vihar are tormented by fundamentally two kinds of relations of exploitation—the employer/employee and the landlord/tenant. The undercurrent of both these forms of exploitation is their status as a 'migrant worker'. With increasing contractualization, workers move industries as well as cities very frequently. Thirty-five-year-old Mohammad Naeem and his much younger nephew Waseem belong to village Paru in the Muzaffarpur district of Bihar. The family owned little land which was further fragmented and shared among Naeem's father and seven of his uncles. Naeem followed his grandfather and father to Calcutta, where he joined their business of supplying tea from wholesalers to retailers. As tea market crashed in 1997–1998 (which Waseem attributes to the corrupt practices of tea suppliers), some of Naeem's relatives who worked in the construction field got him into the construction sites of Hyderabad. He worked as a supervisor in Hyderabad, and later in Tamil Nadu where he could earn ₹2,000–3000 extra. The promise of higher earnings took him to Bombay where he spent nearly two years. The crisis in real estate affected the construction industry badly, which made Naeem to make yet another decision to move from the city and also the construction sector. He came to Gurgaon some two years back and, unlike other workers, has managed to bring his family—four children and his wife—along.

Both Naeem and Waseem are contract workers, who are assigned the task of supervising the loading and unloading of trucks at gate number three of Maruti factory in Gurgaon. For the kind of work that usually stretches to more than 12 hours a day, they earn ₹7,500 a month, a portion of which is deducted as provident fund.

The Inter-State Migrant Workmen Act promulgated by the central government in 1979 provided for a series of protection to the migrant workers. It assured wage equality and made provisions for additional earnings such as displacement and journey allowances to workers recruited from outside the state. The Act required the labour contractors (often called sardars in North India) to make available suitable residential accommodation, medical facilities and protective clothing to the workmen during the period of their accommodation.[17] Neither Kailash Sharma who had a much longer migration history nor the more recent ones displayed any awareness of these entitlements. In constant search of a better labour price, the workers often switch employers; however, they end up losing their provident fund savings as employers generally delay the process of transferring the funds. Approaching the workers' unions is rarely helpful, as according to Waseem, even though they promptly take the matter to the labour courts, the procedure is so tedious that it becomes counter-productive and a costly affair.

The workers' colonies that are home to migrants are also sites of dehumanization and otherization. The landlords—usually from locally

---

[17] Neither Kailash Sharma who migrated to Delhi a long time back, nor the more recent migrants were aware of their entitlements provided by the Inter-State Migrant Workmen Act. It is argued that the collusion among the state government, labour officers and the principal employers has allowed the Act to remain an ineffective one. In 2011, a Standing Committee of the Indian Parliament found that the state governments maintained almost no data on the number of migrant workers in each state, neither did they have any information about the licensed/unlicensed contractors in the states. It found that the Union government had failed to ensure that the contractors and employers 'mandatorily register the workers so that they could avail of social benefits under the Act'. Government of India, *The Inter-State Migrant Workmen (Regulation of Employment and Conditions of Service) Act, 1979*. Available at: http://hrylabour.gov.in/docs/labourActpdfdocs/Inter_State_Migrant_Act.pdf (accessed on 5 September 2016); Ministry of Labour and Employment, *The Inter-State Migrant Workmen (Regulation of Employment and Conditions of service) Amendment Bill, 2011*, Twenty-Third Report, Standing Committee on Labour (2011–2012), Fifteenth Lok Sabha, Lok Sabha Secretariat. Available at: http://164.100.47.134/lsscommittee/Labour/computer-bill.pdf1.pdf (accessed on 2 October 2016).

dominant castes such as Jats and Ahirs—collectively increase rents at will; the workers are compelled to make their grocery purchases from the shops run by the landlords, often, at exorbitant rates. The workers, despite their long stays in these colonies, are denied the necessary residential proof for procuring the ration card and enrolling in electoral rolls. For the migrant in any case, securing entitlements in a world that is alien to him is an uphill task. Curiously, none of the workers interviewed, irrespective of the duration of their migration, have been successful in securing the BPL card. Virendra Prasad explained,

> First you have to surrender your Card at the village. Then you have to provide residential proof of staying for long in the city. Then you need a high government official or the local councillor or the MLA to vouch for your honesty. Every step has its own impediments.

Separately, Muqeem, who runs a small tyre repair shop and has lived in Gurgaon for nearly 35 years, echoed the same reason for failing to procure either the ration or the voter's identity card.

In both, the workplace and the 'non-place', that is, the workers' colonies, the identity is shaped by the commonality of experiences of exploitation. Thus, unlike Auge's 'non-place' that is ephemeral and superficial, the dilapidated colony does have deeper political meaning for the workers. It is the site of everyday politics of solidarity, survival and negotiations and sharing of experiences. But there is rarely any active resistance. The migrant is bereft of his citizenship in his place of work and stay. 'Home' in contrast with 'house' is then idealized as a space that would confer the worker, his/her full citizenship. As Waseem put it, and others who had gathered around him tended to readily agree, 'If we are in our village, in Bihar, we can fight. Here we can't even argue. We submit and accept everything. We keep to ourselves. *Kya karein, majboori hai* (what to do, it is a compulsion).'

The 'home' is then the location for active mobilization and politics in which the migrant sees hope and acts accordingly. This includes his right to practise his religion, which Waseem felt was difficult to exercise in a place like Gurgaon. The city had grown enormously in size, but there was rarely any mosque in the newer areas of Gurgaon where

Waseem and his other Muslim friends could offer their Friday namaz. They recalled how in their village, when the local mosque needed repair, they all contributed towards its restoration. A similar kind of collective effort was not possible here; Waseem rued, 'This is not our place, we cannot make any claim. Although our God is everywhere, the "locals" will never tolerate the coming up of a mosque.'

Although physically separated by no less than a thousand miles, the workers attempt to resurrect the 'home' outside the home and live it through the solidarity networks that have emerged. Usually, such networks surface among workers of the same village, district or region—and echo the familiar world of symbols, gestures, experiences and meanings. As Naeem explained,

> On Sundays, we go and meet people of our village who live nearby. We enquire about each other's well-being, about kin back home. We also help each other out in seeking employment, in dealing with their landlords or in negotiating for wages. We may not meet each other at the village, but here we regularly get to see each other, and are very cordial. None of us here is so highly educated, none of us are officers, we all are labourers here.

The resurrected home, unlike Hobsbawm's heimat, does not merely offer emotional solace, a site of remembrance, but fills the void that inertness of politics produces. Such solidarities are alternatives to politics outside the 'home'. Muqeem travels to his village, Basudeo Patti in Muzaffarpur district, every time the panchayat or assembly election is held. Many others who were interviewed, including Naeem and Waseem, though could not afford to buy the train ticket to make the journey to their villages to cast their votes, do take an active interest in the politics at 'home' and contribute to making collective choices. In Paru, Naeem and Waseem enlisted their community's support for the local Yadav candidate who for the last 15 years had not found favour.

In the life of a migrant worker, the house and the home emerge as two distinct spheres of existence. Nevertheless, both are valued. The house is marked by its temporality, which while being no less power laden is politically inert. The worker ceases to be a full citizen within the house, while he idealizes the home to reclaim what he seems to have lost in the house. It is difficult however to separate the two, the house and the home, into neat compartments. Experiences may vary, but migrant locations, the travails apart, also leave the workers with certain sense of accomplishments and meanings of life. On the other hand, the home, like Habermas's heimat, could also be a social construction rather than a real memory. For anthropology, a truly migrant perspective could be one that seeks to see 'home' and migrant locations, not in a relationship of opposition but simply a mode of being.[18]

---

[18] In this regard, Paul Carter, in *Living in a New Country*, is instructive as he makes a call to 'disarm' anthropology of the 'genealogical rhetoric of blood, property and frontiers' and argues for adopting an 'authentically migrant perspective' based on an 'intuition that the opposition between here and there is itself a cultural construction, a consequence of thinking in terms of fixed entities and defining them oppositionally'. Paul Carter, *Living in a New Country: History, Travelling and Language* (London: Faber and Faber, 1992), 1. I also draw support from Sanjay Srivastava's discussion on home and *ghummakkadi* (wandering), who expresses his discomfort with the fixity of nativity, belongingness and attachment that Indian social science seems to frequently rest on. As Srivastava writes, 'I believe that there also existed quite complex notions of home and belonging, and multifaceted perspectives on spaces of passage as residence.' Sanjay Srivastava, 'Ghummakkads, a Woman's Place, and the LTC-walas: Towards a Critical History of "Home", "belonging" and "attachment"', *Contributions to Indian Sociology* 39, no. 3 (2005): 379.

# Section B

# Social Hegemony and Politics

# Chapter 4

# Illiberal State and the Myth of a Civil Society*

R. Thirunavukkarasu

### INTRODUCTION

The oft-repeated proposition that the Indian State and its liberal democratic character are or have been since independence quintessentially a welfare state and also an aspiring inclusive state remains quite disputable given the increasing intensity of violence against marginalized communities, especially Dalits. The larger argument that the anti-colonial struggle precipitated the emergence of liberal and democratic values in India and these values became the nucleus of India's modern polity acquired academic and political consensus for considerable time. In fact, democracy and nationalism are perceived in India's case as coterminous. The robust assertion that 'the character of India's democracy had to be liberal not only because of its commitment to civil liberties but also

---

\* An earlier version of this chapter was published as 'Illiberal State and the Myth of a Civil Society: Justice Sampath Commission Report on Paramakudi Police Firing', *Review of Development and Change* 22, no. 2 (July–December 2017): 88–108. Available at: https://doi.org/10.1177/0972266120170205 (accessed on 23 August 2020).

because of its vision of equality and social justice'[1] emboldened many not only to be critical of either liberal or democratic values but also the character of the State too. The co-terminality between nationalism and democratic values in scholarly writings is severely questioned in recent times, and the assumption that nationalism in India ensured the emergence of the nation has also been strongly disputed.[2]

As Ernest Gellner has emphatically asserted, 'Nationalism is not the awakening of nations to self-consciousness; it invents where they do not exist.'[3] Thus, the process of inventing a nation and democratizing the State must have been far the most important obligation of the anti-colonial movement; what India has however achieved as a post-colonial country at both the political (State) and social–cultural (nation) realms requires dispassionate scrutiny.

If nationalism is expected to invent a nation, it is highly pertinent to delineate the contours of that imagined community. While a common homeland is quite an obvious requirement along with common lingua franca, establishing a culturally sanctioned comradeship and socially approved solidarity would remain irreducible, axiomatic premises upon which the nation is actually invented. India's anti-colonial struggle was expected to invent a nation; instead, aggregated communities of people where graded inequality has been eulogized as a cultural treasure was deemed to be designated as a nation. A nation and its inherent normative principles must ensure self-esteem for all its members as a political virtue. Self-esteem is not a matter of subjective good to be treated privately; John Rawls in no uncertain terms declares self-esteem a public matter and the just distribution of self-esteem is one of his primary concerns.[4]

---

[1] Rajeev Bhargava, 'Democratic Vision of a New Republic', in *Transforming India: Social and Political Dynamics of Democracy*, eds., Francine Frankel and Rajeev Bhargava (Delhi: Oxford University Press, 2000), 26.

[2] See G. Aloysius, *Nationalism without a Nation in India* (Delhi: Oxford University Press, 1997).

[3] Ernest Gellner, *Thought and Change* (London: Weidenfeld and Nicolson, 1964), 158.

[4] John Rawls, *A Theory of Justice* (Harvard: Belknap Press, 1971), 440.

In the Indian case, anti-colonial struggle did spring up self-esteem to the most deprived sections but not self-respect, as the country has been perennially shrouded in the tyrannical fabric of caste.[5] Scholarly literature on Indian nationalism and its logical inference nation expectedly offered differing perspectives. While Cambridge historians declared that the Indian national movement was largely constituted by power and profit-mongering groups and cliques,[6] the subaltern historiography found the nationalist movement quite elitist in sharp contrast to the struggle and aspirations of the vast subaltern masses whose interests were distinct and different from those of the upper echelon of the society.[7]

Marxists assessed the movement as essentially bourgeoisie enterprise with strong patronage coming from feudal gentry. This unholy alliance between industrial bourgeoisie and feudal gentry prevented the anti-colonial movement from becoming a national liberation movement and made it a mere pressure group against the British rule to achieve political and economic benefits for the two reactionary groups.[8] These major perspectives effectively summed up what we have achieved; it was not exactly a nation but merely a coronation of feudal oligarchies and dominant caste/class interests. Interestingly, the State was perceived to be a modernizing force, especially by the liberals who played a pivotal role in the anti-colonial movement; that was the reason perhaps the term 'nation building' was massively popularized by the State machineries during the first three decades of independent India. The larger question however remains: What kind of a post-colonial State is it?

The consistency with which Marxists have treated the State demands special mention. For them, State always remains an instrument of class domination. The post-colonial State assumes a cardinal obligation, assert Marxist scholars, to expand global capitalist development endeavours.

---

[5] Gopal Guru, 'Liberal Democracy in India and the Dalit Critique', *Social Research* 78, no. 1 (2011): 99–122.

[6] Anil Seal, *The Emergence of Indian Nationalism: Competition and Collaboration in Late Nineteenth Century* (Cambridge: Cambridge University Press, 1968).

[7] Ranajit Guha, 'On Some Aspects of the Historiography of Colonial India', in *Subaltern Studies*, vol. I (Delhi: Oxford University Press, 1982), 1–8.

[8] A. R. Desai, *Social Background of Indian Nationalism* (Bombay: Popular Prakashan, 1954), 175–176.

Their broader assessment was premised upon the colonial context. In fact, it was the elites who insisted on having 'interventionist state' as Desai categorically stated 'the plea for an interventionist state was the result of growing discontent of the Indian capitalist class towards the metropolitan class and metropolitan commodities dominated by the capitalists'.[9] As the result of two-century old colonial rule, the newly emerged native dominant classes—a large section of them—extended their support to the Congress party, which tacitly endorsed the capitalist path of development. This nascent national bourgeoisie with its burgeoning anti-feudal and anti-imperialist political rhetoric was actually keen on expanding the capitalist path of development.

This political situation had effortlessly made State intervention a necessary condition for further expansion of capitalism.[10] The emergence of State-sponsored capitalism especially in India had dual task to perform. Apart from the major task of expanding the capitalist path of development, the post-colonial State had to manufacture a grand consensus in favour of sociocultural values of the dominant classes/castes. In other words, accumulating indigenous capital without external dependency became the paramount task of the post-colonial State for which ensuring a strong approval in terms of sociocultural values became a vital functional prerequisite for the dominant castes/classes.[11]

India's dominant castes/classes largely succeeded in acquiring sociocultural legitimacy for the new political dispensation by maintaining a tactical coalition of different classes and by providing regular concessions to the exploited subaltern masses. These administrative solaces however did not alter the structural positions of the subaltern masses.[12] The national bourgeoisie's tactical alliance with the landed gentry and their almost iron fist grip in independent India's policymaking processes

---

[9] A. R. Desai, *Indian's Path of Development: A Marxist Approach* (Bombay: Popular Prakashan, 1984), 49.

[10] Ibid., 76.

[11] Berch Berberoglu, 'Introduction', *International Review of Modern Sociology* 33 (special issue; 2007): 1–6.

[12] For more, see Prabhat Patnaik, 'Imperialism and the Growth of Indian Capitalism', in *Studies in the Theory of Imperialism*, eds. Roger Owen and Bob Sutcliffe (London: Longman, 1976).

especially in the formidable bureaucracy unambiguously prove the strengthening of the dominant castes/classes. The post-colonial Indian State effectively remained the vanguard in protecting interests of the dominant castes/classes. With its massive apparatus, the State not only mobilized resources for these dominant castes/classes but also enacted laws to protect their interests.[13] The quick and flourishing growth of Indian entrepreneurial groups and commercial associations was singularly indebted to the post-colonial State's interventionist policies. This formidable hegemony of dominant castes/classes was further accelerated by the liberalization policies since early 1990.

The market-friendly economic reforms were carried out as the domestic fiscal condition worsened; hence, the Indian government was left with no option but to adhere to the structural adjustment policies instructed by the World Bank and the International Monetary Fund (IMF). Such a move was believed to have opened up the Indian economy to the forces of globalization. Sociological or social anthropological significance of studying the changing character of the State is to reflect upon certain cultural dimensions embedded in it. Bringing in the cultural dimension to study the post-colonial State, especially in the globalized era, certainly emboldens us to highlight the uniqueness of the State; otherwise, one may end up equating every State on par with Western liberal democratic state as the perfect template. The cultural dimension of the State entails studying the everyday nuanced practices of State institutions and of the representations that circulate through such practices.[14] Contrary to the popular opinion, State is not felt by its citizens only during major events such as wars or elections. The everydayness of the State is quite visible and vivid in many material objects such as currency, medicines/hospitals and post offices.[15]

When market-friendly policies were implemented, they had a tremendous impact on the power structure, especially at the local levels.

---

[13] For more, see Ralph Miliband, *The State in Capitalist Society* (New York, NY: Basic Books, 1967).

[14] C. J. Fuller and Veronique Benei, *The Everyday State and Society in Modern India* (New Delhi: Social Science Press, 2001).

[15] Akhil Gupta and Aradhana Sharma, 'Globalization and Postcolonial States', *Current Anthropology* 47, no. 2 (2006): 277–307.

The post-1991 Indian society witnessed not only the end of License Raj but also the massive entrepreneurial empowerment of many communities. The unhindered flow of liquid currency in turn facilitated the elevation of many such communities' cultural assertions. These communities' assertion and subsequently domination over marginalized subaltern masses resulted in the 'imagination' of their cultural pasts. Such imaginations further facilitated the manufacturing of icons, narratives on velour and betrayals.

The task of the post-colonial State especially in the liberalized economic order is not only to encourage entrepreneurial and commercial acumen of the newly emerged dominant caste groups but also to endorse the cultural narrative of their past. The resistance from subaltern groups against these narratives effortlessly made them anti-State; this necessitates the State to unleash its violence in the most brutal way. What was expected of India becoming an incredible civil society with the arrival of market stands nullified; instead, the State has retained its oligarchic character. This chapter intends to display and demonstrate the perfect union of interest among the increasingly coercive state as a representative of feudal, non-modern, oligarchic interest groups and dominant castes. Publicly executing unarmed Dalits in a Tamil Nadu town for their simple, basic rights to revere their leader is certainly a point to justify the changing nature of the state.

## PARAMAKUDI POLICE FIRING

Ramanathapuram district in southern Tamil Nadu has witnessed several brutalities and violence against Dalits for well over a century, and it has intensified since the early decades of the 20th century. The Pallars/Mallars/Devendra Kulavelalars, as the Dalit community is known here, constitute 18.4 per cent of the district's population according to 2011 Census. The atrocities committed by the Thevar/Maravar caste groups against the Dalits in many parts of Ramanathapuram district acquired a new dimension of notoriety with the brutal murder of Mr Immanuel Sekaran way back on 11 September 1957 in Paramakudi town. Mr Immanuel Sekaran having served in the Indian Army was well informed of the egalitarian principles of the modern polity and was quite instrumental in mobilizing Dalits against the violence unleashed by the Thevar/Maravar caste groups. His brutal death turned out to be the moment of not only commemoration or tribute but also an instance of Dalits' political assertion.

Every year, on the day of his martyrdom, Dalits from various parts of southern Tamil Nadu gather in Paramakudi to pay their tribute to this brave leader. The steep increase in the number of followers thronging Paramakudi to pay their respect to Mr Immanuel Sekaran's memorial on 11 September every year clearly indicates the growing assertion of Dalits, especially in southern Tamil Nadu. This event itself effortlessly becomes a statement of Dalit political assertion besides several Dalit leaders' speeches at the memorial site. The symbolic and substantive significance of this event needless to say had indeed unsettled the otherwise known/projected dominance of the Thevars/Maravars in this area. The commemoration ceremony in honour and memory of Mr Immanuel Sekaran on 11 September 2011 turned violent. This violence is significant for more than one reasons. This is simply incomparable with the violence unleashed by the Thevar/Maravar groups alone; the state unmasked itself and shed all its liberal and egalitarian pretentions. The police opened fire on the unarmed Dalit protesters gathered in Paramakudi on 11 September 2011, which left several Dalits killed and many more wounded. Two days later, the Tamil Nadu government formally announced the setting up of a commission of enquiry under the chairmanship of Justice K. Sampath. The enquiry commission of Justice Sampath conducted its proceedings and submitted its report and recommendations on 7 May 2013 to the state government. This essay intends to explore and scrutinize the larger contours of Justice Sampath Commission report.

## THE CONTEXT

The atrocities and violence Dalits have been subjected to by Thevars/Maravars are an integral part of this district's modern history. The Ramanathapuram Sethupathi dynasty, who ruled this track of land, were lords during the old Pandiyan rule. Thus, a sense of aristocracy is usually invoked by Thevars/Maravars. Eulogizing their valour and bravery has become the new political normalcy. As late as in the 1970s, the Tamil Nadu government in its official publication said,

> The Ramanathapuram Kingdom which was under the rule of Nayakas of Madurai was mostly inhabited by the Maravars—a very fine race of men, active and athletic with a greater degree of manliness than any other race in South India.[16]

At the turn of the 20th century when the subcontinent was slowly but steadily beginning to embrace certain fundamental tenants of modernity, a sense of liberal values, egalitarian principles became the foundational principles of the new social order and the modern polity. The transformation of being the subjects of the imperial rule to the citizens of a republic began to shape itself. Dalits were no longer willing to let the rein of feudal terror unleashed by Thevars/Maravars sustain. They were determined that the subjugation must end and any attempt to inferiorize their self must be thwarted. This is not merely an assertion of a humiliated/exploited community pleading for dignity. It is more of a declaration that equality has become the new political ethics, and this is non-negotiable. The moment of rebellion was systematically articulated, and subsequently a fresh lexicon of praxis was drafted by Mr Immanuel Sekaran.

Mr Immanuel Sekaran was born in 1924 in Paramakudi to Mr Deivanayakam and Mrs Gnana Soundari. His father was a school teacher and believed to have founded an organization for the welfare of and to protect the dignity of his caste—Pallar/Mallar/Devendra Kula velalar. Mr Immanuel Sekaran joined the Army when he was 21 and after his short service as havildar in the Army came back to Paramakudi and began working towards strengthening the organization which his father was quite instrumental in creating. On the fateful day of 11 September 1957, near his residence, he was hacked to death by a group of persons believed to be from Thevar/Maravar caste. The inconsolable community in the neighbouring areas began flocking at his funeral.

---

[16] Director of Information and Public Relation, Ramanathapuram District, *Tamil Arasu* II, no. 16 (February 1972): 11–18, Madras.

He was just 33 at the time of his death. Every year, the community began to observe his martyrdom no less than with religious devotion. The preceding moments of his death unambiguously are believed to display the caste arrogance of Thevars/Maravars.

Way back in 1957, the district collector of Ramanathapuram sought to strike a reconciliatory note as the plight of Dalits became quite unbearable at the hands of Thevars/Maravars in the district. The meeting was convened at Mudukulathur taluk office on 10 September 1957. On behalf of Dalits, Immanuel Sekaran, J. Vedamanickam, Peter Perumal and Alandur Kambar participated. Similarly, on behalf of the Thevars/Maravars, a few prominent figures came in; among them, U. Muthuramalingam Thevar (Member of Parliament) and T. V. Sasivarna Thevar (MLA) were well-known faces. While finalizing a peace accord, Muthuramalingam Thevar announced that Mr Immanuel Sekaran was unworthy of a person to sign on par with his stature. This led to heated arguments, and Mr Immanuel Sekaran stood by his grounds. Subsequently, the district administration officials had to intervene to finalize the accord. The animosity had reached a new height. That night, Mr Immanuel Sekaran stayed back in Mudukulathur itself and the next (11 September 1957) morning he reached his home in Paramakudi; on that night after his dinner while standing near to his residence, he was brutally hacked to death by people believed to be Muthuramalingam Thevar's followers.[17] The next few days, this area witnessed one of the worst riots and brutal murders. On 13 September, Dalits were murdered in Arunkulam village; the next day (14 September), when police personnel came to the protection of Dalits, they were brutally attacked by Muthuramalingam Thevar's followers. As a result, police opened fire which resulted in the killing of a few Maravars. The next one week, this district began witnessing continuous riots, looting, arson and damage of both private and public properties.[18] What popularly called or came to be known as 'Mudukulathur riots' created a permanent scar in the minds of Dalits.

---

[17] T. S. Chokkalingam, *Muthukulathur Payangaram* [Mudukulathur Atrocities] (in Tamil; Kavin Publishers, 2008), 138–139.

[18] Ibid., 76–77.

## THE TRAGEDY ON 11 SEPTEMBER 2011

The district administration maintained that it had provided enough measures for both followers and political leaders to come and pay their tribute to Mr Immanuel Sekaran memorial. A detailed time table had been issued by the district administration in order to facilitate peaceful conduct of the proceedings. One of the prominent Dalit leaders of southern Tamil Nadu Mr John Pandian originally hailing from Tirunelveli district was an influential leader among Pallar/Mallar/Devendra Kulavelalars. He became quite active politically way back in the mid-1980s itself. However, he unsuccessfully contested in Ramanathapuram constituency in 1991 assembly election as a Pattali Makkal Katchi (PMK) candidate. In 2000, he launched his Tamizhaga Makkal Munnetra Kazhagam (TMMK; Tamil People's Progressive Federation).[19]

According to the district administration, Mr John Pandian sought permission to pay his respect at Immanuel Sekaran memorial and was given time between 1.45 PM and 2.45 PM to pay his tributes. The intelligence wing of the district police claimed that it had credible information that Mr John Pandian planned to visit Pacheri village on his way to Paramakudi to console the family members of a young boy—Palani Kumar.[20] This young Dalit school boy was murdered by people believed to be from Thevar/Maravar caste on 9 September 2011 on the allegation that Palani Kumar wrote objectionable comments about Muthuramalingam Thevar on the wall. This had caused unusual restlessness in the neighbouring areas. If John Pandian had chosen to visit Palani Kumar's family on his way to Paramakudi, the police claimed that it would vitiate the already volatile situation in the district.

Thus, the police sought district collector's permission to invoke Section 144 of IPC to prevent Mr John Pandian from entering Ramanathapuram district itself. This prohibitory order was issued by the district administration on 10 September 2011 at 10.30 PM. A copy of

---

[19] He was convicted in a murder case in Coimbatore and sent to life imprisonment; upon his subsequent appeal in the Supreme Court, he was later acquitted after serving eight years in prison.

[20] Dinakaran, *John Pandian in Preventive Custody* (12 September 2011): 3, Madurai edition.

this order had been passed on to the neighbouring Tirunelveli district administration too. On 11 September 2011, when Mr John Pandian began his journey to enter the Ramanathapuram district, he was put under preventive custody. This message spread like wild fire and changed the scenario in Paramakudi. All that went very peaceful till 11 AM abruptly changed to utter chaos. Nearly 500 supporters of Mr John Pandian congregated at the Five Roads Junction in Paramakudi. This venue is vital as this particular road (NH49) is the major link of Madurai–Rameswaram highway. The unarmed protesters simply wanted their leader Mr John Pandian to be released immediately and be allowed to pay his respect to *Thiyagi* (Martyr) Immanuel Sekaran. While a contingent of police force and its top officials tried to convince the protesters to disperse, the protesters first began quarrelling with police officials. The police claimed that the protesters went berserk; a total mayhem set in.[21] Many newspapers and television news reports claimed that senior police officials on the spot tried to pacify the agitating protesters and the protesters were in no mood to relent. Suddenly things went out of control and the police first began canning the protesters and subsequently used tear gas shells. Finally, the firing took place as claimed by several newspapers.[22] The highhandedness of the police and disproportionate use of power and weapons resulted in the killing of 6 unarmed Dalit protesters.

## THE ENQUIRY COMMISSION

The outrage from different political and civil organizations was along the expected lines. The Jayalalithaa government formally announced the setting up of an enquiry commission to look into the issue. The state government in its notification on 13 September 2011 declared the constitution of an enquiry commission under the chairmanship of Honourable Justice K. Sampath to look into the following issues:

---

[21] Janashakti, *Riots Broke Out in Paramakudi* (13 September 2011): 1, Chennai edition.

[22] Daily Thanthi, *Police Opened Fire in Paramakudi* (12 September 2011): 1, Madurai edition; Dinakaran, *John Pandian in Preventive Custody*, 2011; Malai Murasu, *Six Killed in Paramakudi Police Firing* (12 September 2011): 1, Madurai edition; Tamil Murasu, *Riots in Paramakudi; Police Firing; 7 Protesters Killed* (11 September 2011): 1, Madurai edition.

1. Causes/reasons for the police to open fire on the protesters, which led to the loss of life and damages to properties
2. The law and order problems emerged as a result of the police firing
3. To ascertain whether appropriate force had been deployed and whether proper precautionary measures were followed before firing
4. To ascertain whether there were excesses committed by police officials; if so, commission is mandated to offer its valuable advice to police personnel
5. To recommend preventive measures to be taken in order to avoid such incidents in future

From the time of the notification, the commission was expected to submit its report within two months. It assumed its official responsibilities on 15 September 2011, and two lawyers had been subsequently appointed to facilitate the commission's task. Major newspapers' southern editions carried advertisements on 9 and 30 November 2011, asking people to depose before the commission and if need be submit their affidavit pertaining to the Paramakudi police firing incident. When some of the affected people resented to the state government's decision to probe the incident with Justice Sampath Commission and sought CBI enquiry for impartial investigation, the commission considered their concerns and appointed a lawyer to appeal on behalf of those people before the commission.

## HOW DOES THE COMMISSION VIEW THIS INCIDENT?

The commission takes cognizance of both immediate causes and historically well-entrenched rivalry and animosity between Dalits and Thevar/Maravar caste. As a result, the district administration takes extraordinary precaution during two important events in a year. In September, Thiyagi Immanuel Sekaran martyrdom day, and in October, Thevar Guru Puja, are two tension-generating events according to the district civil and police administration. Simple words or action from either side could vitiate the situation to go out of control. While deposing before the commission, District Collector V. Arun Roy provided the details of the administration's preparedness. He said that he had visited the memorial site well three months before on 18 June 2011 itself to ascertain the initiatives to be taken by the administration.[23]

On 29 August 2011, he convened an all-party and all-association meeting to solicit their valuable suggestions to conduct the Immanuel Sekaran martyrdom day proceeding very peacefully. Different organs of the district administration conducted regular meetings to ensure that 11 September remains peaceful. On t10 September, the district collector visited and supervised the preparation for the event and on that evening, according to Mr Arun Roy, the district police superintendent informed of Mr John Pandian's plan to visit Pacheri village to console Palani Kumar's family. The district police cautioned the collector that John Pandian's visit and his usual character of making inflammatory speeches would definitely worsen the law–order situation.[24]

While concurring with the spirit of district police chief's warnings, the collector issued prohibitory orders against Mr John Pandian from entering Ramanathapuram district, and that if Mr Pandian desired to do so, he could be arrested forthwith. When ascertaining the veracity of district SP's caution regarding Mr John Pandian's plausible entry and the inevitable law and order problem, district collector's observation before the commission was very important.

> Mr John Pandian has been well known for his inflammatory speeches as early as 1989 itself; the caste riots which claimed many lives and left many innocent people helpless in Theni was largely the result of Mr John Pandian's hate speeches.[25]

The district administration firmly believed that Mr John Pandian was the troubling figure and that preventing him from entering the district was absolutely necessary to protect law and order in the district. This highly prejudiced, partisan attitude towards a Dalit leader speaks volumes about the nature of our political and administrative structure. Had Mr John Pandian been allowed to proceed to Paramakudi, in all

---

[23] *Justice Sampath Commission Report*, vol. I, 17.
[24] Ibid., 18.
[25] Ibid.

likelihood there would not have been any untoward incident happening. The administration could have provided enough protection and persuaded him not to make any inflammatory speeches. Instead, the administration simply resorted to prevent him from entering the district itself. The legacy of the colonial mindset of demonizing the underprivileged people and their leaders is reconfigured today.

Mr John Pandian's plan of visiting a Dalit school boy's family was the nucleus of the entire fiasco. On 9 September 2011, Palani Kumar was brutally murdered by a gang of people from Thevar/Maravar caste. The allegation was that Palani Kumar had scribbled objectionable comments about Muthuramalingam Thevar on the wall. The commission took cognizance of this incident and its intensity too. However, it did not attempt to probe the matter in detail as it was not its mandate. But an independent committee of civil rights activists found that the alleged wall was not accessible to Dalits, as the wall was located well within Thevar/Maravar caste people neighbourhood; thus, entering Thevar caste neighbourhood for a Dalit boy was not as easy as one might think, as the caste arrogance among the Thevars/Maravars was well known; second, the alleged scribbling was at such a height that Palani Kumar could not have even got his fingers there. It is important to note that on the eve of Mr Immanuel Sekaran's day of martyrdom, attacks and killings of Dalits had become quite recurrent.[26]

## THE COMMISSION AND THE POLICE

The highhandedness and excessive use of force unleashed by police personnel on 11 September 2011 in Paramakudi was indeed a matter of profound concern. The commission, while recording police officials' version, did not seem to have aired the popular resentment especially the victims' anger against its officials' unwarranted excess of force on that fateful day. Ramanathapuram range DIG Sandeep Mittal, District Superintendent of Police Kalirajan Mahesh Kumar and Deputy Commissioner of Police, Chennai Adyar (on special duty specifically

---

[26] Anand Teltumbde, 'Jayalalithaa's Sacrificial Lambs', *Economic & Political Weekly* 46, no. 46 (2011): 10.

for Immanuel Sekaran martyrdom day), Dr Senthil Velan, along with a brigade of police personnel and officials from civil administration had deposed before the commission. As many as 210 government officials—from both police and civil administration—had recorded their statements before the commission. While an overwhelming majority of them had declared that they did not witness the police firing, without any major exception, all of them had confessed that the police firing was the last resort to bring back normalcy and the police had to open fire purely for their self-defence.[27]

Here, Dr Senthil Velan's affidavit needs special attention. Being at the centre of the controversy, this IPS officer declared that he did not witness the police firing; however, he confessed to have 'seen' the incidents.[28] Here we presume that the commission considers 'violence' as 'incidents' which is different from firing. Commission's efforts to differentiate the two are highly perplexing. Having served in Kamuthi range as additional superintendent of police (2006–2007) and later as district superintendent of police (2008–2009), Dr Senthil Velan claimed that he had profound experience in conducting both Immanuel Sekaran and Thevar Guru Puja functions in the past.

He said that he reported to the DIG on the previous day (10 September 2011) and upon receiving his further instructions, he took charge of monitoring 35 spots during Immanuel Sekaran memorial procession. He declared that he received district SP's message of John Pandian's supporters blocking the road at the crucial Five Point Junction around 11 AM and rushed to the spot immediately. He said that he took enormous care while addressing the agitating masses; he was quite committed not to hurt their sentiments.

In his affidavit before the commission,[29] a few observations by Dr Senthil Velan are worth mentioning. He said that the protesting agitators wanted their leader Mr John Pandian's immediate release; otherwise, they would 'cancel' the entire function. Second, the agitators claimed that John Pandian's arrest was carried out at the behest of

---

[27] *Justice Sampath Commission Report*, vol. I, 115–274.
[28] Ibid., 175.
[29] Ibid., 175–179.

Dr Krishnasamy, the leader of Puthiya Tamilagam (another popular leader of Pallars/Mallars/Devendra Kulavelalars).[30] Third, he said that there was a strong rumour deliberately circulated by some vested interest groups that the police arrested John Pandian just to kill him in 'fake encounter'. Dr Senthil Velan firmly denied such baseless allegations and also strongly refuted that the entire firing was carried out at the behest of Mrs Sasikala Natarajan (a close aide and confidante of Chief Minister Jayalalithaa).[31] While one may set aside these allegations as baseless, beneath such rumours and conspiracy theories lay the structural tensions and cultural conflicts. The entrenched subjugation of Dalits actually emboldens them to trust such rumours.

The sociological point is: Why did people believe that the police may organize a fake encounter against John Pandian? The deepening distrust that the police have created either deliberately or perhaps unwittingly among Dalits is something that demands a thorough scrutiny. The police were perceived by the marginalized sections of our society as a legitimate agency to exercise brutal violence over them. While the State declares arbitrary entitlements for the privileged castes, any agitation by marginalized communities is perceived by the State as a law and order problem. However, the real issue is about dignity and honour. When the police force acts solely at the behest of the State's interest, Dalits and other marginalized sections obviously become the 'other'; the 'other' inherently possesses strong with anti-State interests and acts against the State interests. Thus, violence against Dalits and other marginalized sections acquires new dimensions—both social and political.

The next rumour/conspiracy which Dr Senthil Velan strongly denied is the role (both direct and indirect) of Mrs Sasikala Natarajan in the firing. One may easily write off this allegation as baseless and

---

[30] Dr Krishnasamy is a Coimbatore-based general physician; he founded his own party Puthiya Tamilagam and was elected as an MLA in the past. It seems quite unambiguous that both Dr Krishnasamy and John Pandian are political rivals.

[31] Many Dalits allege that the firing was orchestrated by Thevars (Sasikala Natarajan is from Kallar caste which claimed allegiance to Muthuramalingam Thevar's leadership in the recent past) to punish them for speaking for dignity and honour.

absolutely concocted as there is no actual/substantial evidence to prove it beyond any ambiguity. Be that as it may, the crucial point is why did not Dalits simply reject such rumours? It is quite obvious that Mrs Sasikala Natarajan symbolically and substantively represents crude power, the power of her own caste group and similar feudal forces. Needless to add, the All India Anna Dravida Munnetra Kazhagam (AIADMK) is the party of such feudal forces—Thevars/Maravars in southern districts, Kallars in Kaveri delta districts and Gounders in western districts of Tamil Nadu. Sasikala Natarajan, neither elected to any office nor holding any official position, remains an extra-constitutional authority; Dalits trusting such rumours that she may be instrumental in the police firing speaks the nature of our contemporary political culture.

One of the stunning points of Dr Senthil Velan's statement is the blatant caste prejudice that prevails among the children in these areas. School children have colour bands in their wrist, with each colour symbolizing each caste.[32] The actual practice of caste begins at the tender age itself, and the school atmosphere further aggravates caste prejudice. Our schools and classrooms, instead of ensuring inclusive social order, facilitate the reproduction of disgusting feudal virtues and caste hatred.

More than Dr Senthil Velan's statements, Ramanathapuram range DIG Mr Sandeep Mittal's role in the violence and his statements before the commission require thorough scrutiny.

- Mr Mittal said in his statement that he received a confidential message from the district SP regarding Mr John Pandian's clandestine plan to visit Pacheri village to console Palani Kumar's family; the SP also conveyed him that John Pandian and his followers looked determined to visit and declared that 'they would not give any guarantee for public safety and peace in that area'.[33] (The interesting point here is that when the district SP Kalirajan Mahesh Kumar recorded statements before the commission, he did not mention a single word about what transpired between them.)[34]

---

[32] *Justice Sampath Commission Report*, vol. I, 179.
[33] Ibid., 180 (emphasis mine).
[34] Ibid., 173–174.

- Mr Mittal further said that local Dalit leaders met and discussed with the district SP to withdraw cases against John Pandian; however, the SP informed them that such action of withdrawing cases against rioters would simply erode the trust/confidence people had in police. (The commission noted this as evidence no. 198 and retained the document with itself and did not make it public.)
- Mr Mittal noted that the founder of Thiyagi Immanuel Peravai—an organization in honour/memory of Mr Immanuel Sekaran—Mr Chandra Bose came to police control room around 12 noon. The discussion that both Mr Chandra Bose and Mr Mittal had was not mentioned in the report. (The commission report said, 'It is unable to guess what transpired between them.')[35]
- The commission in its report noted that it was not able to declare the details of the discussion Mr Mittal and Mr Chandra Bose had due to official secrecy. The nature and content of the discussion till date is shrouded in secrecy. However, Mr Sivakumar, Inspector of Police, Paramakudi, in his statements before the commission claimed that Mr Chandra Bose very strongly threatened Mr Mittal of very serious consequences if Mr John Pandian was not released immediately during their meeting.[36]

What is obvious here is that the police and the state administration had exerted pressure on Dalit organizations not to react to Palani Kumar's brutal murder. Was the murder of a young school boy a deliberate attempt to vitiate the already surcharged ambiance in the Paramakudi area? The circumstance in which Palani Kumar was murdered was itself quite dubious; there are enough reasons to believe that it could have been a deliberate attempt to provoke the Dalits on the eve of Immanuel Sekaran's martyrdom day. What Mr John Pandian attempted was a correctional mechanism—the state should have intervened and instilled credible, sustainable confidence among Dalits in this area.

The commission virtually endorsed all that the police officials had said regarding the antecedents of the firing. Let us elaborate this point now: (a) Palani Kumar's murder should not be linked with the hate

---

[35] Ibid. (emphasis mine).
[36] Ibid., 157.

politics in this area. (b) Mr John Pandian's initiative to visit the bereaved family was uncalled for and it could have vitiated the atmosphere in Paramakudi. (c) Since Mr John Pandian decided to visit Pacheri village and to console Palani Kumar's family, 'law and order' had become an important issue, whereas Palani Kumar's murder was an 'isolated' incident. (d) Mr John Pandian had become a threat to peace and law and order. (e) Mr John Pandian's arrest was necessary and inevitable in order to preserve peace. (f) The agitating Dalits were hooligans (they were drunk and unwilling to listen to police and civil officials), mindlessly indulging in violence—least bothered about people's lives and damages to property. (g) In order to maintain peace and ensure smooth functioning of that day's events, police firing was necessary. After the police firing, normalcy was restored.

The logic and the narration are quite stunning and equally disturbing. What becomes so obvious is that the administrative ethics of the state apparatus actually displayed vulgar feudal virtue and caste arrogance. The endless list of atrocities committed by the Thevars/Maravars in this region against Dalits had neither social/cultural solace nor administrative remedy for the victims. Dalits' cultural icons were not allowed to be divinized; if attempted, the caste arrogance of the regressive forces would simply jeopardize it; if need be, these forces could convert the entire event into a serious law and order problem. A few days before (7 September 2011), Dalit transportation workers' union had put up flex boards in Paramakudi depicting Mr Immanuel Sekaran as *Deivathirumagan* (Divine Son); local Thevar/Maravar leaders objected very strongly against the use of the word, which apparently denotes their icon Muthuramalingam Thevar. The near perfect union of interest between the Thevar/Maravar groups and the local administration was quite evident as the Dalit organization was forced to remove those flex boards.[37] More than the resources, honour, dignity and even language also remained out of bounds for Dalits. In any ethnographic narration of a Dalit's life in general and in Tamil Nadu in particular, one could witness that both humiliation and indignity are organically embedded in their lived experience.

---

[37] Muthukaruppan Parthasarathy, 'Paramakudi Violence: Against Dalits, Against Politics', *Economic & Political Weekly* 46, no. 44 and 45 (2011): 15.

## THE COMMISSION AND THE VICTIMS

A few came forward to register their statements before the commission. Of them, Mr Pasumalai, a lawyer by profession practising in Paramakudi, came as the first person to record his statements in the report. His observations are very important.

- Around 11.15 AM, when the news of John Pandian's detention reached, as many as 100 people gathered at the Five Point Junction and began their road blockade. By rising slogans for his immediate release, Mr Pasumalai claimed that not a single police person came forward either to negotiate with the agitators or to dissuade them from gathering. He alleged that the police force deliberately made mischievous and dubious silence so as to vitiate the situation. More than anyone, the police personnel knew that under such surcharged atmosphere more people congregating would inevitably make the atmosphere tensed.
- One of the repeated allegations against the protesters was that they had indulged in setting many vehicles including the *Vajra* (water cannon) on fire. But Mr Pasumalai claimed that many police personnel, not in uniform, had indulged in setting government vehicles on fire, including the *Vajra*.
- Mr Pasumalai further claimed that neither Dr Senthil Velan nor Parmakudi town police inspector Mr Sivakumar was keen on holding any discussion with the agitators.
- Mr Pasumalai strongly insisted that the police personnel did not follow the Supreme Court's mandatory procedures before opening fire on unarmed agitators—no cautioning before canning the protesters, no use of water cannon, no mandatory use of firing rubber bullets, warning shots in the sky and more importantly not shooting below the knee. Therefore, for him, it was a blatant violation of the Supreme Court's orders and thus nothing but a cold-blooded murder.

However, the commission summarily rejected many of Mr Pasumalai's allegations.[38] The commission instead attributed ulterior motives to his

---

[38] *Justice Sampath Commission Report*, vol. I, 276.

allegations. It further said that the video records unambiguously prove that Mr Pasumalai's allegations were unfounded since the police did start with canning the protesters as crowd seemed unruly after a point. An independent fact-finding team found that the canning was carried out by the police not only against the so called 'unruly' protesters but also indiscriminately and more brutally carried out against ordinary people who had nothing to do with the protests; local shopkeepers and the passer-by were also attacked.[39]

The best example is Mr Kumar (DW-3), a washerman, who had nothing to do with Immanuel Sekaran memorial procession; he simple was witnessing police chasing the protesters but suddenly found himself beaten mercilessly by police personnel. He claimed that he fell unconscious within a few seconds of police attack and later found himself getting treated at Madurai government hospital. He further accused that the government hospital in Madurai did not provide him adequate medical care; hence, he moved to a private hospital. He further asserted that the compensation that the state government provided to him (₹30,000) was not sufficient for him. He stated before the commission that the medical treatment for nearly three weeks and subsequently the loss of income during those days incurred a lot of money for him.[40] Similarly, the cases of Mr Jagadesan (DW-6) and Mr Isravel (DW-7) are worth mentioning. Mr Jagadesan was a Tamil Nadu State Transport Corporation bus conductor and Mr Isravel was a cobbler. Both had nothing to do with the protests but ended up being beaten up by police very brutally.[41] In other words, the police brutality was in its full swing.

## THE COMMISSION AND ITS RECOMMENDATIONS

Of the many suggestions the commission duly recognized, one of them is the general apprehension about having statues in public places.

---

[39] Henri Tiphagne, 'Paramakudi: A Police Engineered Violence and Firing', People's Watch. Available at: http://roundtableindia.co.in/index.php?option=com_content&view=article&id=3682:peoples-watchs-interim-report-on-paramakudi&catid=122:atrocities&Itemid=138 (accessed on 24 August 2020).

[40] *Justice Sampath Commission Report*, vol. I, 279.

[41] Ibid., 282–283.

The commission quoted the Supreme Court judgment, which pleads not to have any religious places or icons' statues in public places.

- The commission virtually endorsed many people's plea that statues of leaders who have had explicit and open association with political parties or caste groups must be removed.[42]
- No individual must be encouraged to have his favourite leader's statue erected at any public place at his whim. The culture of having statues of political figures is indeed the reason for caste conflicts in many parts of the state.
- The state government must refrain from naming transport corporations or districts after local caste leaders.
- The state government must take necessary action to remove all statues of religious/caste leaders erected in public places without any hesitation. Most of the time, damaging/disfiguring the statues causes severe tension in the area; thus, peace/harmony and law and order become a liability in those areas.
- Therefore, the state must evolve a comprehensive policy towards having statues of public figures in common places.
- The state must refrain from conferring official status/honour to caste leaders' birthday or anniversary. This leads effectively to every caste/religious group demanding a similar protocol from the state. Similarly, the state must strongly act against forces which instigate caste hatred at the time of celebrating their leaders. Inciting violence must be prevented without further delay.

When the commission offered its suggestions to the law-enforcing agencies including the police force, it made no mistakes. The commission advised the police force that it must not mind unnecessary criticisms such as 'highhandedness and unwarranted excess use of force'.[43] It further went on to give a clean chit to the police in Paramakudi that the police force was absolutely non-partisan in discharging its professional duty.

All along, the commission maintained in its report that it was inevitable to open fire against the unruly protesters as they went simply berserk

---

[42] *Justice Sampath Commission Report*, vol. II, 750–751.
[43] Ibid., 753.

damaging government and private properties, gravely assaulting police personnel. The commission euphemistically eulogized police firing by implying that had the police not opened fire, the human casualty would be much more; therefore, less number of casualty would always be better than a mayhem. Similarly, the commission looked at the entire episode mostly from the prism of administrative apparatus; the everyday agony of being an 'inferiorized and tortured' self of being a Dalit had effectively been set aside. The administrative remedy was what the commission referred to often in its two-volume report, but barely two pages were devoted to suggest what could be done in Ramanathapuram district in order to improve the quality of life.[44] The suggestions are no less than a cliché: establishing colleges particularly medical colleges, providing employment opportunities and creating small-scale industrial units.

Expectedly, many civil society and Dalit organizations found the commission's clean chit to the police not surprising. The Tamil Nadu Untouchability Eradication Front termed the report an 'attempt to protect the erring police personnel'. The general secretary of Thyagi Immanuel Peravai, P. Chandra Bose, said that Dalit organizations were not surprised at the outcome of the probe. He added that various judicial enquiries ordered by successive state governments in the past, including the ones relating to the Keezhvenmani massacre of 1968, the Kodiyankulam rampage of 1995 and the Thamirabarani tragedy of 1999, had absolved the police and other government personnel of guilt.[45]

It was not a surprise when the then chief minister of Tamil Nadu Jayalalithaa strongly defended the police action in Paramakudi. She said that the police opened fire only in self-defence and to quell the violence unleashed 'by a few persons for their own political gains'. She declared that the 'protesters indulged in large-scale violence and torched police vehicles. Police opened fire in self-defence to protect public property as they threw petrol bombs and pelted stones.'[46] Her subsequent

---

[44] Ibid., 780–781.
[45] *Frontline*, 29 November 2013.
[46] *The Times of India*, 12 September 2011.

compassionate moves—offering government job to one member of each of the families and increasing the compensation to 4 lakh to the kin of those killed—did not bring in confidence among Dalits.[47]

While almost all major political parties in the state have condemned the police firing, especially the excess police committed, Jayalalithaa's very strong unwavering defence was along the expected lines. In terms of electoral performance, Jayalalithaa's AIADMK enjoyed stronger support in the southern districts. Both Thevars/Maravars and Dalits had been voting for AIADMK since the time of party's iconic, most charismatic leader late M. G. Ramachandran. Jayalalithaa not only supported Thevar/Maravar castes but also conferred official honour to the Thevar icon Muthuramalingam Thevar. In other words, she was well prepared to sacrifice Dalits' welfare to appease Thevars/Maravars.[48]

## DECIPHERING THE POLITICAL MEANING OF JUSTICE SAMPATH COMMISSION

When the police opened fire on the unarmed Dalit protesters just to bring back 'normalcy' on 11 September 2011 in Paramakudi, the state insisted that it was inevitable. Justice Sampath Commission itself found and documented in its report well over hundred cases of violent caste conflicts from 1991 to 2011 in Ramanathapuram district.[49] All those cases were registered in police stations and a few were about police firing which claimed several people's lives. The overwhelming majority of those victims were Dalits. The intensity of caste conflict and the brutal caste arrogance of Thevars/Maravars were more evident here. Nowhere in Tamil Nadu was the police firing frequent as it had been in Ramanathapuram district. Any conflict between Thevars/Maravars and Dalits would invite the police to intervene, and the police usually came down very heavily on Dalits as the commission's documented list of conflicts suggested.

---

[47] *The Indian Express*, 29 November 2011.
[48] Teltumbde, 'Jayalalithaa's Sacrificial Lambs', 10–11.
[49] *Justice Sampath Commission Report*, vol. II, 810–862.

The crux and the nucleus of commission's arguments are quite clear and loud. According to the commission, the conflict between the dominant castes Thevars/Maravars and Dalits resulted in violence; hence, the state had to necessarily intervene in order to bring normalcy and peace. The commission neither recognized nor concurred that it was not merely violence. It was a struggle for Dalits' dignity and honour. It was a struggle to eschew exploitation faced by Dalits at the hands of the dominant castes. It was indeed a crusade for equality. It was certainly appropriate to characterize Dalit assertion as an effort to actualize the virtue of citizenship. The tyranny of caste exploitation and feudal sociocultural values prevent basic constitutional promises to Dalits which each Indian is entitled to. Therefore, it was a brave struggle for equality of opportunity, dignity and honour.

Ever since India began embarking upon a journey of a free market economy, the cheer leaders of laissez-faire declared that the modern notions of civil society would now flourish in India too. The underlying assumption is that only the liberal market-driven economy alone has the ability/potential to provide and sustain 'civil society'. We have long been told that the tyranny of caste would be neutralized if market takes a primary role in our economy. The free flow of capital from both from domestic and overseas (FDI) would simply weaken the tentacles of the traditional value structure; such a transition in a way would ensure the emergence of a good 'civil society'. It is quite clear now that even the nascent capitalist economic order would guarantee to arrive at a good 'civil society'.[50] The number of cases against Dalits[51] in Ramanathapuram district since 1991 (from the time of liberalization in India) would unambiguously prove that we are no way nearer to a good civil society.

Instead, we have every reason to believe that market liberalism has indeed strengthened the state and its coercive law-enforcing agencies. It does not mean that in the pre-liberalized India, there were no caste atrocities against Dalits; that is not only naive but absolutely an inappropriate proposition. Caste atrocities against the marginalized

---

[50] John Hall, 'The Nature of Civil Society', *Society* (May–June 1998): 32–34.
[51] *Justice Sampath Commission Report*, vol. II, 810–862.

groups, especially Dalits, have always persisted in India. However, the nature of violence and indignity that Dalits encounter every day in post-liberalized India acquired a unique dimension. The heightened caste pride among the dominant castes is quite visible more than ever; caste pride and arrogance have become the new ethics in everyday life. This effectively leads to further inferiorization of Dalit self. However, the assertion of Dalits is not only ridiculed but also more ferociously retaliated by the dominant castes, especially Thevars/Maravars. Hence, Ramanathapuram district has witnesses more anti-Dalit atrocities with increased intensity in the recent past than ever before.

The larger questions however remain intact. Does our formal and constitutional freedom/equality ensure substantial freedom/equality to every social group/caste/community in India? Have we restricted the spirit of democracy only to voting? How far could 'organizational pluralism' or 'accommodative character' of Tamil Nadu political landscape remain quite indifferent to Dalit aspirations? These questions inevitably emerge after reading the commission's report.

The commission's mandate is quite clear: to probe the Paramakudi police firing. What remain quite implicit and hidden beneath this text are several politically significant questions mentioned above which the commission perhaps deliberately has not openly answered. But the entire report of the commission actually becomes the answer to these questions. The implicit meaning of the report clearly declares that our democracy is not inclined towards an inclusive social order. The report without munching words makes it abundantly clear that freedom/equality is quite relative not substantive. The accommodative character of Tamil Nadu's modern political landscape no doubt did accommodate all caste groups for electoral dividends, but the substantial power has been retained by the dominant castes. This remains a paradox.

Dalits' assertion is for the substantive democracy not for the nominal one. Dalits' assertions such as commemorating Immanuel Sekaran's martyrdom day aim at just distribution of sociocultural and economic power within the body-politic. What has been provided to Dalits is a limited/restricted notion of freedom/equality not substantive freedom/equality. That is why dominant castes concede that Dalits can perform their local rituals within the sociocultural boundaries of their everyday life. But when Dalits aspire to commemorate their 'leaders' publicly, that very act is perceived by the dominant castes as an attempt for substantive freedom/equality.

Therefore, to say that substantive democracy/freedom/equality is denied to Dalits is almost a cliché now. What is more significant is what happens when Dalits are determined to seek those values in their everyday life. The dominant caste groups by virtue of all kinds of resources at their disposal become the political class à la ruling class; thus, Dalits' determination for substantive democracy/freedom/equality is no longer against the dominant castes. It is indeed against the state itself. Therefore, state being the legitimate agency to exercise violence over its people will be geared up to 'restrict/restrain/contain' anti-state forces. Needless to say, here it implies Dalit assertion.

Thus, Dalits' determination for substantive democracy/freedom/equality actually goes against the interest of the state itself. The state obviously now has its political duty to discharge. Dalits have to be 'contained'; this leads to state/law-enforcing agencies to unleash disproportionate violence against Dalits. Paramakudi police firing is actually the reply from the state that Dalits cannot seek substantive freedom/equality akin to other dominant castes. In the public sphere, Dalits have to be contained if they believe that they can be on par with other dominant castes. Public sphere in Paramakudi is essentially a space where the dominant castes' culture/social values/morals remain the nucleus; it is not a thorough fare. Dalits cannot trespass. When Dalits as citizens of this country embark upon a trajectory to wade through the nuanced public sphere, the state finds it untenable and almost a criminal act. Police firing in Paramakudi on 11 September 2011 was actually the answer from the state that Dalits must not seek substantive freedom/equality in today's political landscape. Any violation would be dealt with brutal violence and cold-blooded murder. But what is equally important is the way the so-called punishment is handed over to Dalits. More than the brutality, the way it was 'performed' by the law-enforcing agency requires further elaboration.

One of the finest philosophers of the 20th century, Michel Foucault, in his *Discipline and Punish*, argues that modern Western capitalist societies with their modified notions of puritan philosophical worldview discontinued pre-modern practices of public executions. In the name of individual liberty and decency, the convict is sent to the gallows behind the metal doors of prisons, which are highly restricted to only a few people. The pre-modern style of public executions had resulted in popular upsurge against the autocratic decree of the king. The Western capitalist system believes in secrecy as an important political virtue.

Dalits here have to live in a paradox. Politically, a modern constitutional democracy (restricted to Dalits though), socioculturally a highly feudal oligarchy, constitutes the modern body-politic in India. Thus, the pre-modern public executions are carried out today where the feudal oligarchy need not worry about any popular upsurge. The modern nomenclature of 'law and order' effectively wraps up any further debate. Paramakudi police firing was nothing but public execution of Dalits by the feudal caste oligarchy with the modern state apparatus. Justice Sampath Commission while absolving the police of any wrongdoing simply endorses that public execution of Dalits too.

# Chapter 5

# Deconstructing the Practice of Manual Scavenging
## Critical Insights

### Shaileshkumar Darokar

## INTRODUCTION

India's expansive occupational diversity is framed around sociohistorical categories that are layered and bounded by a rigid social hierarchy framed around notions such as 'skilled/unskilled', 'purity/pollution', 'dignified/stigmatized' and 'touchable/untouchable'. These hierarchically structured binary conceptions that are organized around caste have reproduced themselves in various socio-economic spheres to this very day. Occupations that fall within the domains of polluted, stigmatized and untouchable, which are generally performed by the manual scavenging castes, are now being denoted as humiliating occupations. All these occupations have their roots in religiously sanctioned caste-bounded activities that are politically affirmed by tradition, birth or descent. Caste groups that are imprisoned into these occupations are often subjected to a lethal form of social exclusion, having to bear the brunt of an all-pervasive sociopsychological humiliation.

Out of the multiple, often dehumanizing (polluted/stigmatized) caste occupations, the scavenging community(s) remains the most adversely affected and socially excluded group. Occupying the lowest position in the caste hierarchy, and made perennially dependent on dominant caste groups, they are, by any yardstick, the most peripheralized within the marginalized caste in the Indian society.

Manual scavenging is a caste-based hereditary occupation, which is predominantly linked to a very complex form of forced labour. It involves the direct removal of human excreta from dry latrines and sewers, using their bare hands and basic tools such as thin boards, buckets and baskets lined with sacking. Following which, the manual scavenger has to carry the collected excreta on their head for disposing to a designated area.

In caste-afflicted India and other countries within South Asia in which caste has permeated, the term 'scavenger' connotes 'untouchable' or 'polluting', especially to those higher up in the ascending scale of the system. Such is the pejorative nature and physical practice of scavenging that it took the UN Special Rapporteur to state that

> The degrading nature of this work is an extreme case and is very much tied up with the inequalities of a deeply ingrained caste system and the lack of choice in finding other types of work.[1]

Critical scholars attempting to confront the theoretico-conceptual status quo of manual scavenging have begun to explore the ethical dimensions of the dehumanizing effects of the occupation and interrogate subjects such as human dignity, dignity of labour, destruction of ethics and even aesthetical genocide. Fundamental questions are being raised pertaining to the intricate relationship among life, livelihoods, occupation, self-respect and beauty. Scholars such as Barbara Harris-White (*India Working*), Ashwini Deshpande (*The Grammar of Caste*) and S Thorat (*Blocked by Caste*) have established in their research the high concentration of Dalits in menial, unclean and dead-end jobs (jobs with no mobility), where 90 per cent of such jobs are general(ly) 'reserved'

---

[1] Catarina de Albuquerque, *On the Right Track: Good Practices in Realising the Rights to Water and Sanitation* (Lisbon: UN Special Rapporteur on Water and Sanitation, February 2012).

for Dalits. They opine that struggles against the caste-based occupation norms do not seem to stimulate dynamism and mobility in the light of a complete absence of economic and social equality in India.

## MANUAL SCAVENGING: DECONSTRUCTING THE CONSTRUCT

Locus classicus, scholarly engagement on the subject of manual scavenging traces its roots to early sacred texts and religious scriptures. Bindeshwar Pathak[2] and Gita Ramaswamy[3] trace the genesis of manual scavenging to the *Narada Samhita*, which mentions the disposal of human excreta as one of the 15 duties assigned to slaves. Similarly, in *Vajasaneyi Samhita*, the authors note that 'Chandals and Paulkas have been referred to as slaves for the disposal of human excreta.'

Across the Indian subcontinent, categories such as 'scavengers', 'sweepers' and '*safai karamcharis*' denoting the occupation of a person/community are historically connoted by different caste names in different regions. However, in India, the 'removers of night soil' and the 'cleaners of latrines' belong to a well-defined social group which has been included under a general nomenclature called 'Bhangi'.[4]

In an anthropological account of *The Tribes and Castes of Bombay*, R. E. Enthoven[5] proffers that Bhangis were found almost in every district of the Bombay Presidency. However, many of them resided in Bombay (now Mumbai), Poona (now Pune), Ahmedabad, Surat and a region called Kathiawar (now in Gujarat). He held that the theories concerning the origin of the term 'Bhangi' point to people identified as broken or outcaste or as a caste of scavengers and sweepers. The 'caste' was conceived as the dregs of the Hindu society and contained an admixture of outcastes who have fallen to this level owing to offenses

---

[2] Bindeshwar Pathak, *Road to Freedom: A Sociological Study on the Abolition of Scavenging in India* (New Delhi: Motilal Banarsidass, 2000, new edition).

[3] Gita Ramaswamy, *India Stinking: Manual Scavengers in Andhra Pradesh and Their Work* (New Delhi: Navayana, 2011).

[4] Shyamlal, *The Bhangi: A Sweeper Caste, Its Socio-economic Portraits* (Hyderabad: Sangam Books, 1992), 11.

[5] R. E. Enthoven, *The Tribes and Castes of Bombay*, vol. I (Delhi: Cosmo Publications, 1920), 105.

against the rigid social code of higher castes. While different Hindu texts identify them as the descendants of a Brahmin sage, in many other references to them, they are identified as offspring of a Brahmin widow from a Shudra father.

It is argued that the term 'Bhangi' is derived from the Sanskrit word *bhang* meaning 'hemp', and from the habit of the Bhangi to take 'bhang'.[6] Others trace its meaning to the word 'broken'. There are ample evidences in India's history of the rise and fall of tribes during waves of foreign and native invasions. It is proposed that those who did not accept the ways and culture of the conquering tribes broke away from the society and were called Bhangis.

In North India, the exonym for night soil removers is *Mehtar*, meaning 'prince' or 'leader'. Writing on the dynamics of caste among sweepers and scavengers in the Central Provinces (CP), Russel and Hira Lal[7] specifically mentioned the term 'Mehtar'. In their opinion, the present sweeper caste in CP was made up of diverse elements, and the name Mehtar, generally applied to it, is a title referring to a prince or leader. They pointed that in CP, sections of the Ghasia, Mahar and Dom castes are also engaged in sweepers' work and are greatly amalgamated with Mehtars. The name Mehtar is generally applied to sweepers in most provinces and taken as the designation of the caste, although the sweepers are known by different names in each province. According to Shyamlal,[8] the Persian term Mehtar could have been used to ridicule them.

In Punjab and Uttar Pradesh, the term used is Valmiki. This identity, it is argued, was adopted to gain some self-respect, drawing their history of being followers of Valmiki Rishi, the author of the epic Ramayana. From a religious perspective, the religion of the sweepers is centred

---

[6] B. N. Srivastava, *Manual Scavenging in India: A Disgrace to the Country* (New Delhi: Concept Publishing Company, 1997); Shyamlal, *The Bhangi*; Stephen Fuchs, *At the Bottom of Indian Society: Harijan and Other Castes*, (New Delhi: Munshiram Manoharlal Publishers, 1984).

[7] R. V. Russel and Hira Lal, *Tribes and Castes of Central Provinces of India*, vol. IV (Delhi: Cosmo Publications, 1916).

[8] Shyamlal, *The Bhangi*, 11.

on the worship of two saints: Lal Beg or Bale Shah and Balmiki or Valmiki, the author of Ramayana. Russel and Hira Lal point out that

> Balmiki was originally a low caste hunter called *Ratnakar*, however, he could not find any animals to hunt and started to rob and kill travelers. One day he met Brahma and wished to kill him but Brahma convinced him of his sins and directed him to repeat the name of Rama until he is purified of his sins. *Ratnakar* repeated the words 'Ram, Ram' sixty thousand years at the same spot till Brahma returns. Brahma named him as *Valmiki* (from valmik, an ant-hill) and told him to compose Ramayana in seven parts, containing the deeds and exploits of Rama.[9]

The saint Lal Beg is widely worshipped in Punjab by sweepers. The religion of Lal Begis appears to overtly resemble the Kabir Panthis and other reforming sects. Probably, the objective is to acquire a status which may elevate them from the utter degradation of their caste.[10]

## DECONSTRUCTING MANUAL SCAVENGING DURING MUGHAL AND COLONIAL RULE

In Punjab, the scavengers are known as Chuhra, and the term is derived from their work of *chura jharna* (to sweep scraps). It may be pointed out that the real construction of identity and its contestation began in the late 19th and early 20th centuries. For instance, Chuhra, the untouchable caste, used multiple strategies to seek freedom from subjugation and oppression. Vijay Prashad notes that the Chuhras were reported as both scavengers and agriculturists in British records.[11] He further expounds that in the last decades of the 19th century, the Chamars and Chuhras had lost access to customary rights and could not be retained as village servants.[12] The Chuhra community, in particular, attempted two paths to liberation: (a) conversion to Christianity and (b) migration to

---

[9] Russel and Lal, *Tribes and Castes*, 225–226.
[10] Ibid., 226–227).
[11] Vijay Prashad, *Untouchable Freedom: A Social History of Dalit Community* (New Delhi: Oxford University Press, 2000), 28.
[12] Ibid., 33.

cities. Christians in Punjab, during this period, increased by 400 per cent, mostly among the Chuhras, who migrated to cities such as Delhi, Shimla, Jalandhar, Amritsar and Lahore. The statutory identification of the Chuhra community with sanitation as sweepers was evident during the colonial period. They migrated as workers but remained as sweepers and menials through their services.

During the 1931 Census, J. H. Hutton clubbed the Bhangi, Chuhra, Halalkhor, Mehtar and Lal Begi under the category 'scavengers'. They inhabited different provinces and presidencies of British India. N. R. Malkani observes in his *Clean People and an Unclean Country* that 'urban scavenging has resulted in the creation of a Bhangi Caste which is untouchable, unseeable and unapproachable.'[13] Augmenting his argument, he states, 'The Bhangi is essentially a recent product of urban life, first created as an occupation by Moslems and later in British rule made into a hereditary caste.' Gita Ramaswamy[14] also makes similar observation, emphasizing that manual scavenging expanded phenomenally under the British rule, particularly in the mid-18th century, which marked the beginning of industrialization and urbanization in the subcontinent. Enthoven[15] affirmed the above arguments noting that

> Many Bhangis in the northern part of the Presidency appear to be immigrants from the United Provinces. It seems probable that in many cases Bhangis originally came to this Presidency as camp followers with the armies from the north.

Pertaining to the historical concretizing of a separate caste, Srivastava[16] asserts that the practice of sweeping and scavenging disposal of human excreta by humans entered India with the advent of Muslims (Mughals). It is argued that the system of bucket privies was designed and constructed during the Mughal era for their women in purdah (veil), as they were not allowed to go in open for defecation and thus the war

---

[13] N. R. Malkani, *Clean People and an Unclean Country* (New Delhi: Harijan Sevak Sangh, 1965).
[14] Ramaswamy, *India Stinking*.
[15] Enthoven, *The Tribes and Castes of Bombay*.
[16] Srivastava, *Manual Scavenging in India*, 17–18.

captives were forced to clean the bucket privies. These captives were not accepted into their own caste of origin and by larger society and thus formed into a separate caste.

Another dimension was brought into the debate by Russel and Hira Lal[17]; they pointed out that

> It can only be definitely shown in a few instances that the existing impure occupational castes were directly derived from the indigenous tribes. The Chamar and Kori, and the Chuhra and Bhangi, or sweepers and scavengers of the Punjab and United Provinces, are purely occupational castes and their original tribal affinities have entirely disappeared.

## ATTEMPTS TO BRING ABOUT HINDU UNITY: REVISITING THE POLITICAL STRATEGY

It was the political strategy of the Hindu conservatives to demonize Muslims and, in the process, position themselves as the saviours of Dalits, thus avoiding the subdivision and 'disunity' among the newly consolidated Hindu identity. The Arya Samaj founded by Dayananda Saraswati underlined the linguistic and racial purity of the Aryans and described the Samaj as a society of Aryan race (upper castes). The Dalits were excluded from this but were later offered to improve their caste status through *shuddhi* or purification.[18] Similarly, different factions within the fold such as All India Achutuddhar Committee and Shraddhananda Dalitudhar Sabha began working for spiritual well-being, religious protection and socio-economic uplift of the depressed classes. Viewed in retrospect, such attempts were fundamentally political yet existed under the guise of religion.

By the 1920s, the movements positioned around an 'adi' status, or aboriginal inhabitants of the land, began to emerge among Dalits. There were several attempts to enumerate themselves in the 1931 Census as Adi-Dharmis, Adi-Hindu, Adi-Dravida, etc. Their arguments were

---

[17] Russel and Lal, *Tribes and Castes*, 76.
[18] Romila Thapar, *The Aryan: Recasting Constructs* (New Delhi: Three Essay Collective, 2008), 40–41.

simple; Dalits were the original inhabitants of this land and were conquered and enslaved by the Aryans and circumscribed as untouchables. The Adi-Dharmis in Punjab, under the leadership of Mangu Ram, protested against the attempt of Arya Samajis to incorporate and forcefully retain them as Hindus. They asserted that they were not Hindus.[19]

By the 1930s, Ambedkar had a clash with Gandhi over the contentious issue of a separate electorate for Dalits. The Adi-Dharmi Mandal and Balmiki Sabha (Chuhras) of Jalandhar sent their signature in human blood to London. This was a radical symbolic expression of two simultaneous processes: (a) their support to Ambedkar who they asserted was their leader and (b) their support to Ambedkar's statement that Dalits were a separate entity, which was cast out by the Hindu society.[20]

## DECONSTRUCTING TWO CONTRADICTORY PERSPECTIVES

There were two contradictory perspectives that the leaders during the time held about how to conceive the scavenging community and engage with them and finally how to emancipate them. The first perspective can be identified as the 'reformist' perspective and the second as the 'abolitionist' perspective.

### The Reformist Perspective

The Chuhra began to call themselves Valmikis and by the 1930s had clashes with Chamars over the caste heritages. The Chamars were the followers of Ravidas and the Chuhras claimed Valmiki as their guru. The clash was around the status and precedence of the guru.[21] These differences were cashed upon by the Arya Samajis to win over the Chuhras to Hinduism. *Shree Valmiki Prakash* written by Amichand in

---

[19] Braj Ranjan Mani, *Debrahmanising History: Dominance and Resistance in Indian History* (New Delhi: Manohar, 2005); Gail Omvedt, *Dalits and the Democratic Revolution: Dr Ambedkar and the Dalit Movement in Colonial India* (New Delhi: SAGE Publications, 1994); Vijay Prashad, *Untouchable Freedom: A Social History of Dalit Community* (New Delhi: Oxford University Press, 2000).

[20] Prashad, *Untouchable Freedom*, 87.

[21] Ibid., 90.

1936 became the staple track of the Valmiki community. The track highlighted the conversation between Ram Sevak and a Valmiki man who carried out a sustained attack on Adi-Dharmi movement and their leaders, supposedly responsible for separating Dalits from Hindus.

It was enforced upon the Chuhras that Brahmins did not allow others to read the vedas, whereas Ramayana was open for all, from the Brahmins to Chandalas, and hence, Valmiki was chosen as a guru by the community. Even Thakkar and Harijan Sevak Sangh were involved in this politics.[22] In this context, some Dalits succumbed to the Arya Samajist strategy and power play.

Prashad[23] noted that in a meeting of Dalits and Arya Samaj, the Arya Samaj *updeshak* (missionary) sought pardon from them and sought friendship with them. This meeting was presided over by Mangu Ram at Shimla. In response to this, Dalits asserted that they would not be swayed by hollow promises and occasional theatrics. N. L. Varma, an Arya Samaj follower, asserted during the meeting that he himself carried refuse from the latrines before the meeting, to which Chunni Lal, an Adi-Dharmi Dalit, retorted, 'You cannot accomplish the work fully well unless you do it for at least ten or fifteen days.'

In the light of this often very contentious historical reality, the recent campaign Swachh Bharat Abhiyan (SBA) is the classic example of such an attitude. The campaign is principled on a reformist framework. While paying no heed to the 'rights of being' of the traditional sanitation workers (safai karamcharis), technicalities of sanitation are instead given priority, plus the health of workers is noted as an important component within its framework. In the perspective of SBA, more toilets equal cleanliness and more healthy workers equal a clean India. Prashad, in 1998, called such an approach to resolving the age-old practice as reformist, where a policy is posited in such strategic ways as to make the inhuman and poor working conditions of the 'scavengers'/'safai karamcharis' more tolerable rather than destroying the very system that generates it.

---

[22] Ibid., 92–93).
[23] Ibid., 87–88).

## The Abolitionist Perspective

Standing directly opposite to the reformist conception is the abolitionist approach. Ambedkar openly contested the reformist approach. His was an argument that challenged the very premise of the occupation, bringing to bear the very idea of social life itself rather than drawing the same conclusions as the reformist thinkers. His argument, often witnessed in tumultuous exchanges with Gandhi, who he viewed as being a mere reformist, was that

> *You* (Gandhi) appeal to the scavenger's pride and vanity in order to induce him and him only to keep on to scavenging by telling him that scavenging is a noble profession and that he need not be ashamed of it.[24]

To Dr Ambedkar, this was an inhuman proposition, pointing out that such glorification of manual scavenging was pejorative, unfounded and, not to say the least, laced with lethal repercussions. Reformism, in the view of Ambedkar, was nothing more than a sanitized conception of sanitation itself, strategically framed to obscure the controversial nature of manual scavenging and the very problematics of untouchability.

In his *The Untouchables: Who Were They and Why They Became Untouchables*,[25] Ambedkar proposes a theory of the origin of untouchability popularly known as the 'broken men' theory. Here, he argues that historically, among primitive societies, certain tribes began to settle down and cultivate, while others remained nomadic and warlike. The nomadic and warlike tribes began attacking settled tribes who were wealthier and had grain, which the warlike tribes wanted. The settled tribes were unable to defend themselves as they had lost their warlike spirit. As a result of this condition, the settled tribes employed

---

[24] B. R. Ambedkar, 'What Congress and Gandhi Have Done to Untouchables', in *Dr. Babasaheb Ambedkar Writings and Speeches*, vol. 9 (Mumbai: Government of Maharashtra, 1990), 292–293.

[25] B. R. Ambedkar, 'The Untouchables: Who Were They and Why They Became Untouchables?' in *Dr. Babasaheb Ambedkar Writings and Speeches*, vol. 7 (Mumbai: Government of Maharashtra, 1990; originally published in October 1948 by Amrit Book Co., New Delhi.

the 'broken men', who were defeated nomads and were willing to become mercenaries of the settled tribes. However, these 'broken men' were not allowed to be part of the main settlement and were kept away. Ambedkar insisted that the 'broken men' were the followers of Buddhism. These 'broken men' were treated with contempt and were imposed upon with worst forms of disabilities, including untouchability and menial jobs. Bhagwan Das,[26] in his seminal work *Main Bhangi Hun*, reiterates Ambedkar's above thesis, noting

> Main Bhangi hun. From the primitive time, I am the original inhabitant (indigenous) of Bharat land and did not accept the slavery and fought against the invaders. I did not bow down before the kings and Purohits nor did I worship their gods. I am part of the social group that safeguarded this freedom of the natives. My story starts from that day when the Aryan kings attacked the pious country like Bharat and made us slaves by removing crown from my head and forced upon my head the basket of refuse.

As can be discerned, the abolitionist perspective challenges the confinement of scavengers in a system in which institutionalized inequality is legitimized by religious scriptures, and in which the fundamental basis to relate with the 'other' is premised on forms of reciprocal repulsion. In the place of the reformist agenda, the abolitionist perspective instead presents struggle and resistance against manual scavenging as a means out of historical degradation and caste subjugation.

## DECONSTRUCTING THE CONTEXT OF MANUAL SCAVENGING IN MAHARASHTRA

In the year 2005, the Government of Maharashtra sanctioned a research project to study the prevalence, extent and nature of practice of manual scavenging in the state, under the Mahatma Phule Backward Class Development Corporation Ltd (MPBCDC). Most of the data presented in this chapter is based on a study carried out by this author and his colleagues in the Tata Institute of Social Sciences. The study covered all

---

[26] Bhagwan Das, *Main Bhangi Hun* (New Delhi: Gautam Book Centre, 1996), 10.

the districts and talukas, urban local bodies (ULBs; municipal corporations and municipal councils) and places whose population is 10,000 and above. Aiming to ascertain the numbers of dry latrines and manual scavengers, the study covered 2,753 households identified as engaging in manual scavenging with 4,182 individuals who are directly involved in different forms of manual scavenging.

Scavengers in Maharashtra are known as Mehtars, Bhangis, Balmiki, Rukhi and Lal Begi in local and regional languages and *aswachha* (unclean), *safai kamgars* and manual scavengers in a bureaucratic parlance. Of the total 59 castes listed as Scheduled Castes (SCs) by the Census of Maharashtra, Mahar (Neo-Buddhists), Mang/Matang, Bhambi (Chambhar/Chamar) and Bhangi together constitute almost 92 per cent of the total SC population in the state.[27] Mahars are numerically the largest SC with 57.5 per cent, followed by Mangs/Matangs 20.3 per cent and Bhambis (Chambhars) 12.5 per cent of the SC population of the state, whereas Bhangis with nearly 2 per cent (186,776) are the fourth largest SC population of the state. Under the entry Bhangi, there are 10 subgroups, namely Bhangi, Mehtars, Olgana, Rukhi, Malkana, Halalkhor, Lal Begi, Balmiki, Korar and Zadmalli.[28] The population of Bhangis is highly urbanized, accounting for nearly 92.7 per cent in the said area. They are employed by both public and private/informal sectors in the state such as the cantonment boards, municipal corporations, municipal councils, railways, airports, government/private hospitals, private housing societies/chawls and commercial establishments. The members of these castes are traditionally known as untouchables or outcastes and form the lowest stratum of the society. Their traditional occupations revolve specifically around the removal of dead animals, handling dead bodies on the funeral ground, drum beating, cleaning/sweeping road/lanes in villages/towns and the manual removal and cleaning of human excreta.

Unlike other SCs such as Mahar (Neo-Buddhists), Mang/Matang and Chambhar, Bhangis, being a moving population, were not the part

---

[27] Census of India 2001.

[28] Scheduled Castes and Scheduled Tribes Orders (Amendment) Act, 1976, provided by the Registrar General of India.

of traditional Maharashtrian village structure. However, being migrants from various parts of India initially brought by the Britishers, they had settled down in urban and semi-urban areas of the state in the first half of the 20th century.

## DEMOGRAPHIC PROFILE OF SCAVENGING CASTE GROUPS AND THEIR MIGRATION PATTERNS IN MAHARASHTRA

In Maharashtra, the untouchable groups (Mahar, Matang, Chambhar, Dhor, etc.) had never performed the task of manual removal of human excreta. However, it is believed that during pre-independence period, the native Muslim Mehtar or Bhangi was the only (religious) group engaged in manual scavenging. As the Britishers laid the foundation of railways and developed certain areas as cantonment towns (Mumbai, Deolali in Nashik, Ahmednagar, Pune, Aurangabad and Kamptee in Nagpur—cantonment towns having military base), the Bhangi/Mehtar or Valmiki especially from the northern parts of India migrated to Maharashtra and to other southern parts of the country and settled in urban and semi-urban trading centres, including these cantonment towns. The Bhangis, Rukhis, Vankars and Meghwals from Gujarat migrated to Mumbai, Pune and Nashik in Maharashtra. All these castes as referred to above are the migrants from Rajasthan, Haryana, Uttar Pradesh, Madhya Pradesh and Gujarat.

According to field observations and data collected through focus group discussions (FGDs), the earliest migration into Maharashtra was that of Gujratis (Meghwals and Vankars). This first wave of migration dates back to the mid-19th century (the famous 'Chhappania Akal', the famine of 1856) and early 20th century. Meghwals are numerically a strong 'untouchable' caste, spread all over Gujarat. They were also known as Dhed, Mayavanshi and Vankar. They were never traditional scavenging communities, but in the absence of other scavenging castes in some villages they were expected to perform this task also. During the same period, Bombay was rapidly becoming the centre of trading activities of British. With the establishment of the Board of Conservancy in Bombay in 1845, a process of systematic 'solid waste management' and recruitment of scavengers/Halalkhors had begun. Due to close proximity to Bombay, Meghwals, Vankars and Rukhis, who migrated to the city, were employed as conservancy workers. They also migrated to nearby cities such as Nashik, Pune and Aurangabad. Since then, they are settled in the state and are engaged in various forms of scavenging.

Other scavenging communities migrated from North India, especially from Haryana, Rajasthan, Uttar Pradesh, Bihar, Punjab, Delhi and Madhya Pradesh, in large numbers. They have a significant presence in various cities/towns of Maharashtra. Although they are known by different names in their respective states as Mehtars, Bhangis and Chuhras, they prefer to identify themselves as Balmiki/Valmiki and have also been notified as such in states like Maharashtra.

The Valmikis, unlike other untouchable groups, occupied a very low status in the traditional caste hierarchy in their place of origin. They performed the most obnoxious traditional occupation in the historical caste structure. They were mainly engaged in polluted, inhuman occupations at the landlords' houses in the village. Being at the bottom of the hierarchy without any access to land, education or any other dignified occupation, they were made completely dependent on their patron landlords for their livelihood. As a result, they were subjected to a greater degree of humiliation and subjugation by the caste-Hindus. In this context, migration perhaps was a preferred option as a means to escape caste-based exclusion. Nonetheless, manual scavenging largely remains a caste-based or descent-based occupation even in urban areas, and while migration has freed them from the immediate clutches of the landlord, it has not helped them much in ridding themselves of caste-based discrimination.

## Zone-wise Concentration by Caste and Category

An important component of the study reveals a critical dimension of manual scavenging. It was found that not only SCs but other groups such as Scheduled Tribes (STs), Denotified Tribes (DNTs), Nomadic Tribes (NTs), Other Backward Castes (OBCs) and General are found engaged in manual scavenging, although their percentage is negligible.

Hoping to provide a deeper understanding about the said context, some data that unravel specific social categories that are engaged in this occupation are presented.

## Scheduled Castes

According to the study, of the total identified sample of 2,753, a total of 87.7 per cent belong to SCs. Zone wise, the Konkan region accounts for more than one-fourth, that is, 29.6 per cent, followed by Pune 17.2 per cent, Aurangabad 16.1 per cent, Amravati 13.8 per cent, Nagpur 13 per cent and Nashik 10.1 per cent.

## STs, DNTs and NTs

Among the STs/DNTs/NTs, data reveal that only 0.9 per cent ST households are found engaged in scavenging. More than half (58.3%) of them are in the Konkan region followed by one-fourth (25.0%) in Amravati. This is perhaps because of their high population in these regions. To be more specific, they belong to the Mahadev Koli, Gond, Kolam and Katkari tribes. Besides these communities, there are a few who may fall into DNT and NT categories such as Kunchi Karve, Bhoi, Kaikadi and Vanjari. The traditional occupation of these STs, DNTs and NTs is not scavenging; however, the likelihood of their own socio-economic marginalization (conceived as a possible push factor) and the easy access to urban settings and employment opportunities available (conceived as a pull factor) can perhaps be accounted as reasons for these communities to join these occupations.

## Other Backward Castes

Of the total identified sample, 1.8 per cent of the OBCs were found engaged in this occupation. Their presence was more prominent in the Konkan zone (nearly three-fourths), whereas their percentage was negligible in other zones. It is important to note that the Konkan division includes Mumbai Metropolitan Region (MMR) and has as many as six municipal corporations. The OBCs were mainly absorbed as employees in these ULBs, hospitals and railways. They come from OBC castes such as Teli, Mali, Kunabi, Kumbhar, Sonar and Dhangar. While their traditional occupation was never scavenging, according to the data collected it was found that significant numbers of people from this category are getting into this occupation and their percentage is slightly high in urban settings, especially in MMR and other big cities. One reason for this could be the cut-throat competition for government jobs among the educated unemployed across the sections. As a result, many Shudra castes falling under the OBC category are attracted to such government jobs. Second, the relative accesses for this category into the administration of these institutions entering as a safai kamgar/sweeper could also be a means to finally get absorbed into other (dignified) departments and/or in due course be promoted as a supervisor through their political connections and influence.

## General Category

Of the total identified sample, 9.6 per cent of the aswachha safai kamgars/scavengers fall under the General category. Among them, 81.5 per cent are Muslims, 0.4 per cent are Christians and 18.1 per cent are Hindus other than SC, ST and OBC. The important point here is that even the Muslims have been included in the list of General category, which is a controversial issue. As per the Constitution, only Hindu, Sikh and Buddhist religions qualify to be included into the SC list, whereas Muslim and Christian do not. However, field observations suggest that Muslims have been performing this occupation since time immemorial, and majorities of them are even more backward than their Hindu counterparts. Another important aspect is that within Muslim Mehtars, Lal Begi and Sheik are two distinct endogamous groups, and intermarriages between these two are not allowed. Among Lal Begis, some are still Hindu and others have embraced Islam. Although they form the most significant part of the underprivileged section of our society, they are still deprived of many government programmes meant for the upliftment of the scavengers.

Among the Hindu General category, people use their political influence at the local level to grab a few posts of safai kamgars, generally meant for the communities traditionally performing these occupations. It is observed that the General category persons entering this profession never perform these filthy tasks. They rather prefer to work as supervisors or sanitary inspectors and then try to become clerks or simply subcontract out their task to somebody else from scavenging castes. Advancement in technology and government measures to completely abolish the dry latrines (at least from urban and semi-urban areas) has brought some positive changes in the nature of this occupation. As a result, persons from the General category do not seem to mind joining as a safai karamchari and thus sweep roads for a few days and then switch over to some other tasks within the same department in due course of time.

## DECONSTRUCTING THE PRACTICE DIMENSIONS OF SCAVENGING

Manual scavengers in Maharashtra are engaged in five major activities of manual scavenging. 'Water-borne latrine' from among other scavenging activities in Maharashtra is the largest practice of manual scavenging, where 43.4 per cent (1,800) of scavengers are manually cleaning excreta. 'Open defecation' (as a part of community toilet block or roadside) is prevalent in the case of 29.80 per cent (1,239). 'Open gutters/drains' account for 24.7 per cent (1,025). 'Manholes', 1.5 per cent (63), are prevalent mainly in cities such as Mumbai and Pune. Only in a very few cases, 0.9 per cent (55), the 'dry latrines/*topli sandas*' are in practice. Incidentally, a large share of them belongs to the Aurangabad zone or region, especially the cantonment area, with 89.09 per cent (49) of the cases.

The nature of manual scavenging has changed over the years. In Maharashtra, the existence of dry latrine/dabba latrine is found only in few areas of Marathwada region, namely Aurangabad, Jalna and Beed. However, the community/public toilet blocks or the water-based/water-borne latrines provided by ULBs in certain localities in semi-urban and urban areas are not adequate and not properly maintained. The practice of defecating in open, alongside road, open gutters, drainages, open space and around toilet blocks has been found prevalent. This requires the manual scavenger as an employee of ULBs or any other government organization to manually remove/clean and dispose of human excreta and other waste.

The practice of scavenging and employment of manual scavengers by the local government authorities and private households has been banned under the Employment of Manual Scavengers and Construction of Dry Latrines (Prohibition) Act, 1993. This Act was enacted in Maharashtra from 26 January 1997. It declared employment of manual scavengers engaged in manually removing human excreta an offence and thus banned the construction of dry latrines, advocating in the process the conversion of existing dry latrines into water seal latrines. The study revealed that only 36 per cent of the respondents are aware of this Act. Not a single case is registered under the Act till government brought in a new legislation, Prohibition of Employment as Manual Scavengers and Their Rehabilitation Act, in 2013. This clearly reflects the apathy of the State in the implementation of this Act.

Further, as a strategy to eradicate this practice, it was identified as important to liberate and rehabilitate the manual scavengers in other dignified occupations. This resulted in the government launching the National Scheme for Liberation and Rehabilitation of Manual Scavengers and Their Dependents (NSLRM) in March 1992. However, the lukewarm implementation and complete lack of coordination between the training and the financial organization under the scheme hardly bore any fruit; instead, it rendered the scavengers unemployed and marginalized even further. According to the data from the study, only 28 per cent of the respondents were aware and only 8 per cent had benefited from this scheme in Maharashtra.

## THE INDIAN CONTEXT

Around 60 per cent of all open defecation in the world takes place in India.[29] To address this problem, the Government of India had launched a programme called the Total Sanitation Campaign (TSC) in 1999.

---

[29] Jairam Ramesh, 'India Is World's Capital for Open Defecation: Ramesh'. Available at: http://www.news18.com/news/india/india-is-worlds-capital-for-open-defecation-ramesh-491314.html (accessed on 24 August 2020).

The campaign became only partially successful and was restructured to make it more people-centric and renamed as Nirmal Bharat Abhiyan (NBA) with a goal of eradicating the practice of open defecation itself by 2022. Maharashtra along with Kerala, Himachal Pradesh and Haryana is on its way to achieve the goal of open defecation-free state in the next two years. However, all such programmes seem to have been unable to effectively tackle the problem of providing adequate sanitation to the masses at large, which is directly responsible for prevalence of practice of manual scavenging in the country. The Census of India 2011 data pertaining to the nature of latrine facilities reports approximately 7.4 lakh households spread across the country where 'night soil is removed by humans'. This excludes such households where 'night soil is disposed into open drain' (approximately 12.33 lakh) and those where 'night soil is serviced by animals' (approximately 4.93 lakh). Nevertheless, the likelihood that these households will engage manual scavenging services in the future is highly probable. Further, it is approximated that 25 lakh households persist in using dry (non-flush) latrines and will probably employ manual scavengers to clean them. However, there are few states and union territories that do not report any presence of manual scavenging; these are Chandigarh, Sikkim, Goa and Lakshadweep.

The Census figures only throw light on various types of latrines and the modes in which human excreta is removed (by human) or serviced (by animal); however, it does not give the exact numbers of manual scavengers in each state. For the population of manual scavengers, we have to rely on Census 2011 and the data given by various ministries of the central government. According to *Annual Report 2009–2010*, Ministry of Social Justice and Empowerment, Government of India, the population of manual scavengers in Maharashtra is 64,785. Of these, 19,086 are rehabilitated and about 45,699 are yet to be rehabilitated.

The Census India 2011 data with regard to sanitation facility in Maharashtra is equally important and relevant in this context. Although it does not give exact population of manual scavengers in Maharashtra, it does provide the magnitude of the problem of sanitation facility and manual scavenging in the state. Table 5.1 reveals the condition of sanitation in both rural and urban areas in the state with types of latrines. If viewed carefully, except the latrines connected to 'piped water system',

**Table 5.1.** Sanitation Facility in Maharashtra (Rural/Urban), Census of India 2011

| State | | | Total No. of Households | % of Households Having Latrine Facility within Premises | | | | | | | | | % of Households Not Having Latrine Facility within the Premise | |
|---|---|---|---|---|---|---|---|---|---|---|---|---|---|---|
| | | | | | Type of Latrine Facility within Premise | | | | | | | | | |
| | | | | | Flush/Pour Flush Latrine Connected to | | | Pit Latrine | | | Service Latrine | | | Alternative Sources | |
| | | | | | Piped Sewer System | Septic Tank | Other System | With Slab/ Ventilated Improved Pit | Without slab/ Open Pit | Night Soil Disposed into Drain | Night Soil Removed by Humans | Night Soil Serviced by Animals | Jointly | Public Latrine | Open |
| Maharashtra | T | | 23,830,580 | 53.10 | 34.58 | 44.18 | 3.07 | 15.63 | 0.88 | 1.22 | 0.1 | 0.4 | 0.44 | 46.90 | 27.58 | 72.4 |
| | R | | 13,016,652 | 38.00 | 5.88 | 50.41 | 5.96 | 35.21 | 1.78 | 0.42 | 0.1 | 0.3 | 0.34 | 62.00 | 10.00 | 90.0 |
| | U | | 10,813,928 | 71.27 | 53.00 | 40.18 | 1.22 | 3.06 | 0.31 | 1.73 | 0.1 | 0.4 | 0.50 | 28.73 | 73.23 | 26.8 |

*Source:* Table prepared by analysing data from Census of India 2011.

all other types of latrines invariably need to be cleaned/removed and disposed of by humans. In the light of the same, the problem of manual scavenging therefore persists.

The population of the castes engaged in manual scavenging profession in the state of Maharashtra is highly urbanized (92.7%). With the process of rapid urbanization in the state, the problem of manual scavenging seems to be more aggravating in urban and semi-urban areas rather than in rural areas where villagers prefer open fields for defecation. The circular issued by the Social Justice & Special Assistance Department, Government of Maharashtra, on 4 March 2013 with regard to the survey of insanitary latrines reveals that there are 171,688 households spread out in 256 towns/cities. The data is based on the Census 2011 and mainly includes the statutory towns in Maharashtra.

However, the Census 2011 data on sanitation reveal the challenges that rural Maharashtra has to face. It indicates that only 38 per cent of households in rural Maharashtra have latrine facility within the premises. Remaining 62 per cent households have no latrine facility and, therefore, have to resort to alternative sources, namely using 'public latrine' accounting for 10 per cent and 'open field' accounting for 90 per cent. The most striking fact that has emerged from this data is that there are 4,291 households where night soil is removed by human. In addition to this, there are 12,528 households where night soil is serviced by animals. Presence of both these categories, in other words, also suggests the engagement of manual scavengers for cleaning/removing and disposing of human excreta.

Further analysis of Census 2011 data and district-wise coverage of rural sanitation is shown in Table 5.2.

## IMPLICATIONS FOR INTERVENTION: CHALLENGES FOR REHABILITATION IN ALTERNATIVE LIVELIHOOD AVENUES

The prevalence of the practice of manual scavenging is confined mostly to urban and semi-urban areas in the state. As a result, manual scavengers are located more in these areas; this is evident from Census 2001 demographic data showing Bhangi as a highly urbanized caste from

**Table 5.2** Sanitation Facility in Rural Maharashtra, 2011

| State/UT | Total No. of Households | Households Having Latrine Facility within Premises | | | | Households Not Having Latrine Facility within Premises | | |
|---|---|---|---|---|---|---|---|---|
| | | % of Households Having Latrine Facility within the Premises | Service Latrine | | | % of Households Not Having Latrine Facility within the Premises | Alternative sources | |
| | | | No. of Households Where Night Soil Is Removed by Humans | No. of Households Where Night Soil Is Serviced by Animals | | | % of Households Using Public Latrine | % of Households Using Open Field |
| Maharashtra | 13,016,652 | 38.00 | 4,291 | 12,528 | | 62.00 | 10.00 | 90.00 |
| Nandurbar | 270,533 | 22.32 | 0 | 177 | | 77.68 | 4.74 | 95.26 |
| Dhule | 298,915 | 18.69 | 48 | 421 | | 81.31 | 24.33 | 75.67 |
| Jalgaon | 618,314 | 22.59 | 32 | 449 | | 77.41 | 21.36 | 78.64 |
| Buldana | 445,247 | 29.07 | 16 | 286 | | 70.93 | 1.62 | 98.38 |
| Akola | 247,752 | 30.93 | 75 | 376 | | 69.07 | 1.30 | 98.70 |
| Washim | 217,490 | 27.55 | 28 | 281 | | 72.45 | 1.39 | 98.61 |
| Amravati | 424,563 | 41.14 | 148 | 305 | | 58.86 | 2.16 | 97.84 |
| Wardha | 210,284 | 47.17 | 141 | 149 | | 52.83 | 1.67 | 98.33 |
| Nagpur | 324,568 | 46.06 | 105 | 514 | | 53.94 | 2.53 | 97.47 |

| | | | | | | |
|---|---|---|---|---|---|---|
| Bhandara | 223,299 | 55.75 | 529 | 311 | 44.25 | 1.27 | 98.73 |
| Gondiya | 241,802 | 47.55 | 22 | 131 | 52.45 | 1.29 | 98.71 |
| Gadchiroli | 218,935 | 22.19 | 107 | 308 | 77.81 | 1.50 | 98.50 |
| Chandrapur | 352,643 | 29.08 | 439 | 222 | 70.92 | 1.43 | 98.57 |
| Yavatmal | 513,041 | 21.75 | 172 | 503 | 78.25 | 1.11 | 98.89 |
| Nanded | 487,624 | 19.23 | 80 | 233 | 80.77 | 1.01 | 98.99 |
| Hingoli | 195,143 | 26.90 | 0 | 103 | 73.10 | 1.25 | 98.75 |
| Parbhani | 256,063 | 13.33 | 0 | 219 | 86.67 | 0.83 | 99.17 |
| Jalna | 318,563 | 29.21 | 69 | 131 | 70.79 | 2.28 | 97.72 |
| Aurangabad | 419,120 | 19.77 | 15 | 483 | 80.23 | 1.74 | 98.26 |
| Nashik | 661,977 | 29.27 | 217 | 691 | 70.73 | 12.47 | 87.53 |
| Thane | 526,397 | 39.70 | 124 | 616 | 60.30 | 15.34 | 84.66 |
| Raigarh | 376,520 | 50.93 | 157 | 326 | 49.07 | 46.51 | 53.49 |
| Pune | 744,114 | 61.76 | 646 | 1,206 | 38.24 | 13.50 | 86.50 |
| Ahmednagar | 717,718 | 39.09 | 147 | 475 | 60.91 | 5.00 | 95.00 |
| Bid | 446,114 | 15.38 | 15 | 311 | 84.62 | 1.37 | 98.63 |
| Latur | 359,858 | 24.85 | 11 | 327 | 75.15 | 0.98 | 99.02 |
| Osmanabad | 294,816 | 22.19 | 16 | 290 | 77.81 | 3.44 | 96.56 |

*(Continued)*

(Continued)

| State/UT | Total No. of Households | Households Having Latrine Facility within Premises | | | Households Not Having Latrine Facility within Premises | | |
|---|---|---|---|---|---|---|---|
| | | % of Households Having Latrine Facility within the Premises | Service Latrine | | % of Households Not Having Latrine Facility within the Premises | Alternative sources | |
| | | | No. of Households Where Night Soil Is Removed by Humans | No. of Households Where Night Soil Is Serviced by Animals | | % of Households Using Public Latrine | % of Households Using Open Field |
| Solapur | 583,706 | 32.11 | 106 | 493 | 67.89 | 5.53 | 94.47 |
| Satara | 518,187 | 70.12 | 294 | 397 | 29.88 | 49.76 | 50.24 |
| Ratnagiri | 333,645 | 67.18 | 124 | 169 | 32.82 | 52.03 | 47.97 |
| Sindhudurg | 180,494 | 74.41 | 0 | 33 | 25.59 | 39.67 | 60.33 |
| Kolhapur | 556,628 | 74.43 | 242 | 947 | 25.57 | 63.84 | 36.16 |
| Sangli | 432,579 | 60.48 | 166 | 645 | 39.52 | 28.33 | 71.67 |

*Source:* Table prepared by analysing data from Census of India 2011.

among the SCs. They account for nearly 93 per cent urban population. While working out strategies to effectively deal with livelihood issues of the manual scavengers in the state, the following aspects are suggested:

1. *Identification of families of manual scavengers in rural Maharashtra*: There is a need to initially target only those districts with maximum numbers of households reporting latrines within premises (as per Census 2011) where night soil is being removed by humans and those latrines which are serviced by animals. Building rapport with *bastis* (localities) of manual scavengers at district headquarter/town or taluka level in order to collect information about scavengers residing in nearby villages is critical. The possibility of occurrence of manual scavenging in small villages is very remote, as most of the people here use open fields for defecation. In such cases, one could select a Census town (having population of up to 5,000 and 75 per cent male population engaged in non-agricultural activities) and explore the households of manual scavengers as carried forth by the Social Justice & Special Assistance Department, Government of Maharashtra, or access the data that this department has collected through recent survey.

   The list of households where night soil is removed by humans can be accessed through village-level Census house listing in order to locate the manual scavengers attending such latrines. As far as rehabilitation of manual scavengers and their dependents in dignified livelihood avenues is concerned, the whole community (set of 10 castes/sub-castes) must be targeted across the state. Targeting only women and that too only from rural areas will never serve the purpose. Rural–urban, male–female, youth, elderly, children, regular, non-regular (on contract/contractual labourer), employed and unemployed members should be included and targeted for the rehabilitation, training and dignified employment avenues.

2. *Livelihood issues and possible strategies to tackle them:* Rehabilitation of scavengers should not be looked in isolation from liberation. It has to be comprehensive and must include (a) alternative dignified and sustainable employment for at least five years; (b) in absence of guaranteed employment, a provision of 'release money' as stipend (remuneration) till some dignified and sustainable employment

is ensured; (c) uninterrupted education of children at least up to matriculation has to be ensured; and (d) housing schemes such as Indira Awas Yojana (rural areas) and especially Valmiki Ambedkar Awas Yojana (VAMBAY) meant for the scavengers' households in urban slums should be given priority.

Hereditary occupation should be replaced by skill-based occupational choices so as to discourage the young generation from taking up parents' hereditary occupation. Young members of the family (of age group of 15–25 years) must be targeted for professional/technical or vocational training. And creation of better career options and livelihood opportunities for the younger generation must be emphasized. For employment after the training, public sector undertakings (PSUs; Indian Railways and many such organizations) should be targeted.

It is observed that the members of the community are often encouraged for piggery (rearing pigs) and are given financial help only for this purpose. There is a stigma attached to this activity, and therefore this should be discouraged and other dignified avenues of livelihood should be explored.

The government must emphasize introducing mechanization in sanitation so as to completely eradicate manual scavenging and reduce the inhumane, undignified and unsafe practices in manual sanitation work in general. Further, the government must draw expertise from NGOs such as Navasarjan and Dalit Shakti Kendra in Gujarat, Garima Abhiyan in Dewas, Madhya Pradesh, and National Safai Karmachari Andolan (SKA), Delhi. They have done exemplary work in liberating manual scavengers and rehabilitating them into dignified occupations.

## CRITICAL ANALYSIS OF APPROACHES TO ELIMINATING MANUAL SCAVENGING

There are broadly four distinct approaches which one can distinguish on the approaches to addressing the problem of manual scavenging. The first finds their source in Akbar and Mahatma Gandhi where an attempt is made to change people's attitude on manual scavenging. The second could be framed as the 'constructive social service approach', which is being exemplified by the Sulabh International movement which views the problem primarily as a sanitation or health issue. The third could be posited as the 'relief approach', adopted by the government through its numerous policies, schemes and programmes and the fourth as the 'radical approach' which aims at the total elimination of manual scavenging and liberation of manual scavengers from this dehumanizing practice.

The 'first' approach which is exemplified by Akbar and Mahatma Gandhi tries to change public attitude towards manual scavengers.[30] For example, Akbar altered the identity of the scavengers to Mehtars, meaning 'prince', 'leader' or 'noble people'. This was followed by Mahatma Gandhi when he applauded the manual scavengers for their services to the society, calling them the 'mother of society'. While there were some positive repercussion to each of these attempts, the problem with this approach is that it is premised on 'unfair inclusion' or 'adverse inclusion' of the manual scavengers, attempting in the process to integrate them unfavourably without questioning the practice of manual scavenging itself.

The 'second' approach could be called the 'constructive social service approach'. This is exemplified by the Sulabh International movement, which views the problem of manual scavenging primarily as a sanitation or health issue.[31] It tries to substitute dry latrines with inexpensive water closets through low-cost sanitation programmes and emphasizes that 'scavenging is a service and not a duty of any one individual/community, and those who avail this service must pay for it and it could be expensive'. The problem with this approach is that it does not employ modern technology, nor does it exercise pressure on local bodies or individuals to eliminate manual scavenging.

The 'third' approach could be termed as the 'relief approach'. This is seen adopted by the government through their numerous policies, schemes and programmes since the 1950s.[32] After India's independence,

---

[30] Y. Moses, 'A Movement to Eradicate Manual Scavenging in India', *Dalit International News Letter* 10, no. 3 (2005), Waterford, CT.

[31] Ibid.

[32] Ibid.

the most critical concern of the government was the eradication of the inhuman practice of carrying human excreta on the head by certain communities and to wipe out this blot from the Indian society. As a result, the government of India appointed various committees and commissions, which studied the socio-economic conditions of sweepers and scavengers at various times. Some of these committees are V. N. Barve Committee (1949), N. R. Malkani Committee (1957), National Commission on Labour (1966), N. R. Malkani Committee and Bhanu Prasad Pandya Committee (1966) and Task Force (1989) appointed by the Planning Commission, Government of India.[33] The then Prime Minister Mr Narasimha Rao launched a new NSLRM at the very beginning of the era of liberalization and globalization in March 1992. The very next year in 1993, his government enacted the legislation Employment of Manual Scavengers and Construction of Dry Latrines (Prohibition) Act. This made the existence of dry latrines and practice of manual scavenging punishable under the law. His government also brought in the National Commission for Safai Karamcharis Act, 1993, and set up the first National Commission for Safai Karamcharis in 1994. Unfortunately, all these programmes remained confined only to improving the working and living conditions of manual scavengers and failed to address the issue of caste-based slavery and human dignity. Further, the liberation of manual scavengers from degrading and dehumanizing practice did not go beyond policies and schemes. If one looks at it critically, for instance, the final word from independent India's first report of the Scavengers' Living Conditions Enquiry Committee (1949) by V. N. Barve squarely held responsible the manual scavengers themselves for the continuation of practice of manual scavenging. The practice continues, it remarked, 'Because the scavengers have submissively put up with its dirty nature and never raised their voices against it, as if it were ordained for them by birth'. Thus, the social order (varna system) and history were reinforced when the chairman (no less a Brahmin) of India's first commission on manual scavenging turned the onus of scavenging onto the scavengers. It further remarked, 'But they should know that, as human beings and as equal citizens of free India,

---

[33] S. Darokar, 'Manual Scavengers: A Blind Spot in Urban Development Discourse', *Economic & Political Weekly* 53, no. 22 (2 June 2018).

they have a right to insist that the condition of scavenging work shall be such, that it should be capable of being done by any self-respecting person.'[34] In fact, there is never a scope for the working condition of manual scavenging in which they can assert their self-respect as it is hereditary or a caste-based occupation.

It is interesting to note that the Comptroller and Auditor General of India (CAG) has evaluated NSLRM and submitted the report. The CAG in its reports said, 'Achievements so far at best can be described as sporadic, uncoordinated and generally poor, without the strength required for catalyzing the future course.' It pointed out that the estimates of scavengers are somewhat higher than what is given in plan documents, while the numbers of rehabilitated people are lower than what is provided in plan documents. It, therefore, noticed that there was 'lack of correspondence between liberation and rehabilitation, and that there was no evidence to suggest if those liberated from the practice were in fact rehabilitated'. The report further pointed out that as against 600,000 scavengers identified in urban areas, the ministry reported having liberated only 37,340 (i.e., 6.2%). More than ₹6 billion ($138 million) was spent under the said scheme, in addition to the fund spent to help weaker sections/scheduled castes.[35]

The 'fourth' approach that the author posits as the 'radical approach' aims at the total elimination of manual scavenging and liberation of manual scavengers from this dehumanizing practice.[36] This approach heavily draws from Ambedkar's ideology of freedom of mind. Both Gandhi and Ambedkar held extremely divergent views on the subject of manual scavenging. Ambedkar asserted that there was a historically constituted intrinsic relationship between caste and manual scavenging, and any attempt to do away with manual scavenging requires the annihilation of caste, without which its abolition remains merely ideational. Ambedkar was of the firm view that such a paternalistic approach will neither rid the practice of manual scavenging nor change society's

---

[34] V. N. Barve, *State of Bombay*, a report of the Scavengers Living Condition Enquiry Committee (Mumbai: Government of Maharashtra, 1949).

[35] Beck and Darokar, *Socio-Economic Survey of Manual Scavengers*, 2005.

[36] Moses, 'A Movement to Eradicate Manual Scavenging'.

perception of the (caste) occupation. Gandhi however opined that alteration of perception and behavioural change, while it will take time, is bound to occur in the near future. He noted in one of his speeches on the subject delivered on 3 February 1934 in Thandkarancheri,

> I call scavenging one of the most honourable among the occupation to which mankind is called. I do not consider it an unclean occupation by any means. That in performing the cleaning operation you have to handle dirt is true. But, that every mother has to do, every doctor does. But, nobody says that a mother's occupation when she cleans her children or a doctor's occupation when he cleans his patients is an unclean occupation.[37]

In disagreement with Gandhi, Ambedkar asserted,

> Under Hinduism scavenging was not a matter of choice; it was a matter of force. What does Gandhism do? It seeks to perpetuate this system by praising scavenging as the noblest service to society! What is the use of telling the scavenger that even a Brahmin is prepared to do scavenging when it is clear that according to Hindu Shastras and Hindu notions even if a Brahmin did scavenging he would never be subject to the disabilities of one who is a born scavenger? For in India a man is not a scavenger because of his work. He is a scavenger because of his birth irrespective of the question whether he does scavenging or not.[38]

The nature of manual scavenging remains caste-based and hereditary and is exclusively practised from one generation to another by Dalits. Empirically, it seems that this caste-based occupation is 'reserved' fully for Dalits without animosity and protest by those who have the tendency to resist the reservation policy.[39] This radical approach is put in practice by the exemplary work done by SKA (initially in Andhra Pradesh and later at national level); Garima Abhiyan by Jan Sahas, Dewas, Madhya Pradesh; and Dalit Shakti Kendra, Sanand, Gujarat. SKA successfully undertook 'dry latrine demolition drive' in the state

---

[37] Gandhi, *The Collected Works of Mahatma Gandhi*, 104.
[38] Ambedkar, *What Congress and Gandhi Have Done to the Untouchables*, 292–293.
[39] Darokar, 'Manual Scavengers'.

of Andhra Pradesh, and dry latrines were demolished in all the districts of the state by members of Safai Karmachari community.[40]

Similarly, it is evident from the struggles and testimonies of women manual scavengers belonging to Garima Abhiyan, Jan Sahas in Madhya Pradesh, who have been able to leave the practice. It was the courage and struggle of these women that resulted in putting an end to this inhuman practice in many places. It began in Dewas district of Madhya Pradesh in 2001. Initially, a few women belonging to Valmiki and Hela communities began leaving this practice with the help of Garima Abhiyan. Later, it spread to 15 districts of the state and other neighbouring states. Garima Abhiyan called it slavery and with its intervention through social awakening has liberated more than 10,000 women so far.

## CONCLUDING REMARKS

In 2003, SKA led by Bezwada Wilson and S. R. Sankaran filed a writ petition in the Supreme Court for elimination of manual scavenging. It gave details of prevalence of the practice of manual scavenging and perseverance of dry latrines usage across India. The National Commission for Safai Karamcharis pointed out that there remain 96 lakh dry latrines across the country, and it noted that the government/public sector is the highest employer of manual scavengers. Successive reports brought out by the commission even note that manual scavengers are employed by ULBs, military engineering services, Indian Railways and other PSUs.

Thus, attempting to deconstruct a historically constituted occupation, such as manual scavenging, which is socially embedded in layers of rigidly structured inequality and humiliation, is a challenge. Marking its prevalence, nature and extent in Maharashtra while rupturing embodied widely accepted social notions again, while imperative, is a difficult task. Nonetheless, I consider it important to assert that the moment is ripe for retheorizing fundamental questions pertaining to the said subject.

---

[40] Moses, 'A Movement to Eradicate Manual Scavenging'.

The urgency to engage with more fundamental questions is duly felt in the light of a series of policy-related actions by the Indian State to confront and rid caste-based manual scavenging from India. Even though most of the State Acts and policies do not seem to have made any qualitative impact on people's lives, the attempt is noteworthy. Beginning with the Employment of Manual Scavengers and Construction of Dry Latrines (Prohibition) Act, 1993, and Prohibition of Employment as Manual Scavengers and Their Rehabilitation Act, 2013 and schemes such as NSLRM, TSC, National Safai Karamcharis Finance and Development Corporation, Nirmal Gram Puraskar Yojana, Self-Employment Scheme for Rehabilitation of Manual Scavengers and SBA, the Acts and programmes of the Government of India in general and of different states in particular remain nondescript. In many ways, they seem to have miserably failed to eradicate the inhuman practice of cleaning toilets and lifting human excreta by hand assigned mostly to some caste groups.

Based on the recognition of the above concrete conditions, I will attempt to state a few propositions on the concrete conditions of manual scavenging. Many of the occupations that are marked as impure and stigmatized have always been caste/descent-based and are performed predominantly by members of Dalit communities. Whereas government officials, politicians and judiciary (predominantly upper caste) have rarely shown any genuine commitment to its eradication beyond loud policy pronouncements when cornered by facts and figures, there is however a perennial denial of its social existence among those who wish to free themselves from the responsibility of their daily excreta produce.

A number of reports that examine the issue of manual scavenging, published by civil society organizations and reputed institutions like the Tata Institute of Social Sciences, point to a fact that both the central and state governments seem unaware that it is perpetuating manual scavenging, being its highest employer. This social condition is often viewed as fundamentally violating basic human rights of many voiceless citizens of the country. In an interesting report of the Malkani Committee (1969) in the wake of Gandhi Centenary Year, the Bhangi Kashta Mukti programme was launched by providing scavengers with wheelbarrows, subsidy to households to convert dry latrines into flush-out latrines, etc. The policy that informed the programme purported to address the issue of indignity, stigma associated with scavenging and consequent practice of untouchability against manual scavengers by eradicating unsanitary conditions around them. Most such welfare policies/programmes of the State are informed by a belief that the inhuman state of manual scavengers and safai karamcharis is likely due to physical and unhygienic conditions, rather than 'sociocultural' or 'ritual' impurity imposed on their lives by the caste system.

It is also to be noted that the state and central governments for a long time were even reluctant to redefine the term 'manual scavengers'. This was because they feared that they would have to circumscribe these workers into the framework of other work such as sewerage workers, morgue attendants, garbage worker, and railway's and hospital's sanitation workers, who themselves work in extremely hazardous conditions. The State has neither tried alleviating the vulnerability of manual scavengers who put their own lives at risk while sanitizing towns and cities nor has offered entitlements such as housing, health care and social security to them. This is not to find fault with the said conditions but only to pithily assert that in India, the practice of manual scavenging is still perceived as a normal occupation which is the social obligation of a caste.

Although many political leaders have presented the case as a 'national shame' and articulated the need to eradicate the practice, inappropriate as it may be, political parties and civil society alike have rarely shown the seriousness and courage to take a drastic action on the matter. Imbued and deeply rooted in caste, manual scavenging keeps persisting. This is one of the main reasons for the inability to secure any theoretical advancement that can provide deeper insights and bring dynamism in the said reality. Nonetheless, this should not be the reason for not attempting to raise the debate about manual scavenging to a valid place in both social and moral discourses.

In conclusion, the production of real concrete numbers that throws light on the spread and extent of the practice of manual scavenging is vital. But even with stark facts staring shone brightly on the concrete conditions of peoples, we are still confronted in every sociopolitical realm by State apathy, caste hatred or even the scavenger's fatalistic acquiescence to the said occupation. We live in a society where caste encapsulates our whole being, where social solidarity is established and structured on historical peripheralization and reciprocal repulsion. The commonsensical attitude that stems from such malicious historiosocial conditions often suffers from an epistemic sightlessness that binds caste groups into rigid islands of oppression. In such concrete conditions, while one has a sense of oneself and one's location, one is blind to the experiential conditions of others. This complex psycho-epistemic condition often manifests in the public domain as normative duties and political responsibilities assigned by history in its political interplay.

While those in the higher echelons of the caste structure deem the production of waste a natural bodily process that everyone experience, the same caste is totally apathetic to the responsibility of cleaning the same once it turns to dirt, because as per the scriptural law, it is the God-ordained duty of the lower caste to religiously partake in its cleansing. So pervasive is this religiously bounded attitude among the higher caste that even the mention of this social act of taking responsibility for one's own waste is often conceived as epithetical.

It is within such circumscribed conditions that the practice of untouchability is produced and reproduced. The theory, if articulated in commonsensical ways, would refer to a notion that reads as follows: 'Whereas it is my God designed natural duty to produce waste, it is however the religiously ordained responsibility of the untouchable to clean the dirt.' We are a long way from achieving the fundamental alteration of the caste system, and probably a freedom from the very idea of caste, especially its narrow colonizing mindset and its inhumane practices. Nonetheless, this should not deter those who believe in the historical struggle for self-worth, self-respect, dignity and freedom of mind to attempt its political disruption and ultimately its social annihilation.

## BIBLIOGRAPHY

Ambedkar, B. R. 'The Triumph of Brahmanism'. In *Dr. Babasaheb Ambedkar Writings and Speeches*. Vol. 3. Mumbai: Government of Maharashtra, 1987.

Beck, H., and S. Darokar. *Socio-economic Survey of Manual Scavengers in Maharashtra*. Mumbai: TISS for Mahatma Phule Backward Class Development Corporation Ltd, a Government of Maharashtra undertaking, 2005.

———.'Socio-economic Status of Scavengers Engaged in the Practice of Manual Scavenging in Maharashtra'. *The Indian Journal of Social Work* 66, no. 2 (2005): 223–236.

Census of India. 'List of Scheduled Castes in India'. Available at: http://censusindia.gov.in/Tables_Published/SCST/ST%20Lists.pdf (accessed on 24 August 2020).

Gandhi, M. K. *The Collected Works of Mahatma Gandhi* (electronic book), 104. Vol. 63. New Delhi: Publications Division, Government of India, 1999.

Law Publishers. *Employment of Manual Scavengers and Construction of Dry Latrines (Prohibition) Act, 1993*. Allahabad: Bare Acts, 2004.

Census of India. 'List of Scheduled Castes in India'. Available at: http://censusindia.gov.in/Tables_Published/SCST/ST%20Lists.pdf (accessed on 24 August 2020).

Ministry of Social Justice and Empowerment. 'State-wise Population of Manual Scavengers in India'. Available at: http://socialjustice.nic.in/srmsapp1.php (accessed on 23 November 2020).

# Section C

# Social Hegemony, Media and Culture

# Chapter 6

# Understanding the Ideological Nature of Caste Violence in Tamil Nadu
Particularism and Universalism

Karthick Ram Manoharan

Caste violence has been a recurring event in the political landscape of Tamil Nadu in post-independence India. The Ramnad riots of 1957, which saw clashes between the Thevars, a Most Backward Caste (MBC), and the Pallars, a Scheduled Caste (SC), led to loss of dozens of lives on both sides. The Kizhavenmani massacre of 1968 saw 44 Dalit labourers being burnt alive by upper-caste landlords, and in retaliation Gopalakrishna Naidu, the key orchestrator of this gruesome incident, was murdered several years later, allegedly by individuals affiliated to radical left and Dravidian outfits. In 1998, six Dalits including the panchayat president of Melur were killed in Melavalavu by Thevars who were angered that the panchayat had been converted to a reserved constituency for the SCs. Recently, in 2012, Vanniyars, an MBC group, protesting against inter-caste marriages between Dalits and Vanniyars, went on a riot in Dharmapuri, burning hundreds of houses in Dalit hamlets. The progress of science, technology and modernity, it appears, has not affected the 'primordial' identity of caste and caste-related violence.

But what many observers find even more perturbing is that such caste violence occurs in a state that has had a legacy of progressive non-Brahmin and anti-caste assertion. This has led some to comment that this non-Brahmin political assertion that began with the Justice Party was only anti-Brahmin and not anti-caste as such. The general accusation is that the rhetoric of anti-Brahminism was initiated and deployed by upper non-Brahmin castes so as to become a new power bloc, marginalizing the rest in the process. Such criticism is of course ignorant of the rich history of contestation of Brahmin secular and cultural hegemony by thinkers such as Iyothee Thass,[1] which reveals that opposition to Brahminism was not just an affair of elite non-Brahmin castes but of the Dalit imagination as well. Reductive criticisms also mischievously try to cover up upper-caste anxieties about the non-Brahmin movement, using the Dalit card to dismiss a complex and diverse non-movement, which was not a single linear trajectory but an evolving politico-historical field where several agents from different strata of society articulated their concerns and grievances at different points in time.

Critics of the Dravidian movement have accused it of several things—being anti-Indian, promoting hatred towards the Brahmins, separatism, advocating a collapse of family values and traditional morality and so on. Of this, one particular criticism stands out in recent times, which is the supposed failure of the Dravidian movement to take Dalit concerns seriously. What is particularly interesting about this criticism is that intellectuals from the left, right and centre of the political spectrum are united in pointing it out. Cho Ramaswamy, a Hindu right-wing critic, says of Periyar, the key ideologue of the Dravidian movement, 'In his crusade against the caste system, however, he did not concentrate on the liberation of the Harijans, perhaps for fear of alienating his followers, mostly from the other castes.'[2] Much earlier, M. N. Srinivas, a sociologist of liberal orientation, commented that the Dravidian movement in Tamil Nadu resulted in the dominant

---

[1] G. Aloysius, *Iyothee Thassar and Tamil Buddhist Movement*, 2nd ed. (New Delhi: Critical Quest, 2015).

[2] Cho S. Ramaswamy, 'E.V. Ramaswami Naicker and C.N. Annadurai'. Available at: http://www.india-today.com/itoday/millennium/100people/durai.html (accessed on 20 November 2013).

non-Brahmin castes gaining power, arguing that these castes have a 'vested interest' in keeping the Dalits poor socially and economically as the latter are their main sources of agricultural labour.[3]

The Dalit Marxist activist Anand Teltumbde makes a grand claim that the Dravidar Kazhagam by 1949 'transformed into a ruling-class lobby that ignored the caste question altogether',[4] while Ravikumar, a Dalit writer with postmodernist leaning, argues that 'The propaganda against Brahmin domination in government services and in the social sphere benefited only the non-Brahmins (who were economically powerful) and excluded the Dalits'[5] and urges the Dalits to not sacrifice their singularity by standing on a common political platform with the non-Brahmin castes.[6] These writers, who otherwise would not see eye to eye on other social issues, have a commonality in their criticism that the Dravidian movement's political discourse focused solely on empowering the non-Brahmins at the cost of the Dalits.

Recent academic interventions highlight the need for an autonomous Dalit politics in Tamil Nadu,[7] while others point out the tensions within the same, alleging that Arunthathiyar grievances are not addressed by mainstream Dalit politics.[8] Others defend Dravidian politics for its egalitarian pasts[9] and possibilities.[10] Research has also

---

[3] M. N. Srinivas, *Caste in Modern India and Other Essays* (New York, NY: Asia Publishing House, 1962), 91.

[4] Anand Teltumbde, *The Persistence of Caste: The Khairlanji Murders and India's Hidden Apartheid* (New Delhi: Navayana, 2010), 23.

[5] Ravikumar, *Venomous Touch: Notes on Caste, Culture and Politics* (Kolkata: Samya, 2009), 41.

[6] Ibid., 241. It must, however, be noted that of late, Ravikumar has revised his earlier positions and has defended Periyarist and Dravidian politics from his Dalit standpoint.

[7] Hugo Gorringe, *Panthers in Parliament: Dalits, Caste, and Political Power in South India* (New Delhi: Oxford University Press, 2017).

[8] Ravichandran Bathran, 'The Many Omissions of a Concept: Discrimination amongst Scheduled Castes', *Economic & Political Weekly* 51, no. 47 (2016): 30–34.

[9] Sundar Kaali, 'Making of a New Public Sphere', *Seminar*, no. 708 (August 2018): 45–48.

[10] Rajan Kurai Krishnan and Ravindran Sriramachandran, 'Dravidian Futures', *Seminar*, no. 708 (August 2018): 62–68.

recorded the inclusive developmental and social welfare policies implemented by the Dravidian parties in power, which were universal in their reach.[11] But the persistence of violence against Dalits continues to raise questions.

Johan Galtung in his widely cited essay on violence argues that 'Personal violence represents change and dynamism—not only ripples on waves, but waves on otherwise tranquil waters. Structural violence is silent, it does not show—it is essentially static, it *is* the tranquil waters.'[12] It can be argued that as far as criticism of anti-Dalit violence goes, personal violence is focused on but structural violence is ignored. That is, acts of physical violence perpetrated by a few clusters of OBCs against Dalits receive focus, interrogation and condemnation (and rightly so), but little effort is taken to understand the ideological nature of caste violence that is embedded in the structure of the society.

## LOVE, CASTE AND IDEOLOGY: NOTES FROM A TAMIL FILM

It is instructive here to have a look at Balaji Sakthivel's movie *Kaadhal* (2004), which deals with the theme of caste brutality in the wake of an inter-caste marriage. The film is remarkable in the history of Tamil cinema for its frank and brutal portrayal of how caste hurts not just love between two individuals but also the very idea of a universal human community.

---

[11] A. Kalaiyarasan, 'Politics of Dravidian Populism: Understanding Developmental Outcomes in Tamil Nadu', in *Rethinking Social Justice*, eds. S. Anandhi et al. (Hyderabad: Orient BlackSwan, 2020): 231–254; J. Jeyaranjan, 'Tenancy Reforms in Tamil Nadu: A Study from the Cauvery Delta Region', in *Rethinking Social Justice*, eds. S. Anandhi et al. (Hyderabad: Orient BlackSwan, 2020), 255–283; M. Vijayabaskar, 'Emerging Labour Regimes and Mobilities in Tamil Nadu', in *Rethinking Social Justice*, eds. S. Anandhi et al. (Hyderabad: Orient BlackSwan, 2020): 206–230; S. Narayan, *Dravidian Years: Politics and Welfare in Tamil Nadu* (New Delhi: Oxford University Press, 2018).

[12] Johan Galtung, 'Violence, Peace and Peace Research', *Journal of Peace Research* 6, no. 3 (1969): 173.

The movie begins with a couple, Murugan (Bharath) and Aishwarya (Sandhya), eloping from Madurai to Chennai. Just as Aishwarya pleads with Murugan to tie a *thaali* (the sacred marital thread) and make her his lawful wife, the scene cuts to Rajendran (Thandapani), Aishwarya's father, who is revealed to be an influential feudalistic strongman in Madurai. Rajendran is seen to be forcibly breaking up the marriage between a driver and his employer's daughter when he receives a phone call from home that his own daughter is missing. While Rajendran is visibly irate, his younger brother Vellaiyan (Krishna Murthy) is seen to be a sobering influence, who advises him to keep a calm head since the family honour is at stake.

Meanwhile, through the journey of the eloping couple, their flashback is shown through bits. Aishwarya is shown to be a girl from a very affluent background and a darling child of her family. Her father dotes on her and names his house, property and even wine stores after her. A student in her 12th grade, her first encounters with Murugan result in minor accidents for the latter, causing much amusement for her. Murugan corners Aishwarya in a secluded lane and warns her against messing with him and instructs her to behave like a woman. Following this, Aishwarya attains puberty.

With the blossoming of womanhood, love too blossoms for Aishwarya, and she begins pursuing Murugan. After some initial reluctance, Murugan also reciprocates, despite his well-founded apprehensions about her father and family. Although Aishwarya is still in her school, her family fixes her marriage with an affluent relative who is working in America. In the wake of these developments, Aishwarya approaches Murugan and urges him to elope with her. Murugan is reluctant, fearful of her family's influence in the region. Aishwarya assures him that once they see her married and settled happily, their anger will dissipate. The lovers decide to elope to Chennai.

In Chennai, they are helped by Murugan's friend Stephen (Sukumar), who temporarily hosts them in a bachelor's lodging. After a few hassles in the city, the couple get married at a street temple and manage to get lodging. In contrast to the feudal hierarchy and the caste identity tensions of Madurai, Chennai's youth appears to welcome the couple. The supposed caste-blindness of the urban setting is hinted at. Stephen's friends throw a wedding party for the couple and a song runs with lyrics that suggest a horizontal solidarity in urban social spaces. The happiness for the couple is short-lived. Before they can take off on their conjugal life, Aishwarya's uncle Vellaiyan arrives in Chennai.

The shrewd man cajoles the couple to return to Madurai, assuring them that they will be accepted into the family. However, in the journey back home, Vellaiyan compares the educational and economic advantages that Aishwarya has over Murugan. Finally, he asks Murugan what his caste is. At this point, the real face of Vellaiyan is revealed, and the couple are taken forcibly to a family farm, where Rajendran and his henchmen have gathered. First, the women of the family beat Aishwarya; then, the men turn their attention to Murugan. After beating him black and blue, Rajendran compels Aishwarya to remove the *thaali* tied by Murugan. To save Murugan's life, Aishwarya discards the *thaali*.

Years later, Aishwarya is shown to be wedded to a middle-class man, presumably from her own caste, and is seen travelling on a scooter with him in Dindigul with her child. (Of course, this is an indication of her lowered value in the marriage market by virtue of her supposed corruption—consider that she was engaged to a person from a rich family earlier.) As they wait at a signal near a statue of Periyar, she looks at a madman on the road who is revealed to be Murugan. She faints and is admitted to a hospital. Later, without her husband's knowledge, she rushes to the spot where she finds the madman Murugan and begins wailing on the road, asking if love was a crime. Her husband arrives there with their child, comforts her, and takes along Murugan whom he admits in a hospital for the mentally disabled. As they walk back, credits roll and it is revealed by the director that this is a real-life story.

This movie has eerie significance for the contemporary times. In the last three years, three highly publicized 'honour killings' based on caste gathered considerable attention in Tamil Nadu. The caste violence unleashed by the Vanniyars mentioned above happened in the wake of an inter-caste marriage between a Dalit youth Ilavarasan and a Vanniyar girl. Months later, in July 2013, Ilavarasan was found dead on a railway track. While official records state that this was a case of suicide, Dalit sources suggest that Ilavarasan might have been murdered. In June 2015, Gokulraj, a Dalit youth from Salem, was abducted, murdered and decapitated by a Gounder caste outfit for allegedly being in love with a girl from their caste. Much recently, in March 2016, a Dalit man Sankar who was married to a Thevar girl was hacked to death in broad daylight in Tiruppur.

In all these cases, the victim was a Dalit and the perpetrators were from OBC communities. These atrocities received considerable attention in both the English and Tamil media, and condemnations for the attacks were swift. Sadly, the same attention was not given to the murder of a Dalit-Paraiyar girl by her parents for marrying a Dalit-Arunthathiyar boy in 2012.[13] Indeed, the rule of endogamy, and its associated restrictions, is also followed by those SCs who consider themselves to be higher to other SCs. Arunthathiyar groups like the Adi Tamizhar Katchi, acknowledging the stark divisions within the Dalit category itself, have condemned the silence over these crimes.

It is here that a critical reading of Balaji Sakthivel's *Kaadhal* helps. This movie deals with the theme of inter-caste marriage and the crisis that it brings about in the lives of the couple involved. The castes of Aishwarya and Murugan are not revealed but are left to be deciphered. Those familiar with southern Tamil Nadu could infer Aishwarya belonging to the Thevar community—her father's social status and extra-legal activities, the manner of conduction of her puberty ceremony, the specific language and terminology used by her family and so on. However, Murugan's caste is a bit more ambiguous.

Murugan lives with his widowed mother in a slum area. He clearly is from a lower class and a caste lower than Aishwarya's. However,

---

[13] Ravi Chandran, 'The Murder of a Dalit Girl and the Silence Over It' (2012). Available at: http://roundtableindia.co.in/index.php?option=com_content&view=article&id=6001:the-murder-of-a-dalit-girl-and-the-silence-over-it&catid=119:feature&Itemid=132 (accessed on 5 May 2016).

there is no clear indication that he is a Dalit. Anand makes much out of Murugan's house being painted an Ambedkarite blue.[14] This is an unconvincing speculation. In this case, Murugan's house has a calendar that bears a red and yellow logo, the colours used by the Vanniyar Sangam. By Anand's logic, one could also speculate that Murugan is a Vanniyar, which would be a far more interesting hypothesis. Indeed, Vanniyars historically faced quite brutal discrimination from Brahmins and non-Brahmin elites in southern Tamil Nadu as has been recorded.[15]

Besides, when Murugan is attacked by Aishwarya's father, he calls him an 'inferior caste dog'. This only helps us locate Murugan as a relatively lower caste, maybe a Dalit, but not necessarily so. All the same, the movie helps throw light on the tensions of particularity and universality as regards the question of caste. Here is one conversation—between Vellaiyan and Murugan—which is quite explicitly revealing of this theme.

> Vellaiyan: So what type are you?
> Murugan: [Silence]
> Vellaiyan: I asked what type are you…. Couldn't you understand me? What caste are you?
> Murugan: Human caste.
> Vellaiyan: That I can see. The difference between a human and an animal. But even animals have caste. A lion is also an animal. A tiger is also an animal. A donkey is also an animal. Who are you among humans? A lion? A tiger? A dog? A pig? How dare you lay your hands on our girl? We are lions!

The figure of the 'lion' is taken as a symbol by dominant OBC castes in Tamil Nadu and also castes that claim a higher dominant status, like the Pallars. Thevars in particular often use symbols of roaring lions on posters and flags of their community leaders. We can see in this conversation

---

[14] S. Anand, 'Politics, Tamil Cinema Eshtyle' (2005). Available at: http://www.outlookindia.com/magazine/story/politics-tamil-cinema-eshtyle/227523 (accessed on 5 March 2016).

[15] See A. N. Sattanathan, *Plain Speaking: A Sudra's Story* (New Delhi: Permanent Black, 2006) for a detailed account of the same.

that difference/conflict between particular castes is emphasized. Now, what we can see here is the intermediate caste Thevar individual refusing to renounce his particularist caste pride and, likewise, preventing the individual lower caste from transcending his particularity. As you can see, the Thevar character in the movie prefers to identify himself with an animal than with the universal ideal of humanity. On the other hand, the lower caste who asserts his humanity is painfully reminded that he can never be truly human.

Caste, we must understand, at a discursive level is the production and reproduction of particularities. Ambedkar famously said that caste is a graded division of labourers. Even if one section of the labourers manages to move up in the gradation, the system of division still remains, preventing a common narrative from successfully emerging. Castes desiring to move up in the system can only do so by enforcing and committing acts of physical violence on castes inferior to them. Now, this will quickly lead to passing judgements on the intermediate castes, as some writers referred to them as the baton holders of Brahminism. Of course, there should be no reservations in unconditionally condemning anti-lower caste and anti-Dalit violence by intermediate castes, who themselves are 'lower' in the caste order. But is that enough?

What is missing here, what is missing in the entire movie, is the locus of ideology: the figure of the Brahmin. We can see that not even in one scene in the movie is the Brahmin represented, referred to or given a place of importance. One could explain this by arguing that the Dravidian movement disempowered the Brahmins in the political sphere and gave much political power to the backward castes. But beyond the obvious, this is where a Lacanian understanding helps—the Brahmin here is not just a representable figure but operates on the realm of the symbolic, that is, the determiner of the rules and meanings that structure the society. While the figure of the Brahmin itself need not be at the site of the act of physical violence, or even represented in the narrative around anti-lower caste violence as in the film being discussed, it is nevertheless the invisible power that operates the structural violence of caste. And at the core of this is the structuring of castes into fixed particularities. One could thus define Brahminism as a 'system of graded inequality that seals castes in particularist identities and prevents the emergence of any radical universalist politics that could challenge its existence'.[16]

We can observe this in a curious form of neo-Brahminism that is operating in the name of pro-Dalit solidarity, which ingeniously pits Dalits against the intermediate castes. Just for instance, when the Ambedkar Periyar Study Circle controversy was happening in IIT Chennai, RSS ideologues were making statements to the extent that they had no issue against Ambedkar but only against Periyar, who, according to them, was anti-national and anti-Dalit. In fact, it is only in Tamil Nadu to my knowledge that the Hindu Right, Hindu Left and Hindu Centre want to be projected as the saviour of Dalits! It is easy to show Dalits as victims, suffering, pre-modern, etc. This is the perverse logic of neoliberal capitalism, where a particular identity is valourized for its victimhood, fixed in its particularity and encouraged not to rupture the mainstream. More importantly, the identity politics of such marginalized communities is buttressed and encouraged with the confidence that it can never emerge into something larger, something universal.

This is why there is a crucial need now to figure out a newer politics of identity, with universalist possibilities, that contributes to an effective Dalit–OBC caste solidarity and resistance against Brahminism. Such an attempt was made during the Dravidian movement. Yet there were some limitations in the practical operation of this attempt. We shall discuss some of these briefly in the next section that looks at how Periyar addressed the questions of the particular identity of the Brahmin Other.

## PERIYAR AND THE BRAHMINS

Periyar was no friend of colonialism, but like Marx and Ambedkar, who were held in high regard by him, he recognized that modernity, the education system and the rule of law introduced by the colonial

---

[16] Karthick Ram Manoharan, 'Towards a Žižekian Critique of the Indian Ideology', *International Journal of Žižek Studies* 13, no. 2 (2019): 1–22.

system had certain positive fallouts. They might be negotiated with to get greater rights for the Dravidians—the non-Brahmin castes in general, inclusive of the Dalits. He says,

> Though the White man ruled us, he gave us rights; he considered us as human beings; he ate in our homes; he wouldn't take a bath on touching us. The Brahmin is not like that. Doesn't he believe that he needs to take a bath for merely touching us? [...]
>
> We belong to this country. We do the labour that is required for the sustenance of humanity, and then shouldn't we think why we should continue being sons of prostitutes and Shudras to the Brahmins? Why should our women be Shudra women and prostitutes to the Brahmins?[17]

To reject Brahmin sacral power, Periyar strategically advocated conversion to other religions, mainly Buddhism, as he saw it as a rationalist system than a theology. He firmly believed that rejection of Hindu religious authority was important to challenge and demolish caste at a secular level and, in general, he advocated a 'freedom from god' to live an emancipated life.[18] He imagined the Dravidians to be a community of the oppressed—oppressed by nation, caste, gender, religion and economy—he did not seek to blot out one form of oppression to talk about the other. For instance, while talking about workers' rights, he did not ignore caste. Likewise, while talking about non-Brahmins, he paid special attention to the Dalit question. As I have argued elsewhere,[19] he was acutely sensitive to the specificity of Dalit politics and encouraged both religious and secular forms of Dalit militancy. And his attention to questions of caste and class did not lead him to ignore gender, and he placed women's liberation as one of the core pillars of his concept of self-respect.

---

[17] E.V. Ramasamy, *Viduthalai*, 11 December 1967.

[18] Karthick Ram Manoharan, 'Freedom from God: Periyar and Religion', *Religions* 11, no. 1 (2020): 10. Available at: https://doi.org/10.3390/rel11010010 (accessed on 27 May 2020).

[19] Karthick Ram Manoharan, 'In the Path of Ambedkar: Periyar and the Dalit Question', *South Asian History and Culture* (2020). Available at: https://doi.org/10.1080/19472498.2020.1755127 (accessed on 27 May 2020).

So why did Periyar single out the Brahmins as the oppressors? At several places, Periyar criticized the intermediate castes for their assumptions of relative superiority over Dalits. In the wake of the Ramnad riots of 1957, he came out strongly in favour of the Pallars and called for stringent measures to be taken against the Thevar rioters, risking the support of this politically powerful community. He was also wary of certain friends of the Self-Respect Movement who, while being open to criticisms of Brahmins, were unwilling to challenge their own positions of power and privilege. Commenting on this, he said,

> I am aware of the criticism that while the non-Brahmins are bitter about the superiority complex of the Brahmins, they themselves do not grant equality to those below them in the infamous caste hierarchy. There is much truth in this criticism. My only reply is that the Brahmins have to take the greatest blame, because their forebears have been the authors of caste and it is they who have meticulously striven to preserve the system.[20]

Similar to Ambedkar, Periyar located the Brahmin agent at the centre of an ideological system which maintained social hierarchy. While other castes below the Brahmin might also be complicit in the preservation of this hierarchy, it was the discourse of Brahminism which was manifested in the corporeal existence of the Brahmin, which needed to be challenged for any social revolution to be affected. To take from Sartre,

> The 'master', the 'feudal lord', the 'bourgeois', the 'capitalist' all appear not only as powerful people who command but in addition and above all as *Thirds:* that is, as those who are outside the oppressed community and *for whom* this community exists. It is therefore for them and *in their freedom* that the reality of the oppressed class is going to exist. They cause it to be born by their look. It is to them and through them that there is revealed the identity of my condition

---

[20] E. V. Ramasamy, *Social Reform or Social Revolution*, trans. A. M. Dharmalingam (Chennai: Dravidar Kazhagam, 1998), 16.

and that of others who are oppressed; it is for them that I exist in a situation organized with others and that my possible are strictly equivalent with the possibilities of others.[21]

Here, it can be seen how in Periyar's discourse the Brahmin is the 'Third' who creates the identity of the non-Brahmin condition, of that of the Shudras and the Dalits. But here, Brahmin ends up becoming constitutive of the non-Brahmin identity. When the Brahmin is identified as an oppressor, the 'non-Brahmin' literally seeks to indicate a community of non-oppressors. It is to be noted that while there is no attempt at closure of the non-Brahmin identity, by Periyar's emphasis that it remains permanently closed to the Brahmin, it is also recognition of the closure of the Brahmin identity. The non-Brahmin category, equated with the Dravidian, which includes women, backward castes, Dalits, Christians, Muslims and Scheduled Tribes, was meant to form a bloc against Brahminical oppression.

I have critiqued in an earlier intervention some inherent problems arising out of basing an identity on not being an oppressor or on having an inferiorized identity in relation to an oppressive identity, because the oppressor becomes the central figure of one's own identity.[22] To take from a question of Aletta Norval posed in her letter to Ernesto Laclau, 'what are the implications of recognizing that the identity of the other is constitutive of the self'[23] in a condition where the non-Brahmins are in political power where Brahmin hegemony over political discourse has become something of the past? In a compelling observation, Laclau writes, 'As the identity of the newly emancipated groups has been constituted through the rejection of the old dominant ones, the latter continue shaping the identity of the former. The operation of inversion takes place entirely within the old *formal* system

---

[21] Jean-Paul Sartre, *Being and Nothingness: An Essay on Phenomenological Ontology*, trans. Hazel E. Barnes (Oxon: Routledge, 2003), 442.

[22] Karthick Ram Manoharan, 'Anti-Casteist Casteism? A Fanonist Critique of Ramasamy's Discourse on Caste', *Interventions: International Journal of Postcolonial Studies* 19, no. 1 (2017): 73–90.

[23] Aletta J. Norval, 'Letter to Ernesto', in *New Reflections on the Revolution of Our Time,* ed. Ernesto Laclau (London: Verso, 1990), 157.

of power.'²⁴ As Laclau expands from Norval's argument, 'The reference to the other is also maintained here but, as the inversion takes place at the level of the universal reference and not of the concrete contents of an oppressive system, the identities of *both* oppressors and oppressed are radically changed.'²⁵

Commenting on Black identity politics in America, Žižek writes, 'It is not enough to find new terms with which to define oneself outside of the dominant white tradition—one should go a step further and deprive the whites of the monopoly on defining *their own* tradition.'²⁶ That is, one could say in a Žižekian way that it is not enough to define oneself outside the Brahminical hegemonic tradition—one should also prevent the upper-castes from having a monopoly in defining what their own tradition and identity is. But there is another question: Is there anything from the tradition of the Other, something universal, that can be worth retrieving for the formerly oppressed? Fanon writes,

> All elements for a solution to the major problems of humanity existed at one time or another in European thought. But the Europeans did not act on the missions that was designated them and which consisted of virulently pondering these elements, modifying their configurations, their being, of changing them and finally taking the problem of man to an infinitely higher plane.²⁷

Fanon, here, is not decrying European humanism; he is decrying Europe for failing to live up to its humanism. Fanon was a universalist and believed that after the anti-colonial struggle, a genuine universal conversation between the people of humanity, Europe included, was both possible and desirable. European humanism, thus, was not to be rejected but to be brought to fruition. For Periyar, and anti-caste thinkers such as Ambedkar and Jyotirao Phule, there was no such humanistic tradition to be recovered from the Brahminical system. They were not defending a Dalit or Dravidian particularity against a

---

²⁴ Ernesto Laclau, *Emancipation(s)* (London: Verso, 2007), 31.
²⁵ Ibid., 31.
²⁶ Slavoj Žižek, *First as Tragedy, Then as Farce* (London: Verso, 2009), 120.
²⁷ Frantz Fanon, *The Wretched of the Earth*, trans. Richard Philcox (New York, NY: Grove Press, 2004), 237.

Brahmin universality; rather, they were accusing the Brahmin to be incapable of universality, caught in his own particular interests and privileges. Universality to these thinkers could be found only out of the Brahminical system.

## TOWARDS A NEW UNIVERSALISM

Taylor argues, 'My own identity crucially depends on my dialogical relations with others.'[28] Identity also crucially depends on dialogical relations imposed by others. This caste identity of a person, to take from Fanon, is overdetermined from without, that is, one cannot get to freely choose what one's caste identity is. If hell is other people, caste is the hell that the inquisitive Other confines a person. A reply like 'I do not believe in caste' may be accepted, but 'I do not have a caste' is almost always looked on with cynicism much like colour-blindness in the West. Caste works, even if you do not believe in it. Irrespective of the choice of identity that one would like to make for one's Self, one is located by the Other in a hierarchical network of social relationships. It is impossible to avoid encountering this question in India, but is it impossible to evade the caste identity? Periyarism would argue for the possibility of caste identity breaking down by a rationalist struggle and a struggle for rationalism against the enemy located in the particularist identity of the Brahmin Other.

Is the Dravidian movement guilty of 'resentment' in this discourse wherein 'political identity emerges and obtains its unifying coherence through the politicization of *exclusion* from an ostensible universal, as a protest against exclusion'?[29] We need to be careful here; the Periyarist accusation against the Brahmin is not that the Brahmin excludes the rest from universality, but rather that the Brahmin is incapable of universality. The Brahmin identity was fixed. But as long as the Brahmin was sealed in his Brahminhood, so would the other castes remain sealed in their particular identities. The Fanonian plea for subjects to exercise their

---

[28] Charles Taylor, 'The Politics of Recognition', in *Multiculturalism: A Critical Reader*, ed. David Theo Goldberg (Oxford: Blackwell, 1994), 80.

[29] Wendy Brown, *States of Injury: Power and Freedom in Late Modernity* (Princeton, NJ: Princeton University Press, 1995), 65.

agency to transcend their particularisms and work towards universal solidarity is appealing here.

I hold the view that all politics is a 'politics of identification', of the Self and the Other. There can be no politics without identification. 'We know who we are only when we know who we are not and often only when we know whom we are against,' Huntington observed.[30] It is crucial to note that the external Other forges who 'we are' but not who 'I am'. A Hegelian would understand the resolution of the dialectic as a stage where the 'We' becomes a part of the 'I' and 'I' becomes a part of the 'We'. 'We' in a political sense makes sense only with the arrival of 'They', or the Other. Again, the Other as a political entity makes sense only when the Self is perceived as a part of a collective against the collective of the Other. In the political realm, the Other is always a terrible, threatening force who threatens to injure the political interests of the Self that identifies with a collective. In a Schmittian understanding, the individual has no political enemies, but the group cannot survive without a political enemy—the colonized against the colonizer, occupied against occupier, Soviets against Nazis. The enemy becomes a projected Otherness where the Self of different individuals unites under the banner of one identity; that is, the individual Self 'identifies' with a collective fighting against another collective.

The conflict for universalism, conflict against universalism conflict of universalisms emerges at the stage where the Other is identified as the political enemy. Marxism denounces the bourgeoisie for its fake universalism and announces the proletariat as the agent of and for genuine universalism. Nazism identifies the Jews as a sort of a particular—universal—confined to their Jewish identity but nevertheless responsible for universalist conspiracies. Racist politics is always a conflict against universalism. Even when it is targeted against particular identities, like the ethnic conflict in Rwanda for instance, it involves a rejection of universality. A similar argument can be made for caste conflicts and politics that celebrate particularist identities. What is

---

[30] Samuel P. Huntington, *The Clash of Civilizations and the Remaking of World Order* (New York, NY: Simon and Schuster, 2003), 21.

important to note is that the manner in which the Other is constructed determines the nature of the universality of the politics being espoused.

A truly transformative praxis must unsettle the identity of both the Self and the Other, so as to create a new paradigm of discourse where there can be a reconciliation of interests of the actors involved. Nonetheless, an abstract universalism is not possible. To speak of a 'human identity' makes as much sense to politics as to speak of 'God's children', unless the human identity is mobilized to fight an inhuman Other or God's children are mobilized to fight godless children. Given that the understanding of the enemy in the political is still anthropocentric, such a universal can be more harmful than good, and likely to cause as much, if not more, harm than the extremist nationalist ideologies of the previous century.

All universalisms must evolve or adapt to particular contexts. Periyar's promotion of Enlightenment rationalist values was made with the understanding of the particular context of Tamil Nadu, the native social and religious customs. Likewise, all particularisms have a potential for transcendence into a universal.

Pluralism, for it to be functional, must defend the right to challenge and even offend fixed identities. A pluralism must also respect the right to be offended. For it to function in a democratic manner, it must be able to place caste, race, and religious and sexual identities under critical scrutiny. What it cannot and must not tolerate is murder by those who claim to be offended—consider, for instance, the attack on Charlie Hebdo journalists by Islamist extremists—and the legitimation of such acts. But here is the paradox of such a pluralist ethos. Even to defend liberal values, pluralism needs to be illiberal. One can invoke Strauss's concern here, 'whether Tolerance can remain tolerant when confronted with unqualified intolerance.'[31]

A democratic emancipatory politics must not only begin from the assumption that societies are plural, but it should also recognize that the identities of individuals are plural. Likewise, the particularity of

---

[31] Leo Strauss, *Liberalism, Ancient and Modern* (Chicago, IL: University of Chicago Press, 1968), 28.

an identity 'can only fully realize itself if it constantly keeps open, and constantly redefines, its relation to the universal'.[32] The need for and effect of broader coalitions were evident in the 2019 Indian Lok Sabha elections. In these elections, the Hindu nationalist Bharatiya Janata Party (BJP) returned to power at the Centre with a comfortable margin. In Tamil Nadu, however, the BJP-led alliance suffered a severe defeat at the hands of the Secular Progressive Alliance (SPA) led by the Dravida Munnetra Kazhagam (DMK). The SPA won 38 seats out of 39. The Viduthalai Chiruthaigal Katchi (VCK), the most prominent Dalit party in Tamil Nadu, was a part of the SPA. The VCK leader Thirumavalavan, who contested from the Chidambaram constituency, faced a tough campaign against him by Vanniyar outfits. The Vanniyars comprise a sizeable population in this district. However, thanks to the DMK's extensive counter-campaign among the Vanniyars appealing to the community to vote for him, he was able to win, albeit by a narrow margin.[33] Thirumavalavan's victory showed that political solidarities between Dalits and backward caste communities were not only desirable but also absolutely necessary, and also that with strategic alliances and actions, it could ensure victory for progressive forces.

Ambedkar, Periyar, Phule, Kanshi Ram, the Dravidar Kazhagam and the Dalit Panthers, all imagined solidarities between the oppressed castes—Dalits and the backward castes—to be crucial to the goal of annihilation of caste. But the rise of caste particularist politics, within a general political atmosphere of Hindutva ascendancy, exacerbated the rift between not only the backward castes and Dalits but also the castes that comprise Dalits themselves. While the Dalit critique is definitely important to address questions of exclusion and marginalization, a completely isolationist Dalit politics is not only unproductive but also unfeasible. Speaking in a strict empirical sense, Dalits in the state or across India do not have the numbers to capture power all by themselves. Theoretically speaking, the binary of Dalit and non-Dalit

---

[32] Laclau, *Emancipation(s)*, 49.
[33] K. Ezhilarasan, 'How PMK Lost the Battle for Chidambaram', *The New Indian Express*, 27 May 2019. Available at: http://www.newindianexpress.com/states/tamil-nadu/2019/may/27/how-pmk-lost-the-battle-for-chidambaram-1982243.html (accessed on 24 April 2020).

places emphasis on the particular marginality of the Dalit position, foreclosing the possibility of universalism. The rise of ethnic and religious right-wing populism across the world has shown that the vocabulary of progressive universalism is the only effective counter to narrow imaginations of identity. The Dravidian project, with all its problems, imagined a broad coalition of the oppressed communities, basing its discourse not on racial supremacy or hatred but on a demand for the three Rs—recognition, representation and redistribution.[34] At the current juncture, it is most vital to reimagine, and recreate, a Dravidian universality or its appropriate equivalent.

---

[34] Nancy Fraser, Hanne Marlene Dahl, Pauline Stoltz, and Rasmus Willig, 'Recognition, Redistribution and Representation in Capitalist Global Society: An Interview with Nancy Fraser', *Acta Sociologica* 47, no. 4 (2004): 374–382.

# Chapter 7

# Deconstructing the Language of Hegemony

Archana Singh

*Per aaj Janaki sab jaan gayi hai*
*Wah dharti me nahi aakash me jana chahti hai*
*Devaki ki kanya ki tarah bijli si chamak kar sandesh dena chahti hai*
*Tumhari kansiya mansikta ke anta ka*
*Hey Ram, manav manav ke beech bhedbhav karna band karo,*
*Band karo Shambook ka vadh karna*
*Kyoki hum apna savera dhoond lenge*
*Humne ankhoo me suraj bharna sikh liya hai*
*Chand ko muthhi me bharna sikh liya hai*
*Samay ko bandhak banana bhi seekh lenge.*
[But now Janki is aware of everything
Instead of submerging into earth, she wants to fly in the sky
Like the daughter of Devki, she wants to flash like lightning
To convey a message
To eliminate your devilish mentality
O Ram, please stop discrimination among humans
Stop killing Shambook
Because we will reach our day of redemption
We have learnt how to capture the Sun in our eyes
We have learnt to seize the Moon in our fists
We will also learn to make time our hostage.]

*Pida ki Fasale* by Sushila Takbhore

## INTRODUCTION

Nowadays, Dalit women are writing to expose their marginality through autobiographies, poetries and stories. There is a debate regarding the democratic attitude of Dalit patriarchy. Dalit-Bahujan male intellectuals like Kancha Ilaiah have valourized Dalit-Bahujan patriarchy as essentially democratic.[1] According to Guru,[2] Dalit women justified the case for talking differently based on external factors (non-Dalit forces homogenizing the issue of Dalit women) and internal factors (patriarchal domination by male Dalits).[3]

Dalit women writers have used various expressions and strategies in recreating and rupturing dominant social scripts—those that label them as victims. With the help of various kinds of writings and dissenting language, these socially excluded subaltern communities are creating a counter-public sphere to give voice to their anguish against the everyday sociocultural humiliation faced by them from all the dominant sections. These 'counter-publics' (a term coined by Nancy Fraser) usually emerge in response to exclusion within the dominant publics, as the dominant discourses of society are controlled by these dominant publics, and it deconstructs the language of hegemony which makes them oppressed.

Dalit assertions have emerged to rupture mainstream discourse at a different level all over the country from time to time. It is a mix of different tools like social movements and dissenting writings about caste tyranny. Electoral politics (number game) also forced many political parties to influence Dalit vote bank. Strong Dalit movements emerged in several parts of southern and western India. At the same time, Western feminist movements encouraged Indian women to challenge the mainstream discourse for the negligence of women's issues. Feminist movements of the 1970s made women's assertion visible. But Dalit women could not get space either in the Dalit movement or in feminist movements.

---

[1] S. Rege, *Against the Madness of Manu: B.R Ambedkar's Writings on Brahmanical Patriarchy* (New Delhi: Navayana, 2013).

[2] G. Guru, 'Dalit Women Talk Differently', *Economic & Political Weekly* 30, no. 41–42 (1995): 2548–2550.

[3] Rege, *Against the Madness of Manu*.

In recent decades, India has experienced strong voices of Dalit assertion. But still, neither women appeared as visible leaders in Dalit movements nor did this movement explicitly address the women's questions. Women were part of the Dalit movement, but they may be described as, in Mansbridge words, absorbing the less powerful into a false 'we' that reflects the more powerful.[4]

The Dalit movement was never a single expression but contained various dissenting voices with subtle differences. It challenged the disharmonic and disequilibrious societal structure, with several small dissent and protest movements. This dissent was based on various political, social, economic and cultural issues. One the one hand, these dissents played a crucial role in articulating Dalit resistance and, on the other, it made several unheard voices audible. Overall, the Dalit movement emerged as a strong movement to challenge the hegemonic power structure with their dissenting language.

Although the movement needed to override all identities other than caste, gender, caste and class were issues that always existed as a challenge for homogenization. As a result, the silence on separate women's questions continued with hidden resistances. The trickle-down effect of this dissenting discourse on women's lives cannot be denied. We have to understand it in different ways: the women involved in it, their questions and their impact on their everyday struggle. This can be understood by mapping the political subjectivity[5] of rural Dalit women, their emerging political consciousness and their method to deconstruct the hegemonic language.

## EXPLORING THE BACKDROP

The women about whom I am talking are ignorant of contemporary Dalit and feminist discourses, but they are emerging as powerful leaders.

---

[4] J. Mansbridge, 'Using Power/Fighting Power: The Polity', *Democracy and Difference: Contesting the Boundaries of the Political* 46 (1996): 66.

[5] Political subjectivity is a term used to indicate the deeply embedded nature of subjectivity and subjective experience in a socially constructed system of power and meaning.

Emergence of Dalit women as political subjects in the villages of Uttar Pradesh (UP) is a critical phenomenon. These women are neither literate nor trained leaders nor have any political background. Many undercurrents played an important role in the political awakening of these women, especially in the reign of Bahujan Samaj Party (BSP). The party has focused on symbolic means of mobilization and empowerment, and this has led to the transformation of UP cities, roads and parks into celebratory spaces for Dalits. Access to public spaces played an important role in the emergence of women's consciousness. The community version of heroes and histories fuelled the sense of potential of such women.

I see this chapter as an intervention in a broader discussion: the impact of Dalit and Ambedkarite movement in the emergence of rural Dalit women as political subjects. The micro-narratives loaded with the dissenting language of Dalit women provide a critical insight to understand their method of dissent against various forms of essentialized control and domination. This helps in exploring the meaning and nuances of the voices of Dalit women and also to broaden our horizon of Dalit feminist discourse, which represents only literate and middle-class educated Dalit women. Rural Dalit women, who have their way of interventions on issues of caste and patriarchy, should be mapped.

This is an attempt to document the trajectory of the emergence of rural Dalit women as political subjects by deconstructing the language of hegemony in their everyday life. We should understand the strength of the dialogical relationship between Dalit icons and their followers, which empowers, awakens and consolidates the community member as a political subject from among whom future leaders of the movement will emerge.

## EMERGENCE OF DISSENT

The radical and very important departure in the life of Dalit women in India began in the 1920s with the intervention of Dr Ambedkar, who with his modernist insights aroused the sense of self-esteem among his community women and inculcated in their mind the consciousness of their rights. Ambedkar has become an inspiring symbol, a symbol of hopes and aspirations for India's Dalit women, the most subjugated and disadvantaged. From the very beginning, in Mooknayak and Bahishkrit Bharat, oppression of women remained one of the core concerns of Ambedkar and his movement. He encouraged the involvement of women in all social struggles. In Mahad Satyagraha, women participated in large numbers. Ambedkar said on the eve of Mahad Satyagraha,

> Women must attend parishads. The task of ending untouchability is a woman question. You have given birth to us and you know how people grade us and treat us even lower than animals. When you know this all how would you answer people who will raise questions about why you gave birth to us at all? What is the difference between the children born to Kayastha and Savarna women sitting in this meeting and us? You must think and realize that you have as much character and purity as a Brahmin woman. The courage and will to act that you possess, even the Brahmin women lack. Then why must children born to you be insulted?[6]

Such movements have a phenomenal impact on transforming the lives of Dalit women. For Ambedkar, education was a means of liberation from dominant structures of caste, class and gender as well as to reconstruct a new social order. Ambedkar had realized the potential of Dalit women leaders a long time ago.

He helped Dalit women deconstruct the language of hegemony and recreate the popular perception of Dalit women as *abala* in dominant discourse. The vigour of Ambedkar's icon, as an instrument of dissent and protest against hegemonic domination for decades, changed the lives of these women. The way he revolutionized the social life of Dalits, especially women, is incredible.

In UP, the scenario is still different. It is still under feudal dominance where social structure creates inequality and deprivation based on caste and gender. But it has a long dissenting tradition of Bhakti saints like Kabir and Ravidas, and many popular icons like Uda Devi, Jhalkari Bai and Matadin Bhangi. Dissent was always in the air despite

---

[6] U. Pawar and M. Moon, *We Also Made History: Women in the Ambedkarite Movement* (New Delhi: Zubaan, 2000).

its feudal settings. Indeed, caste movements were not quite evident in UP, which did not witness powerful anti-caste Dalit movements in the colonial period unlike the southern and western parts of India.[7]

This area did not remain untouched by the impact of Ambedkar and caste movements of his time. The effects crept silently into this area, though this is not properly documented. Adi- Hindu Movement of Swami Acchutanand was a pioneer to make Dalit community of this area assert themselves as original inhabitants of India. Dalits, especially Chamars, resisted against many unjust traditions that snatched away their dignity. Women themselves protested against an inhuman tradition for Dalit women, Raat Basna (staying at night). Under this practice, Chamar women were summoned by upper-caste families for cutting the umbilical cord of the newborn baby and spend six days with the mother and the child in their service. During these six days, she had to do all menial work to keep both the mother and the child clean. Because of this filthy and inhuman job, these women suffered humiliation and were treated as untouchables.[8]

Chamar leaders organized and sensitized their people of their right to lead a dignified life with self-respect. A village near Allahabad, Jugrajpur, witnessed strong protest (Nara-Maveshi Movement) against these practices and faced severe repression by upper castes and few other Dalit castes.[9] Both men and women participated in this struggle. Women liberated themselves from this inhuman practice through their dissent.

The leadership of Dalit women and policies of protective discrimination at local governance have disturbed the power equations which opened the ways of their entry in politics, although village-level studies no longer provide a privileged 'window' on processes of social change in India.[10] BSP and Mayawati marked the beginning

---

[7] S. Pai, *Dalit Assertion and the Unfinished Democratic Revolution: The Bahujan Samaj Party in Uttar Pradesh* (New Delhi: SAGE Publications, 2001).

[8] Interview of Advocate Guru Parsad Madan, writer–activist, Allahabad.

[9] B. Narayan, *The Making of the Dalit Public in North India: Uttar Pradesh, 1950–Present* (New Delhi: Oxford University Press, 2011).

[10] O. Mendelsohn, 'The Transformation of Authority in Rural India', *Modern Asian Studies* 27 (1993): 805–845.

of a new era in Dalit politics by proclaiming her Chamar identity to the masses in public rallies, even though 'Chamar' in North India is used with circumspection as it is often used as a term of abuse. Dalit cultural assertion in North India has also taken place through what I have termed a strategy of asserting 'presence in time',[11] the forging of new Dalit histories.

Mayawati in one of her speeches asserted,

> *Jis samaj ka itihhas nahi hota hai, wah samaj kabhi shasak nahi ban pata hai, kyoki iitihas se prerna milti hai, prerna se jagriti aati hai, jagriti se soch banti hai, soch se taqat banti hai, taquat se shakti banti hai aur shakti se shasak banta hai.*[12] (A community without history cannot be the ruler community. This is because history gives inspiration, inspiration awakens people, awakening constructs thoughts, thoughts help in acquiring power and power makes a community the ruler.)

In BSP regime, the claim for access to public spaces through Ambedkar statues in villages gave women the courage to claim their access to them. Women started organizing meetings to worship Ambedkar statues, sing songs, recite poems on Baba Saheb and recite Bhim Chalisa. Even on the occasion of marriage, they start the ritual with worshipping Baba saheb and sing songs loaded with messages of Baba Saheb. '*Baba saheb ne hume sir utha ke khade hone ki himmat di*' (Baba saheb has given us strength to live with dignity). Posters and pamphlets with the messages of Baba Saheb played a major role in sensitizing Dalit public. Women participated in large numbers, though no significant women leaders emerged. Women have been marginalized when it comes to lead roles. But in UP, things changed with the leadership of Mayawati. New women leadership is emerging in villages. This is perhaps the most fundamental level at which transformation needs to take place, as it touches on the beliefs and value systems of individuals and is thus the point at which the person does become political in organizations.[13]

---

[11] M. Ciotti, 'Resurrecting Seva [Social Service]: Dalit and Low-caste Women Party Activists as Producers and Consumers of Political Culture and Practice in Urban North India', *The Journal of Asian Studies* 71, no.1 (2012): 149–170.

[12] Pamphlet journey of social change.

[13] Sara Ahmed, 'Engendering Organisational Practice in NGOs: The Case of Utthan', *Development in Practice* 12, no. 3 & 4 (2002): 307.

*Outlook* organized a survey in 2012 where Ambedkar received the highest votes from his followers as a great Indian personality.

Although Ambedkar himself was against worshipping his statues, it worked as a tool for assertion in public spaces in villages and as seats of transformation. True change can only be possible when those who are at the margins participate in the social and political to create reforms. Marginals need to use the site of oppression as a space of resistance, struggle and negotiations.[14] The reason being that marginality is a site that nourishes the capacity of the marginals to resist and help to create a new and alternative world. So villages are the spaces that nourish the resistance and aspiration of Dalit women and from there emerge strong claimants of political power.

Through a different range of activities, these leaders convert individual self-assertion into collective resistance and protest for their community. They are aspiring to share power, control over resources, participate in decision-making and finally change the passive power relations. Power is not a negative, coercive or repressive thing that forces them to do negative activities, but it works as a necessary, productive and positive force in the society (in Foucaultean terms).

BSP women are a perfect example of these full-fledged citizens, despite their low-caste status, and often only a few years of schooling, marriage at an early age, children-rearing and what we would call a vernacular apprenticeship into politics rather than a bourgeois one.[15] Moreover, while caste atrocities have been increased by Dalits' socio-economic mobility and rights assertion, these have triggered these women to resist dominance. Despite their low-caste identity and low literacy, they are creating a vernacular leadership style into politics with a new, strong and dissenting language.

They subverted the upper-caste notions of feminity (*abala nari*) and re-interpreted and reconstructed the whole notion of Dalit identity (*dabe-kuchle log*). The organic intellectuals of the community and their

---

[14] B. Hooks, 'Marginality as a Site of Resistance', *Out There: Marginalization and Contemporary Cultures* 4 (1990): 341–343.

[15] Manuela Ciotti, 'Futurity in Words: Low-caste Women Political Activists' Self-representation and Post-Dalit Scenarios in North India', *Contemporary South Asia* 18, no. 1 (2010): 43–56

popular texts on Baba Saheb helped in their mission to counter the dominant discourses of society, mostly controlled by the dominant public, the upper-caste people. They quote Baba Saheb, educate, organize and agitate.

Nowadays, *mahilaon ka samman aur suraksha* (respect and safety of women) are important issues for all political parties. All these factors make these Dalit women leaders more significant for electoral politics.

## SHARPENING THE DISSENTING LANGUAGE

They are not passive participants in politics but, as active political subjects, are asserting their caste and gender identity with pride. A community leader in Durjanpur village said with pride, '*Ab hume dabane ka jamana gya.... Ab hum eet ka jawab pathhar se denge.*' (No one can oppress us. That time is over; now we are efficient enough to answer anyone.) These changing circumstances have forced upper and middle castes to include them. A 'rural elite' comprising either upper castes or locally dominant intermediate castes is increasingly being forced to share power with Dalits.[16] Jaffrelot,[17] in particular, has argued that a transformation in local power relations in rural UP is significantly advanced on the ground. Now their identity is their strength. They celebrate their autonomy in their community: '*Hum bahar me hawa paani me pale barhe h.... Hume bahar ki duniya ki samajh jyada h.... Humare yaha jameen se neta paida hote h—Baba saheb ... Behan ji.*' (We have been brought up in freedom. We have a better understanding of the outer world. Our leaders emerge from bottom—Baba Saheb ... Behan ji.) They feel that they are more efficient to deal with political matters.

These women play their leadership role in villages in mobilizing women, but they aspire for more. All political parties want to utilize them as a resource for their benefits. These Dalit women are emerging as an important resource of politics. BSP rally has always been

---

[16] C. Jaffrelot, *India's Silent Revolution: The Rise of the Lower Castes in North India* (New Delhi: Orient BlackSwan, 2003); O. Mendelsohn, 'The Transformation of Authority in Rural India', *Modern Asian Studies* 27 (1993): 805–845.

[17] Jaffrelot, *India's Silent Revolution*.

known for women's presence. They have their version of assertions: '*Baba Saheb humare Bhagwan h ... Behan ji humari neta.*' (Baba Saheb is our God ... Behan ji is our leader.) They are bargaining with political parties, going beyond boundaries, without fixing to any particular political ideology or party. '*Humare darwaje sabhi ke liye khule hai.... Hum sab ki sun lete h per kerte apne man ki hai ... jisme humare samaj ka bhala ho.*' (Our doors are open for all. Although we listen to everyone, we do whatever is in our mind. We always aspire for betterment of community.)

They are coming out of their boundaries in a different role. In a village-level meeting, I met Kamala. She said, '*Ab humare samne khade hone ki himmat kisi me nahi hai. Sab rasta bacha ke nikal jate h.... Pehle to humara jeena dubhar tha.*' (Now no one dares to stand in front of us. Now they do not dare to even face us. Previously, our lives were so difficult.) Without any formal training, they are performing well in the political realm and are trying to celebrate the changed scenario. They have learned to deconstruct the dominant discourse and space and celebrate their freedom.

'*Humko koi suraksha ke liye nhi chahiye.... Hum khud hi majboot hai.*' (We do not need anyone to protect us. We are strong enough.) They encourage community women to organize. They encourage their community women to assert for their rights. They sensitize people about state policies to increase their accessibility.

Despite their struggles, atrocities on them, they feel empowered and that is their strength. Neeta of Bani said, '*Ab hume koi ankh utha ke nahi dekhta.... Kisi ke sath galat nahi hota.*'[18] (No one dares to tease us. Now, we do not suffer any atrocities.) They understand their strengths for politics. They know that upper-caste women will not go in rallies and meetings. '*Devi ban ke baithe rehne se pet nhi bharta.*' (We cannot survive by sitting in temple like a Devi.) During rallies, leaders used to depend on Dalit bastis for the crowd. But, now they are not part of the crowd. They are not public. She added, '*Pehle hume sab party lemonchus deke mithai ka kamm karvate rahi, tab hume mithai ka gyan nahi tha per ab*

---

[18] Pamphlet journey of social change.

*hume mithai ka gyan ho gaya hai.*'[19] (Previously, these upper castes used to allure us by giving toffees and use us for big causes. But we have tasted power. No one can fool us.) Now they are powerful and have developed their vision on getting power. '*Humari jati ne bade bade neta diye hai, jaise Baba Saheb.*'[20] (Our community has given great leaders like Baba Saheb). They vehemently criticize the appropriation of their icons by Hindutva forces. 'Now, these upper-caste people are trying to appropriate our messiah—Baba saheb ... Budhha,' she scornfully added, '*Bamhan thakur hume jindagi bhar satye, jab hum Budhha bhagwan ki sharan me chale gaye to ab kehte ki wo Vishnu ke avatar hai.*'[21] (These Brahmin and Kshatriya have tortured us since ancient times and now when we have gone in the shelter of Lord Buddha, they have started claiming that Buddha was the incarnation of Lord Vishnu.) Varshney[22] suggests that although the BSP has not substantially improved the economic position of ordinary Dalits, it is benefitting Dalits at the symbolic, organizational and political levels in many parts of North India. He claims that Dalits are increasingly in a position to challenge the legitimacy of caste discrimination and to engage in everyday politics.

When asked about their priorities as a leader, she said, '*Kaam to karna h per jindage ka mayne khali nal, bijli, sadak hi nahi hai, hum per apne samaj ko age le jane ki jimmedari hai.*' (We have to work but the meaning of life is not only water, electricity, but we also have a responsibility to take our people forward.) The politics of caste is often nurturing the politics of dignity. Its goals are sometimes much more than infrastructure, but more respect, equality of treatment and symbolic gains.

## EXPANDING THE HORIZONS

The story of these Dalit women leaders can be the story of every Dalit women (gendered subaltern) with persistent determinations. They worship Ambedkar, though they are still far behind to follow Ambedkar's

---

[19] Ibid.
[20] Ibid.
[21] Field Diary, Archana Singh.
[22] A. Varshney, 'Ethnic Conflict and Civil Society: India and Beyond', *World Politics* 53, no. 3 (2001): 362–398.

call of 'Educate, Organize, Agitate'. Without getting education in a proper form, they are trying to organize and agitate. Indian politics should now be ready to celebrate the Dalit politics in terms of femininity with its Dalit women leaders. These women leaders do not bother whether they are being seen as Dalit women or as forms of Shakti (in Hindutva connotation). They are trying to capture the political power to empower their community from the clutches of the hegemonic structure, to secure their women from the derogatory identity that spoils their life and ultimately for the emancipation of their community.

BSP movement helped them in not only accessing public spaces to inculcate a political consciousness but also deconstructing the hegemonic language. Mayawati worked as an invigorating potential for these women. 'Mayawati was depicted as a brave and wise leader who is also highly patriotic, having devoted her life to the service of the nation.'[23] Mayawati herself valourizes her potential as a strong and courageous Dalit leader. '*Maine apne aap ko us patthar ke rup me dhal liya hai, jo pani me rehkar bhi pani ke dabav me galta nahi hai, balki nadi ki dhara ko hi badal dalta hai.*' (I have transformed myself into a rock of a river which does not melt by the pressure of water but turns the course of rivers.)

They repetitively quote Mayawati with pride, '*Main Dalit ki beti hun, aur mujhe is per garv hai.*' (I am a daughter of Dalit, and I am proud of it.)[24]

Several public discourses have been constructed around her.

During public meetings with bureaucrats and government officials, [Mayawati] always projects her leadership qualities by highlighting her masculine characteristics of aggression and arrogance. She tries hard to subvert the upper-caste notions of femininity and lady-like behaviour, which are associated with meekness, mildness, subservience, docility and hierarchical form of address.[25]

---

[23] B. Narayan, *Women Heroes and Dalit Assertion in North India: Culture, Identity and Politics* (New Delhi: SAGE Publications, 2006).

[24] Kumari Mayawati, *Mera Sangharshmay Jeevan aur Bahujan Movement ka Safanama* [Autobiography of Mayawati], Bahujan Samaj Party, New Delhi.

[25] Narayan, *Women Heroes and Dalit Assertion*, 159.

Her self-fashioning project has culminated in Mayawati projecting herself as a living goddess.[26]

Dalit women in villages are not only passive participants in politics, but they are struggling to put forward their agenda by doing politics and they celebrate their autonomy in comparison of upper caste women in villages, who are not only obedient housewives but also silent and passive followers of their males. A Dalit woman in village narrated her political participation, '*Hum to kamkaj ke liye bahar nikalte hai, humko duniya ki samjh h, kuan ke medhak ki tarah nahi hai hum*' (We go outside of our domestic realm for livelihood, we understand the social world, we are not frog of well.), she smiled. They celebrate their caste identity and deconstruct all kinds of hegemonies.

An analysis of the practices of the caste basis of violence against women reveals that while the incidence of dowry deaths and violent control and regulation of their mobility and sexuality by the family is frequent among the dominant upper castes, Dalit women are more likely to face the collective and public threats of rape, sexual assault and physical violence at the workplace and in public.[27] It is not so that they are not performing the role of housewives; they are doing all the works such as cooking food and child rearing but are still not confined in the boundaries. For them, *matritva* (motherhood) is not only priority but they also feel, '*Hume apne bachho ko sammanjanak jivan dena hai, unke liye samaj me jagah banani hai.*' (We have to carve a dignified space for our kids; we have to give them a respectful society.) Through their political subjectivity, they are carving dignified spaces for their kids. Their increased participation in politics is a threat for dominant public. The increasing visibility of Dalit women in power structures as sarpanch, as members of the panchayat and in the new knowledge-making processes (such as Bhanwari Devi's intervention through the Saathin programme) has led to an increased backlash against Dalit women.[28] But any such incident could not stop them from moving forward.

---

[26] Ibid., 162.

[27] S. Rege, 'A Dalit Feminist Standpoint', in *Gender and Caste*, ed. Anupama Rao (New Delhi: Zuban, 1998).

[28] Ibid.

## CRAFTING THE LANGUAGE OF FUTURE

All such narratives reveal the discrimination and exclusion which a Dalit woman faces due to their stigmatized identity: caste untouchability and gender instrumentality.[29] Untouchability and patriarchy are devastating for Dalit women. These work as social and cultural tools for the sake of oppression.

Patriarchal caste privilege marks out the woman's body as a privileged space for all types of control, but narratives of rural Dalit women leaders could be seen as an attempt of resistance usually ignored in the mainstream discourse. These voices are borne from the womb of humiliation, negligence and imposed silence. Their hidden and veiled feelings of dissent are fuelled by new political spaces and opportunities, which help them to make claim for dignified survival and quest for identity.

These women are the path-makers having an encouraging illumination for fellow women, and their particular forms of resistance are creating a new path for others. These political aspirants emerge from a subjective pain and agony of Dalit women, who are never treated as humans. Now, these Dalit women community leaders are breaking the shackles of traditional dominant discourses and show their commitment to struggle for their community women. They focus on women without voices. They are changing the 'culture of silence' into the 'culture of voice'. The narratives of these women do not display accusations, anger or dishonour of their identity, but they adopt different strategies at different locations. But all these narratives have a severe kind of resistance. The narratives are not a simple emotional outburst. They are now claiming a life with dignity and self-respect. These women's narratives create a new world of aspirations and dissent. A feminine sensitivity, cultural creativity and dignified caste identity are highlighted in these narratives, which can help create a new resistance theory, which not only deconstructs but reconstructs a parallel discourse of new political subjects simultaneously.

---

[29] G. Poitevin, 'Dalit Autobiographical Narratives: Figures of Subaltern Consciousness, Assertion and Identity', in *Biography as Religious and Cultural Text* (Munster: LIT Verlag, 2002), 77–109.

Dalit icons are *élan vital* (impulse for life) for Dalits, especially women. The Dalit movement instilled the courage to throw off the androcentric and anthropocentric notions among women and empowered them to aspire for a dignified life. Assertion in public spaces, creating heroes and histories, is, on the one hand, making Dalit women conscious to assert their (Dalit) feminine identity in the hegemonic world and, on the other, providing them a space where these women simultaneously resist and subvert the mainstream discourse of the world with the strength of caste subjectivity and feminity.

# BIBLIOGRAPHY

Ciotti, M. Futurity in Words: Low-caste Women Political Activists' Self-representation and Post-Dalit Scenarios in North India. *Contemporary South Asia* 18, no. 1 (March 2010): 43–56.

Ciotti, M. 'The Bourgeois Woman and the Half-Naked One': Or the Indian Nation's Contradictions Personified. *Modern Asian Studies* 44, no. 4 (2010): 785–815.

Chapter 8

# Revitalizing Caste Hierarchies through State, Law and Order and Judiciary

C. Jerome Samraj

## CASTE AND MULTILAYERED INEQUALITIES

The idea of individual rights is alien to caste-based hierarchical Indian society. In India, people are compartmentalized into mutually exclusive groups called caste, and membership to caste is determined only by birth. Dr Ambedkar has aptly described this hierarchical ordering of caste as graded inequality.[1] No two castes are equal, and every caste is either below or above the other. Rights, responsibilities, privileges and denials of every individual are determined by the caste in which he/she is born and its position in the ritual hierarchy. Socio-economic and cultural privileges and restrictions of the people are structured according to the ritual position of their caste, based on the binary of ritual purity and pollution. At the top of the hierarchy are the Brahmins, who consider themselves as ritually 'pure and high', and castes at the other

---

[1] Vasant Moon, *Dr. Babasaheb Ambedkar: Writings and Speeches*, vol. 1 (New Delhi: Dr. Ambedkar Foundation, 2014), 167.

extreme are considered to be ritually 'low and polluting' and treated untouchable. The traditional village social hierarchy had Brahmin (high and pure) or a non-Brahmin (high) caste at the top of the social order, the lower Shudra castes, the artisans, service castes (barbers and washermen), the 'untouchable' castes, and the service castes to 'untouchable' castes forming the bottommost layer of the society. Artisans working with precious metals are considered superior to those who sculpt stone, carpenters, blacksmiths and potters respectively, and among weavers, silk weavers were superior to cotton weavers. Thus, the notion of ritual purity and pollution is the fundamental organizing principle. This considers physical labour, which is the essential component in agrarian production process, as polluting and hence inferior, and the most unproductive priesthood is not only considered to be superior but also sacred. By degrading physical labour as pollution, a vast majority of the agrarian population has been made ineligible to control land, thereby keeping them in a position of dependence. The ritual hierarchy and its embedded graded inequality further manifested in the system of remuneration. Only a few labouring castes were eligible to get wages in kind, while other labourers belonging to the 'untouchable' castes and the service castes were provided left-over food as remuneration. In a context where the ritual notions associate any contact with the 'lower' castes with potential defilement that makes the relative 'high' castes hate to be approached by the 'lower' castes, collecting left-over food from every house in the village to survive hunger, meant nothing less than a severe form of humiliation which each member of the 'lower' castes had to undergo. Thus, a village is a space where this hierarchical idea is socially realized in terms of unequal set of sociocultural and ritual rights governing people's spatial mobility and inter-caste relationships.[2]

The idea of caste, ascription of sociocultural and economic rights to the ritual status of castes, and the related myths about birth in a 'high' or 'low' caste as a result of karma produces a social psyche that accepts 'high and pure' castes innately superior and even sacred, and the 'low' castes as innately inferior. Unequal rights are taught to be the result of 'high' and 'low' birth, enculturing people to understand and accept

---

[2] Samraj Samraj, Jerome C. *The Question of Land to the Dalits: A Historical Perspective.* Unpublished PhD Thesis, University of Madras (2009): Chapter II, 57–61.

their unequal existence as preordained and only way of life. Another crucial aspect inherent in the caste society is the idea of respect. When there is no need for the 'high and pure' castes to treat the castes below with respect and dignity, it is the duty of the 'low and polluted' castes to respect the members of 'high and pure' castes in every aspect of social life. It is the duty of the 'lower' castes to do whatever the dominant castes commanded, and at the same time, they have to withdraw their presence from the public space, as their presence is inauspicious and polluting for the 'high' castes. In contexts where this 'un-see-ability' was practised, it is not that the 'high and pure' castes should not see the 'un-see-able' castes; rather, the members of the 'un-see-able' castes should not show up during the day time, as their appearance would amount to be a sin for the others who happen to see them. Therefore, it is the responsibility of the 'lower' castes to keep themselves away from the 'high and pure' castes, and any breach of the restrictions imposed against them would lead to a severe punishment on the 'lower' castes. A village is a social space where inferiorization of the relative 'lower' caste is manifested through relative menial nature of work and its associated remuneration—its kind, volume and method, spatial segregation, and sociocultural and ritual code of inter-caste conduct backed by unequal system of punishment.[3] In his work on *Ideology and Ideological State Apparatuses*, Louis Althusser states,

> The state is a 'machine' of repression, which enables the ruling classes (in the nineteenth century the bourgeois class and the 'class' of big landowners) to ensure their domination over the working class, thus enabling the former to subject the latter to the process of surplus value extortion i.e. to capitalist exploitation.[4]

It can, therefore, be said that caste-based village society played the role of state in the Indian context.

Thus, people's responsibilities, relationships, rights, privileges and denials are determined based on their caste, and the idea of individual

---

[3] Wendy Doniger, ed., *The Laws of Manu* (Penguin Books, 1991), 182–93.
[4] Louis Althusser, *Ideology and Ideological State Apparatus* (New Delhi: Critical Quest, 2012), 11.

rights is non-existent in the Indian social psyche. The graded inequality that is socially realized through the matrix of inter-caste relationship also acts as an effective surveillance mechanism to monitor every act of every other person. This is because superiority/hegemony of a caste placed above is established by imposing subordinating restrictions on those placed below, and every caste strives to ensure the demarcation of sociocultural ritual, spatial and occupational rights of the castes placed below. Since the un-freedom (subordination) increases as we go down the social order, every caste placed below aspires to enhance their position within the local hierarchy. All these make the village a very rigid and structured social space in which different castes are organized to perform a specific role in the traditional production processes. The colonial state was established on the top of this ritual hierarchy, and the following section attempts to map out the engagement of the local society with the modern state.

## CASTE, ADVENT OF MODERN STATE AND EVOLUTION OF QUEST FOR EQUALITY

Louis Althusser states, 'Every social formation arises from a dominant mode of production.' Further, he says,

> The process of production sets to work the existing productive forces in and under definite relations of production.... In order to exist, every social formation must reproduce the conditions of its production at the same time as it produces and in order to be able to produce. It must therefore reproduce 1) the productive forces, and 2) the existing relations of production.[5]

While this has been the European experience, caste system plays the role of the state in native Indian society, and as we have seen, caste system is at once a social, cultural, economic and political system that fixes people to a specific role in the production process. Caste being an institution that determines the sociocultural, economic and political rights at birth, and fixes people to hereditary occupations, it reproduces

---

[5] Ibid., 3–4.

both the productive forces and the production relations. The colonial state was established on top of this production organization.

The modern Indian State has its origin in the colonial state established by the British colonialists since the 1780s. Therefore, it becomes imperative to understand the process of establishment of the colonial state, and how the local society responded to that. Given the rigid socio-economic and cultural structure in the native Indian society, people's access to the colonial state was determined by the local social structure. While the local caste order was the administrative order of the pre-colonial society, the advent of the colonial state led to the bifurcation of the ideology of caste from the state. During the formative years, the colonial government had to depend upon the already existing local system in order to establish itself as a dominant sociopolitical power.[6] While the colonial rulers needed the sanction of the local elites, the local elites also needed the recognition of the newly established colonial government. Thus, the British officers recognized the local dominant social groups because they were the heads of the local society, and the local society depended on the 'high and pure' castes to interact with the colonial rulers.[7] The existence of a separate state created a situation where there were a set of castes and a state unrelated to the ideology of caste, and every caste had to carve a niche vis-à-vis the state to represent their socio-economic and political demands.

Nevertheless, its functioning was dependent on the local socio-economic structure of caste, which in turn facilitated the intrusion of means and ways of caste into the state and its functioning, making the state a contested sphere. Ever since, the interaction between the caste and the state was mediated by the caste hierarchy. Right from the beginning of the colonial rule, traditionally dominant 'high and pure' castes tried to extend and establish their sociocultural dominance in the official spheres. This is because during the early decades of the colonial rule, the officers interacted only with the dominant sections of the local society, who could decisively influence the making, interpretation and

---

[6] Irschick, *Eugene Dialogue and History: Constructing South India, 1795–1895* (Delhi: Oxford University Press, 1994), 14; Samraj, *The Question of Land to the Dalits*, 65.
[7] Irschick 1994, 21.

implementation of colonial policies to their advantage.[8] The colonial officers' perspective about the local society significantly changed when they got acquainted with communities placed below, and this happened several decades later. By then, the colonial policies had already contributed towards rigidified traditional caste-based property rights. Nevertheless, the very presence of colonial state institutions necessitated, and also created, an official space, which was relatively caste-neutral. The lower castes realized the possibility of a direct negotiation with the colonial state, and since then, different castes across the sociocultural ladder have different aspirations. While the native caste society did not provide any scope of socio-economic or occupational mobility, the idea of individual rights and the associated socio-economic changes and new livelihood possibilities provided the hope for upward socio-economic mobility for the oppressed social groups.

The most crucial change was that the very emergence of urban space and livelihood options also facilitated occupational shift for some members of the oppressed communities. Unlike the traditional temple-based urban space of the precolonial era, the urban space that emerged during the colonial period offered different socio-economic opportunities for different social groups. Service occupations that emerged in urban spaces provided alternative sources of livelihood, notionally free of sociocultural control. This provided the initial opportunities for 'lower' Shudra and 'untouchable' castes to earn their livelihood outside the agrarian organization. Unlike the traditional occupations in the villages, these livelihood opportunities can be termed relatively modern in arrangement, as those who hired these people could only extract their work but could not have social control, and once the work was completed, the workers were relatively free. This happened because the newly emerging urban places were inhabited by migrants from various places that made the caste identities anonymous along with occupational diversification. This in turn rendered the traditional social control unviable, freeing traditionally oppressed communities from everyday marginalization. This relief from everyday oppression together with the separation of cultural from the official sphere created

---

[8] GO Ms. No. 2435, Revenue Department, dated 26 June 1918, Tamil Nadu State Archives.

the much-needed opportunities for the oppressed among the native society to represent their socio-economic and civic disadvantages directly to colonial government.[9] Whenever the 'high and pure' castes tried to alter the policies or its implementation, the leaders from the oppressed social groups untiringly opposed them. These processes resulted in ameliorative measures to help the oppressed communities overcome specific socio-economic and educational disabilities.

None of these changes would have emerged if the British colonial powers had not established a modern state. This can be seen as a transformation of a sociocultural agrarian production organization into the modern state, which marked a significant departure from the traditional cultural economy based on ascribed social status and hereditary occupations into a modern production process in which people can switch occupations based on their achieved status. The current socio-economic changes and the relative progress of people belonging to different castes are outcomes of their relationship with the external source of power. Given the local social hierarchy, if the local dominant sections interacted with the modern state to retain their dominance through the state machinery, the oppressed social groups had to defy the local power structure to interact with the state to earn their independence. It can be said here that the traditional structure has been reproduced in the modern state in terms of inter-caste disparities in socio-economic status, education and employment, which in turn has reproduced the same hierarchy in the state administration. The following sections attempt to contextualize the interaction of different caste groups across the local social ladder in order to understand the unassailable power of caste in determining and subverting the policies of social justice.

## DEFYING RIGHT TO EQUALITY UNDER THE REGIME OF MODERN LAW

As noted earlier, the local social structure determined local communities' interaction with the colonial state and its temporality, and the oppressed communities could interact with the colonial state several decades later, while the dominant social groups interacted with them

---

[9] Samraj, *The Question of Land to the Dalits*, 103–109.

right from the beginning. Given the local social hierarchy, the demands laid down by each caste varied depending upon their relative position in the matrix of caste and its embedded socio-economic and cultural deprivation. For example, if we take the idea of 'right to equality' as a reference point, every social group would have its own set of demands because the traditional restrictions faced by the non-Brahmin 'high' caste is different from that of 'lower' Shudra caste, which in turn is different from the service castes such as barbers and washermen, which in turn is very different from that of the 'untouchables'.[10] While very few demands may be common across the spectrum, communities facing the most extreme forms of oppression remain isolated in their fight for equality. As noted earlier, the relative affluence of one caste is expressed only in terms of subordinating restrictions imposed on the caste below, and therefore the backward classes who face lighter forms of discrimination would stand against the demands of the 'untouchable' communities placed at the bottom. In this context, the traditional dominant social groups use their relatively better access to state machinery, either to prevent, stop or delay the implementation or to subvert the policies enacted in favour of the oppressed social groups. Even if certain policies were enacted, these sections could subvert the implementation of the policies to their advantage. This social tendency isolates the victims when the victims are from the oppressed social group, and their demands never gain political support from other social groups, and in most instances, the dominant social groups oppose the Dalits' quest for equality.[11]

Given the complexities of the local sociocultural structure, officers of the colonial state were very cautious about their policies and wanted to abstain from matters considered cultural. While the colonial state was premised on the idea of individual rights-based modern citizenship,

---

[10] Notes connected with resolutions on matters of general public interest, for the meeting of 3 February 1925, GO No. 180 (a), Revenue (Ordinary Series), dated 3 February 1926.

[11] Akhil Gupta, 'Governing Population: The Integrated Child Development Services Program in India', in *States of Imagination: Ethnographic Explorations of the Postcolonial State*, eds. Thomas Blom Hansen and Finn Stepputat (Durham, NC: Duke University Press, 2001), 66.

enactment of all these were limited by their preoccupation with maintaining 'law and order' without disturbing the 'peace and tranquillity' of the region. As a result, they had a policy to prevent, which would adversely affect the peace and tranquillity of the region. As this law continues to be in effect till date, the dominant social groups never fail to use it to deny the very right to equality promised by the Indian Constitution. To elaborate this further, the hierarchical local social order is, in principle, against the modern idea of 'equality before law', and maintaining law and order in such a sociopolitical and economic context is nothing but revitalizing the social hierarchy. Conversely, any initiative by the oppressed to vie for an egalitarian social space is in itself against the traditional social order and, hence, would 'threaten the peace and tranquillity of the region'. It is this fear that made officers of the colonial state withdraw themselves from intervening in matters considered to be cultural. In fact, it is this preoccupation that still continues to be used as a subversive political instrument to deny the very right to equality promised by the law.

The modern development process, the socio-economic and educational opportunities, and the government's initiatives to foster social justice have resulted in significant socio-economic and political changes. The process of urbanization, development of transport network, rural industrialization and increasing non-farm employment have contributed towards significant changes in the rural inter-caste relationships. Communities that had been traditionally oppressed and socio-economically dependent had then become relatively independent over the years. This socio-economic independence has resulted in them vying to enhance their position in the sociocultural and ritual spheres. Such attempts by the 'lower' castes have led to violent retribution by the dominant castes. This has also been observed by Donner and De Neve, who state, 'Changing caste and class relations are articulated through a politics of space that often (re)creates rather than dissolves boundaries and localities.'[12] Gradually, such oppressive

---

[12] H. Donner and G. de Neve, 'Space, Place and Globalisation', in *The Meaning of the Local: Politics of Place in Urban India* (London: UCL Press, 2006), 13, as cited in Hugo Gorringe, 'Out of the Cheris: Dalits Contesting and Creating Public Space in Tamil Nadu', *Space and Culture* 19, no. 2 (2016): 166.

violence was countered by stiff resistance by Dalits in the form of retaliatory violence that changed the equations of murder on both the sides, and sometimes higher loss on the side of the dominant castes. At this stage, the presence of dominant castes in the state administrative hierarchies made the very functioning of the state biased in favour of the dominant castes.[13] There is an explicit allegiance between the dominant castes and the state that is discernible from a number of instances. While there has been a series of gruesome instances of violence leading to loss of lives and severe loss to property, this chapter engages with three specific instances in which the entire state machinery, the judiciary and the police forces have proved to be inadequate to ensure the constitutional promise of right to equality, and how Dalits were taught to be lesser citizens despite several orders of the judiciary that endorsed their claim for equality. In his analysis of Dalits' contestation for public space, Gorringe states, 'Dalits' temerity in staking a claim to public space, thus, resulted in a reinforcement of caste boundaries.'[14] It is in this light that the legal ordeal undergone by Dalits in three distinct cases is analysed collectively and individually to comprehend the continuing methods through which the socially dominant groups revitalize their hegemony by using the very state machinery which promises right to equality for the oppressed.

## Case I: Dalits' Claim for the Right to Take Out the Procession of Their Deity at Seshasamuthiram

The village Seshasamuthiram in Kallakurichi taluk of Villupuram district lies on the state highway. The state highway bifurcates the village with the residential area of Vanniyars on the western side and the residential area of Dalits on the eastern side of the road. The village inhabits 2,000 families of Vanniyars and 200 families belonging

---

[13] For a detailed discussion on the changing pattern of inter-caste violence, read M. S. S. Pandian, 'Dalit Assertion in Tamil Nadu: An Exploratory Note', *Journal of Indian School of Political Economy* (July–December 2000): 501–517. Also see Gorringe, 'Out of the Cheris'; Grace Carswell and Geert de Neve, 'Litigation against Political Organization? The Politics of Dalit Mobilization in Tamil Nadu, India', *Development and Change* 46, no. 5 (2015): 1106–1132.

[14] Gorringe, 'Out of the Cheris', 170.

to the Scheduled Caste Paraiyar community. There are a few temples in the Vanniyars' residential area including the Murugan temple and Dhrowpathy Amman temple, in which Dalits are not allowed to enter. Dalits themselves constructed a Mariamman temple in their residential area, and they conduct a festival during the Tamil month Aadi (July–August). Dalits used to take the deity on a procession either carrying the deity on the head or in a bullock cart, and start from the first street and walk through the state highway to other three streets inhabited by them. It is pertinent that the five streets where Dalits live are parallel streets with no link/access road/street to reach the other street. The cart is used to reach the other streets only through the state highway. The dominant caste Vanniyars never used to object when the deity was taken on a procession on the head or on the bullock cart. In 2012, Dalits pooled some money from themselves and also accepted the donations of the local MLA and then built a temple car.[15] After the temple car was built, the procession was planned for 6 August 2012, following which the Vanniyars raised their objection against the procession. The police and revenue officials, instead of taking legal action against the people who objected to the temple car procession, convened a peace meeting and pleaded to them; however, the Vanniyars were not willing to withdraw their objection. On 3 August 2012, the tehsildar conducted a peace meeting with the Vanniyars and yielded to their pressure, and the superintendent of police issued an order prohibiting the conduct of temple car procession. The revenue officials went on to cover the temple car with cloth and sealed it, making it immovable. On 5 August 2012, the deputy collector issued another order permitting the procession of the deity in a bullock cart as it used to be before, and the procession started at 7.30 AM under the supervision of the revenue divisional officer, tehsildar/executive magistrate, deputy tehsildar and village administrative officer. When the cart reached the state highway, a mob of about 30 members belonging to the dominant caste stopped the procession and started attacking the people, and Dalits left the bullock cart with the deity on the road and ran to escape the violent attack. All this happened in the presence of all the government

---

[15] https://www.keetru.com/index.php/homepage/2009-10-07-16-54-27/dalit-murasu-aug2015/30087-2016-01-15-11-54-44 (accessed on 25 August 2020).

officials including the superintendent of police, Villupuram district, and inspector of police, Sankarapuram Police Station. However, no action was taken on the mob. Subsequently, one member of the Dalit community launched a complaint at Sankarapuram Police Station, seeking action under the PoA Act; however, the inspector of police refused to register the complaint. In the evening of 6 August 2012, at 4.00 PM, Dalits and members of Viduthalai Chiruthaigal Katchi (VCK), a political party, carried out a peaceful protest in Sankarapuram, which forced the police to register the FIR invoking Sections 147, 148, 188, 341, 506(ii) of the Indian Penal Code r/w and Section 3(1)(x) of the PoA Act. The superintendent of police did not withdraw the order prohibiting temple car procession, and on 27 August, a representation was made to the Villupuram district collector to ensure the right to carry out the temple car procession, which he assured to consider. A decision was made to conduct the procession on 12 September 2012, and Dalits started printing pamphlets, and on 7 September 2012, the superintendent called for a peace meeting with the dominant castes on 10 September 2012. On 8 September 2012, 25 Dalit women from Seshasamuthiram village observed hunger strike against the unlawful prohibition of their temple car procession and condemned the police and revenue officials for supporting the illegal prohibition. On 9 September 2012, the superintendent of police issued an order under Section 144 prohibiting the temple car procession planned on 12 September. Subsequently, Dalits filed an affidavit at the Madras High Court and obtained a stay on the prohibition orders issued by the superintendent under Section 144. On 11 September night, police arrested the 25 women who were on hunger strike and also arrested 17 men who tried to prevent the arrest. Even 6 girls between 14 and 17 years of age, who should have been treated as juveniles, were reported as 22-year-olds and were imprisoned. Subsequently, a writ petition was filed at the High Court seeking a stay on the prohibitory orders under Section 144 issued by the superintendent of police, and on 8 November 2012, the court ordered an interim stay on the superintendent's order dated 9 September 2012.

However, despite continuous initiatives to conduct the temple car procession, Dalits were unable to conduct the procession for the next five years. The dominant castes with the connivance of the police and revenue authorities ensured that they could not conduct the temple car procession.

In an attempt to attract the attention of the chief minister of Tamil Nadu, on 30 December 2013, 79 Dalit families residing at Seshasamuthiram colony collectively represented to the revenue officials that they would leave the temple car in the custody of the tehsildar, as they are prevented from carrying out the procession, and would denounce Hindu religion. They cited that the Vanniyars who follow the same religion act as hurdles against the Dalits' right to conduct the temple car procession, and moreover, no other person from the Hindu religion has condemned their attitude. They would therefore denounce the Hindu religion and embrace another religion that treats all humans as equals. They also expressed their helplessness, as the police and revenue officials failed to ensure their right to equality promised by the Constitution of India, and said that they had lost all faith that the officials would ensure that in the future. Even this attempt was also futile, and the temple car remained stranded in the middle of the streets inhabited by Dalits till 2015. In August 2015, Dalits made another series of attempts to take out the temple car procession. While there was no difference in the attitude of the revenue and police officers, Vanniyars engaged in violence and burnt down the temple car and the Dalit colony, causing severe loss to Dalits. In the clash, the mob threw petrol bombs on the police posse and their vehicles, and a superior police officer who was portrayed as pro-Dalit was attacked. However, there was no counter-attack by the police, and not much action was taken on the attackers.

## Case II: Dalits' Claim for Mandagapadi Abishegam Rites at Palangkallimedu Sri Bathrakaliamman Temple

Denial of ritual rights of Dalits has been a common problem in many villages of Nagapattinam, Thiruvarur region, and this has led to struggles in several villages including Palangkallimedu, Vizhundhamavadi and Vazhuvur. Being prevented from performing mandagapadi rites by the dominant castes, Dalit representatives from Palangkallimedu village in Vedaranyam taluk of Nagapattinam district filed a case in Madras High Court to redeem their right to equality. Officials of the Hindu Religious and Charitable Endowments (HRCE) Department, Adi Dravidar and Tribal Welfare Department, revenue officers of the district represented by the district collector and tehsildar, and the joint commissioner of police were the respondents on behalf of the state of Tamil Nadu. The case demanding the rights to perform mandagapadi and special abhishegam by the Scheduled Castes was heard by the Madras High Court on 11 August 2015, and the court observed that

> Learned Government Pleader produced the proceedings of the Tahsildar, which has taken note of the decision arrived at by the Peace Committee Meeting. A perusal of the same would show that the deity would be taken throughout the village including the streets in which the petitioners' houses are situated. Therefore, a direction is issued to the respondents to make sure the deity is taken on procession throughout the streets of the petitioners' village.
>
> Prima facie, this court is of the view that the petitioner cannot be treated differently. However, this is matter which could be decided only after impleadment of opposite group, who are raising objection. Post after 8 weeks.[16]

While the judiciary is seen as the last resort to protect their right to equality, it is an irony that the court had to depend on the proceedings of the 'peace committee meeting' in which revenue and police officers pleaded to the dominant castes. Further, while the rulings of Khap panchayats have been declared illegal on several occasions, the Madras High Court directing the revenue and police officials to conduct a 'peace committee meeting' made a mockery of such directions. Given the constitutional promise of right to equality, the police should have taken necessary and adequate measures to ensure Dalits' right to equality.

While it was initially posted after eight weeks, it could be understood that this case did not lead to any logical conclusion, which made

---

[16] Writ Petition No. 24720/2015, *The High Court of Judicature at Madras* (11 August 2015). Available at: https://www.mhc.tn.gov.in/judis/madras-do/index.php/casestatus/viewpdf/WP_24720_2015_XXX_0_0_11082015_108.pdf

Dalits file another case (W.P. No. 27580 of 2016), which was however not any more effective in breaking the status quo.

As the court ordered,

> Since the date on which the rituals have to be held are likely to be over this year, no function will be held, but in the next year, the second as well as the third respondents will definitely ensure that the people belonging to the Scheduled Caste Community will be allowed to perform 'mandagapadi' on a particular date and also give further assurance that the procession of the deity will be taken through all places which include the place in which the Scheduled Castes people also reside.[17]

> 5. In the light of the mandate cast upon the concerned authority under Tamil Nadu Temple Entry Authorisation Act 1947 read with rules framed thereunder, the respondents 2 and 3 are under statutory as well as moral obligation to permit the people belonging to the Scheduled Caste community to have a right of worship and perform rituals in connection with the Aadi festival and this court hopes and trusts that the petitioners in W.P. No 27580 of 2016 as well as the petitioner in W.P. No 24720 of 2015 will be alive to the said situation and work out *some compromise* so that at least in the next year during the Tamil month of Aadi, the Temple festival can be performed without any problem or hitch.[18]

The order was dated 9 August 2016, and was posted on 30 August 2016, and both the cases remain pending in the High Court.

An interview with activists and functionaries belonging to VCK revealed that Palangkallimedu is not an isolated case, as there are similar incidences in Vizhundhamavadi, Vazhuvur and other temples in the region. While recollecting the events relating to Thirunelkondacheri, Eelavalavan, a seasoned activist and an office-bearer of VCK party, revealed the practices of untouchability in rituals prevalent in Veerateeswarar temple, Vazhuvur. Dalits belonging to Thirunelkondacheri were prevented from taking water from the

---

[17] Writ Petition No. 27580, *The High Court of Judicature at Madras* (9th August 2016), 2. Available at: https://www.mhc.tn.gov.in/judis/madras-do/index.php/casestatus/viewpdf/wp_27580_2016_xxx_0_0_09082016_3.pdf

[18] Ibid., 2.

Veerateeswarar temple to perform abhishegam for the temple they had built in their village. While Dalits contended that there was a tradition where they took water from the Veerateeswarar temple tank to perform abhishegam in their temple before 30 years, the dominant castes contested that there was no such tradition. However, ignorant of the claimed older tradition, the officers of the HRCE Department, revenue department and police were convinced by the status quo that there was no such practice in the past and did not back the ritual demands of Dalits. When the court wanted clarification from the HRCE Department regarding the existence of such a practice, the officials were said to have responded that they did not have any evidence of such a practice or the lack of it. Being indecisive on the issue, the court ordered a peace committee meeting in the presence of village representatives from both the sides and officials of the HRCE Department and revenue and police departments, in which the Dalits representatives were coerced to agree with the status quo. While the collector of Nagapattinam district had ordered that no community could take water from the temple tank belonging to the HRCE Department and conduct a procession around the temple, the dominant castes subverted this order, as they continued to take out a procession by taking water from elsewhere, whereas Dalits did not have any such scope, and their right to carry out the ritual remained denied.

In this context, it is worthwhile to state here that the idea of constitutional equality does not necessitate any precedence in the past to validate one's claim to a ritual right in the present. Given the practice of caste and untouchability, if the court sticks to erstwhile practices as the basis for a claim to a particular right in the present times, all the claims for equality by the oppressed would never have any historical validity. Ironically, the Madras High Court also ordered the officials to convene a 'peace committee meeting' in the village and ascertain whether there was any such practice before, and report, and in the said meeting, the Dalit representatives are said to have been coerced to agree to the status quo.

While this has been the experience of Dalits with regard to ritual rights, the experiences of Dalits in their struggle for a respectful funeral reveals yet another dimension of the inadequacy of the state and its machinery to ensure the constitutional promise of right to equality to them. The analysis of events surrounding the death of an elderly Dalit woman Kunjamma (wife of Chellamuthu), and the subsequent death of Chellamuthu, reveals the prevailing practices of untouchability and the inability of the state to ensure its constitutional promise.

## Case III: Denial of a Respectful Funeral for a Dalit Elderly in Thirunelkondacheri

While the tussle between the dominant castes and Dalits regarding the ritual rights was going on, Kunjamma (wife of Chellamuthu) of Thirunelkondacheri died. Given the practice of untouchability in the villages, whenever there is a death among Dalits, the dominant castes prevent them from taking the body of the deceased through the public road in the village. This time, Dalits submitted a letter to the panchayat president, requesting to take the body through the public road. The panchayat president had been the president for the past 20 years, and most of Dalits earned their livelihood working in the agricultural lands owned by his family. Even when the Adi Dravidar and Welfare Department attempted to construct a road leading to the cremation ground after acquiring the required lands from the HRCE Department, the local dominant castes filed a case and obtained a stay against it. As the dominant castes opposed the funeral procession through the streets of the village, Dalits refused to carry the body to the cremation ground. As the police and revenue officials compelled them, Dalits left the body on the street, saying they would not carry through the fields, and if the officials wished, they themselves could arrange to carry the body on their own and cremate it. The police had by then arranged for cranes and earthmovers to pave a temporary path to cross the canal and on the third day after the death, the police and revenue officials hired a few labourers from outside and arranged to carry the body to the cremation ground through the agricultural fields crossing an irrigation canal. Given this experience, Dalits were determined not to leave this issue unsettled in the future; however, the subsequent experience of Dalits revealed yet another dimension of the prevailing practices of untouchability.

In January 2016, Chellamuthu (husband of Kunjamma) died at the age of about 105 years, and they wanted to give him a dignified funeral. When this was met with stiff resistance from the members of the dominant castes, the officials of the revenue and police departments failed to ensure a dignified funeral. One of his grandsons approached the Madras High Court secretively, without the knowledge of the officials and others, and sought an order to ensure a dignified funeral. The officials came to know about the case when the court communicated and sought their views on the issue, and later the court issued an order in favour of the deceased, directing the officials to ensure a dignified funeral.

Given the High Court's order, the police and the revenue officials should have arrested those who were opposing to ensure a peaceful dignified funeral for the deceased. The officials of the state could only plead to the dominant castes, and when even the court's order did not seem to have any sanctity against their casteist hegemony, the officials themselves ridiculed the order once again by convincing the relatives of the deceased to give up their right to use their public road for the funeral and take the body through the fields. Never once did the officials thought of carrying out preventive arrest of the members of the dominant castes who were denying the right to equality to other fellow citizens. As the tussle became severe, and the dominant castes were not willing to show any respect to the court's order, Dalits were also worried about another constraint. Given the numerical dominance of the dominant castes, Dalits would have had to bear a severe loss if a violent clash erupted. In addition to that, the constant attempt of the police to convince Dalits to give up their demand demonstrated their attitude towards Dalits and their quest for equality. Dalits could understand that the police officials were not going to ensure protection to them if there erupted a clash. As the situation seemed to be highly volatile and tense, the police started detaining activists and other youth who had gathered in the support of Dalits as a preventive measure. When the funeral procession started towards the contested streets, the police waited till they reached the junction and then took the body by force after carrying out lathi charge and carried the body to the cremation ground through the agrarian fields to perform the final rites.

In addition, an interview with Arulselvan, a functionary of VCK and an activist, revealed how the police dealt with assertive activists. Mr Arulselvan recollected,

It was after my higher secondary exams. A meeting of our people about our ritual right in our temple was being held in the presence of a dominant caste man, who was also the district secretary of AIADMK, the then ruling party. I asked, 'Why can't we talk among ourselves, why should he come and decide things here?' and then there was an unrest and I went home. The next day, two policemen came to my home, and I was taken to the police station, on the charge that I had beaten two people, and they had filed a case under a non-bailable section of Cr. P.C. 506/2. They threatened to inflict on me a case for trading in *ganja* for my involvement in common issues. Since I did not get subdued, they reported my age as 19, and imprisoned me in general prison instead of taking the case to the juvenile justice board. I was detained for four days; both my father (who was also charged) and I were granted conditional bail and had to sign every day at Thiruvarur court which is 60 km from my village. My father was the only bread winner then, and he could not go for work due to this conditional bail, and as a result my younger brother worked as a labourer and gave us ₹50 every day, and the travel would cost ₹36 for both of us, and we used to have one tea each with the remaining money. The case went on for several months, and finally it was dismissed as there was no complaint at all.[19]

Another well-known advocate, activist and documentary filmmaker Divya Bharathi responded that police arrest without any complaint is very common in Tamil Nadu. Given these three instances, the following section attempts to understand the pattern of police action across various instances, so as to understand how caste as a sociopolitical and cultural institution determines and endorses different actions in different contexts.

## OBVIOUSNESS OF CASTE IN THE VARYING ACTIONS OF THE STATE MACHINERY AND THE JUDICIARY

All the cases are explicit practices of untouchability, which the officials of the state could easily handle and downplay by approaching them as a deviation from established customs, and by doing so, the state has in fact given an official sanction to those discriminatory social practices.

---

[19] Interview with Arulselvan, on 19 January 2019.

The discriminatory past in itself becomes a substantiation for the same to continue, as the officials of the state were unwilling to approach the same as a denial of right to equality. In all the cases, the respondents were not the dominant castes, but officials of Tamil Nadu state government, such as police, revenue and HRCE, and the counter-affidavit against the appeal of Dalits had been filed by them. This raises the question: When all individuals have their own process of socialization, how can the state, which believes in the right to equality, ensure that they discharge their responsibility in their official capacity according to the Constitution of India? In all these occasions, never once have the officials attempted to present the case in favour of the Dalits' demand for right to equality, whereas their stand in support of the dominant is so spontaneous. No officer of the state has been subjected to disciplinary action for endorsing the practice of untouchability and justifying discrimination.

While the Constitution of India promises the right to equality before law, the priorities of the revenue department and the law-enforcing agencies are different from that of enforcing the right to equality. Since the idea of equality is alien to our traditional caste-based society, every festival, or system of rights in a village, or ceremonies, is established in such a way that the inequalities are manifested in one form or the other in everything. While Dalits have been historically denied those rights, exposure to modern laws and breaking of traditional caste dependence empower them to vie for a claim for equal treatment in the village. However, every time there arises an issue, the state machinery approaches it from the point of view of the established tradition, and any deviation from that has to be prevented so as to protect 'law and order'. So, irrespective of whether it is preventing a temple car procession, denial of a ritual right or denial of a respectful funeral, the state always attempts to stick to the traditional practices. Even if such practices are grossly discriminatory and illegal as per the Constitution, the law-enforcing agencies adhere to those because both the dominant section and the subordinated section had followed it in the past. However, the socio-economic relationships between the dominant castes and Dalits change over the years, as new livelihood options arise, and once the oppressed communities become economically independent, they try to assert it by way of demanding certain religious rights which they see as an indicator of their upward mobility. For the local dominant social groups, such demands seem to undermine the traditional superiority that they had enjoyed over the years. So, whenever the oppressed communities attempt to demonstrate their material prosperity in terms of an improvised ritual right—be it hosting a day's fest or building a temple car—the local dominant sections see that as an attempt to enhance their ritual position in the village. When the tussle between these two communities invites the intervention of the law-enforcing agencies, the state machinery fails to remember that the traditionally oppressed are now legally entitled to such benefits as the Constitution promises right to equality, and so they try to maintain the status quo on the premise of maintaining law and order, irrespective of whether that amounts to endorsing the practice of untouchability or denial of the constitutional promise of right to equality. Every time such a conflict arises, the state intervention is guided by the established practices. Therefore, it only tries to maintain the status quo in the name of protecting law and order, and the officials invoke Cr. P.C. 107[20] and convene a 'peace committee meeting'.

If we look into the social composition of villages, the 'touchable' castes form the numerical majority, and on most occasions they are socially, economically, politically and culturally dominant than the 'untouchable' castes. Even if a village comprises multiple castes, the idea

---

[20] '107. Security for keeping the peace in other cases.

(1) When an Executive Magistrate receives information that any person is likely to commit a breach of the peace or disturb the public tranquility or to do any wrongful act that may probably occasion a breach of the peace or disturb the public tranquility and is of opinion that there is sufficient ground for proceeding, he may, in the manner hereinafter provided, require such person to show cause why he should not be ordered to execute a bond,[1] with or without sureties,] for keeping the peace for such period, not exceeding one year, as the Magistrate thinks fit.

(2) Proceedings under this section may be taken before any Executive Magistrate when either the place where the breach of the peace or disturbance is apprehended is within his local jurisdiction or there is within such jurisdiction a person who is likely to commit a breach of the peace or disturb the public tranquility or to do any wrongful act as aforesaid beyond such jurisdiction.' Available at: https://indiankanoon.org/doc/1914745/ (accessed on 29 May 2019).

of untouchability would determine the social alliance, and it is a very common pattern that all 'touchable' castes unite in opposing the 'untouchable' castes, and such an alliance makes them the numerical majority.

If we closely observe the sequence of events and the state's interventions, it may be clear that the numerical strength of the contesting social groups proves to be a crucial determining factor. If the right to equality is followed in letter and spirit, all the three issues discussed previously should have been settled by the local administration or, at the maximum, the district-level administration. While the hostility in the village and negligence of the local authorities make Dalits approach the state to ensure their right to equality, the police and state machinery find an easy excuse in the numerical dominance or vulnerability of the contesting social groups to justify their (in)action. When the 'touchable' castes form a formidable social alliance, the officers of the state tend to compromise on the constitutional promise of right to equality and engage in negotiation with the contesting social groups. And in most instances, such negotiations are nothing more than 'Khap panchayats.'

It is in such circumstances that members of the oppressed social groups approach the court, and it is an irony that in the case of Palangkallimedu and Vazhuvur, even the court had yielded to the interest of the dominant castes and called for negotiating through peace meetings. In all the issues that are discussed in this chapter, Dalits exhausted all possible legal means to assert their right to equality, but it is a sad fact that even the mighty state has meekly surrendered to the hegemony of the dominant castes. However, it is also worthwhile to draw parallels from the way the state machinery and the police had reacted in other similar issues:

First, on 29 October 2007, the president of Tamil Nadu Congress Committee (TNCC), Krishnasamy, was attacked by Pallars when he went to participate in the Thevar Guru Poojai, an event organized to commemorate Late Pasumpon Muthuramalinga Thevar, a leader of the dominant Mukkulathor communities. It was later clarified that it was an attempt on another local leader of the Thevar community, and Krishnasamy's car was attacked by mistake, as the attempt happened in the night. Subsequently, a battalion of a special task force was sent to the villages in the vicinity and all the Pallar houses were raided by the police, and a retired schoolteacher died during the raid. In the year 2008, when there was a struggle to demolish the 'untouchability' wall at Uthapuram near Usilampatti in Madurai, the dominant castes attacked the Pallars, and several members of the community including women and children were injured. Subsequently, the leader of the Puthiya Tamilagam party, Dr Krishnasamy, visited the village to meet the members of the Pallar community who were affected in the clashes. Dr Krishnasamy was attacked by the dominant caste Kallars on his way to Uthapuram, and the police did not file any case against that.[21] Subsequently, Pallars from the neighbouring villages organized a protest against police inaction in Usilampatti, and in that protest, the police opened fire and killed a Dalit youth, blaming him for pelting stones on the police officers.[22]

On 11 September 2011, the Pallars gathered in Paramakudi to commemorate late Immanuel Sekaran, a leader of the Pallar community. While it is a common sight to see villagers travelling in carrier vehicles for festivals and marriages, the police stopped the people who came to pay homage to their leader, and subsequently, the situation became tense following the detention of John Pandian, the leader of Makkal Tamil Desam Katchi and a prominent leader from the Pallar community. Subsequently, the police opened fire without any statutory warning and seven Dalits were killed in police firing and several others were severely injured.[23] Subsequently, the Government of Tamil Nadu ordered a judicial enquiry headed by Justice Sampath, who later relieved the police of any charge.[24]

---

[21] https://www.thehindu.com/todays-paper/tp-national/tp-tamilnadu/PT-leader-convoy-attacked/article15334190.ece (accessed on 25 August 2020). Krishnasamy had blamed the police for not providing adequate security.

[22] https://www.thehindu.com/todays-paper/Dalit-youth-killed-in-police-firing/article15335531.ece (accessed on 25 August 2020).

[23] https://www.thehindu.com/news/national/tamil-nadu/paramakudi-police-firing-toll-rises-to-seven/article2446414.ece (accessed on 31 May 2019).

[24] For a detailed analysis about the Justice Sampath Commission, read R. Thirunavukkarasu, 'Illiberal State and the Myth of a Civil Society: Justice Sampath Commission Report on Paramakudi Police Firing', *Review of Development and Change* 22, no. 2 (July–December 2017): 88–108.

Surprisingly, in the conflict in Eraiyur Church alone, the police had opened fire and killed two Christian Vanniyars on 8 March 2008 when they ransacked the church that the Christian Paraiyars built and sought recognition as they faced untouchability in the already-existing church.[25]

It is also worthwhile to recollect the police excesses that led to the death of 17 Pallars in Thamirabarani River in 1997 and police firing in the Panchami Land protest in Chengalpattu on 10 October 1994, killing 2 Dalits and injuring 14 others. Ironically, the police did not resort to any such measures in Seshasamuthiram event when the dominant caste Vanniyars hurled petrol bombs on the police and attacked the police personnel. While Dalits had to bear the brunt of a raid by a battalion of the special task force of the police for attacking Krishnasamy, the then president of TNCC, at the same time, there was no action on those who attacked the Dalit leader Krishnasamy in Uthapuram, and the attitude of the police was even more explicit when they opened fire and killed a Dalit youth in Usilampatti for pelting stones. Thus, these incidents present a clear pattern where the action of the police varies depending upon the community in question. While the police seldom attacks the dominant castes, Dalits always have to fear police excesses at any time. The police force has never hesitated to be violent and lethal when acting against Dalits, whereas they have always been impotent in ensuring the constitutional promise for Dalits, as it necessitates actions against the dominant castes.

While judiciary is seen as the last resort for the people, the incidents at Seshasamuthiram, Palangkallimedu, Vazhuvur and Thirunelkondacheri prove that the orders issued by the Madras High Court have no sanctity for the hegemonic dominant castes, and the police show no interest in implementing the court's order.

When we see the severity of police action against Dalits, and the explicit slack in ensuring their fundamental rights and right to equality, it is very clear that Manu's dictate finds its social life through the modern state and its judiciary. All these make the constitutional promise

---

[25] https://www.maalaimalar.com/News/District/2016/05/30112429/1015264/Today-chariot-festival-in-eraiyur-christian-church.vpf (accessed on 25 August 2020); also see https://www.oneindia.com/2008/03/17/eraiyur-echo-churches-in-cuddalore-villupuram-locked-1205764732.html (accessed on 25 August 2020).

of equality before law and justice a mirage, which is visible from a distance but disappears as we get closer, leaving no hope for the oppressed to recover their dignity and self-respect.

It is a Herculean task for Dalits to remain hopeful and assert their right to equality. Caste as a system makes different castes mutually dependent and antagonistic; it is obvious that the dominant social groups tend to exercise their dominance in various spheres of social life. But the apathy is visible when officials of the state use their official capacity to do the same, and the administrative machinery has no mechanism to check whether the action of the official is as per the constitutional values of equality and justice or not. This, together with lack of knowledge about illegalities of many caste-based customary practices among both the oppressor and the oppressed, makes the idea of justice unknown to common men. The victims belonging to the oppressed communities are denied a fair deal at will by the officers of the state, and it is their indifference and inaction that compel Dalits to approach the court of law. This access to judicial procedures is determined by whether they have minimum knowledge about their rights as equal citizens and their ability to spend their time, energy and resources to hire a legal counsel. However, all the three cases discussed in this chapter have proved that irrespective of what the court orders, the dominant social groups are able to continue their discrimination without an iota of fear of legal repercussions. The orders of the court are nothing more than scribblings on a piece of paper that has no sanctity even for the officials of the state. Thus, it can be stated that caste reproduces itself through the state in multiple ways and means. It can be reproduced by delaying access to state's administrative machinery or welfare measures, or its education and employment opportunities, and thereby reproducing the traditional hierarchy in the modern space. Further, even when the modern space is accessed, caste reproduces itself by subversion of the law, differential implementation or delay in implementation, depending upon the social identity of the individual. Further, the repressive measures also vary depending upon the social identity of the individual, and all these collectively make the state system as hierarchical as the traditional caste system.

It is worthwhile to return to Althusser's summarization of the Marxist theory of state, in which the fourth stage refers to a process where

The proletariat must seize state power in order to destroy the existing bourgeois and state apparatus and, in a first phase, replace it with a quite different, proletarian state apparatus, then in later phases set in motion a radical process, that of the destruction of the state (the end of state power, the end of every state apparatus).[26]

In the Indian context, while we cannot imagine such a process leading to statelessness, the minimum expectation of Dalits would be a dignified social space where their rights are respected by other fellow citizens without the necessity of it being monitored by the state apparatus. But caste as an ideology has corrupted the way in which the state apparatus engages with Dalits' right to equality. Therefore, with all apprehension, fear and hesitation, it can be stated that unless the dominant social groups learn to respect other fellow citizens from vulnerable social groups as equals, the state and the administrative machinery and the legal establishment would continue to remain meaningless for the oppressed and would continue to violate their constitutional promise. Any promise of equality in the future is nothing but an endorsement of the denial in the present. One can understand that it is after being the chairman of the Drafting Committee of Indian Constitution that Babasaheb, Dr B. R. Ambedkar, wrote, 'We cannot enact laws to make people love each other,' and these instances of state failure point that this statement of despair would continue to capture the historical angst of Dalits in the years to come.

## BIBLIOGRAPHY

Lakshmanan, C., and K. Srinivasulu, eds. 'Interrogating Enquiry Commission Reports on Caste Violence'. *Review of Development and Change* 22 (special issue), no. 2 (July–December 2017): 3–16.

Ludden, David E. 'Ecological Zones and the Cultural Economy of Irrigation in Southern Tamilnadu'. *Journal of South Asian Studies* I (new series), no. 1 (1978): 1–13.

The Indian Express, *Row between Dalits, Upper Caste Hindus over Temple Ritual; Nagapattinam Festival Suspended* (31 July 2016). Available at: https://indianexpress.com/article/india/india-news-india/row-between-dalits-upper-caste-hindus-over-temple-ritual-nagapattinam-festival-suspended-2946474/ (accessed on 25 August 2020).

---

[26] Althusser, *Ideology and Ideological State Apparatus*, 14–15.

One India, *One Killed, 2 Injured in Police Firing in TN Village* (4 November 2008). Available at: https://tamil.oneindia.com/news/2008/11/04/tn-one-killed-in-police-firing-near-usilampatti.html (accessed on 25 August 2020).

The Hindu, *Untouchability Still Prevails: Krishnasamy* (29 December 2007). Available at: https://www.thehindu.com/todays-paper/tp-national/tp-tamilnadu/Untouchability-still-prevails-Krishnasamy/article14903870.ece (accessed on 25 August 2020).

The Hindu, *Tension in Ramanathapuram, Sivaganga* (29 October 2016). Available at: https://www.thehindu.com/todays-paper/tp-national/tp-tamilnadu/Tension-in-Ramanathapuram-Sivaganga/article15301493.ece (accessed on 25 August 2020).

The Hindu, *Body of Dalit Youth Buried* (6 November 2008) Available at: https://www.thehindu.com/todays-paper/tp-national/tp-tamilnadu/Body-of-Dalit-youth-buried/article15336232.ece (accessed on 25 August 2020).

The Hindu, *Dalit Youth Killed in Police Firing Near Uthapuram* (6 November 2008). Available at: https://www.thehindu.com/todays-paper/tp-national/tp-tamilnadu/Dalit-youth-killed-in-police-firing-near-Uthapuram/article15335346.ece (accessed on 25 August 2020).

The Hindu, *CPI(M) Seeks Probe into Police Firing* (5 November 2008). https://www.thehindu.com/todays-paper/tp-national/tp-tamilnadu/CPI-M-seeks-probe-into-police-firing/article15335715.ece (accessed on 25 August 2020).

The Hindu, *Bus Damaged, 289 Puthiya Tamilagam Cadres Arrested* (5 November 2008). Available at: https://www.thehindu.com/todays-paper/tp-national/tp-tamilnadu/Bus-damaged-289-Puthiya-Tamilagam-cadres-arrested/article15334601.ece (accessed on 25 August 2020).

The Hindu, *Buses Attacked in Southern Districts, 400 Persons Held* (4 November 2008). Available at: https://www.thehindu.com/todays-paper/tp-national/tp-tamilnadu/Buses-attacked-in-southern-districts-400-persons-held/article15334662.ece (accessed on 25 August 2020).

The Hindu, *TNCC President Stabbed* (30 October 2007). Available at: https://www.thehindu.com/todays-paper/TNCC-president-stabbed/article14866254.ece (accessed on 25 August 2020).

The Hindu, *Violence Mars Thevar Centenary Celebrations* (31 October 2007). Available at: https://www.thehindu.com/todays-paper/Violence-mars-Thevar-centenary-celebrations/article14866879.ece (accessed on 25 August 2020).

The Hindu, *Ramadoss for CB-CID Probe* (1 November 2007). Available at: https://www.thehindu.com/todays-paper/tp-national/tp-tamilnadu/Ramadoss-for-CB-CID-probe/article14867752.ece (accessed on 25 August 2020).

The Hindu, *Tension at Government Rajaji Hospital* (1 November 2007). Available at: https://www.thehindu.com/todays-paper/tp-national/tp-tamilnadu/Tension-at-Government-Rajaji-Hospital/article14867617.ece (accessed on 25 August 2020).

The Hindu, *Cases Registered Against 1200 Persons in Ramanathapuram* (1 November 2007). Available at: https://www.thehindu.com/todays-paper/tp-national/tp-tamilnadu/Cases-registered-against-1200-persons-in-Ramanathapuram/article14867751.ece (accessed on 25 August 2020).

# Chapter 9

# Identity, Representation and Reservation
Dravidian Politics towards Muslims

P. Ramajayam

### INTRODUCTION

Muslims as a religious minority have become an indispensable part of Indian politics. Since independence, the religious character of politics has been undergoing changes within the framework of the parliamentary democratic system apart from secularism and ideological positions of the political forces. Until the 1980s, Muslim religious politics was at the periphery and later in the 1990s it came to occupy the centre stage due to Babri Masjid demolition followed by the rise of Hindutva politics. The religious identity politics of Muslims encompasses and interfaces with many other identities of national, regional, linguistic, ethnicity, traditional, belief systems and social groups. This has been the experience of Indian Muslims who have been engaging with multiple identities within the regional cultural nationalism. Muslims have to play a dual role with pan-Indian national politics and regional and ethno-linguistic cultural identity politics in many states where regional roots are very strong in their sociocultural life.

More than 800 years of continuous Muslim governance in North India has made Muslims addicted to power trappings and the hierarchy of *Ashrafs* (foreign conquerors) and *Ajlafs* (local converts).... Ethnically, North Indian Muslims speak mainly Urdu, a language developed and prospered in the Ganga–Yamuna belt of North India by the civil society, enriched by Persian, Hindi and Sanskrit words.[1]

The geographical, cultural and linguistic diversity among Muslims has ingrained a regional character in its political mobilization. The regional roots of identity have been continuously interwoven, explicitly within the pan-Indian and regional politics. But '[T]he Muslims in the southern states of India, Tamil Nadu, Karnataka, Andhra, Telangana and Kerala, lived on the outskirts of the Muslim empire, and spoke local languages and adopted local Hindu culture.'[2]

In Tamil Nadu, the Muslim identity politics had existed during the colonial struggle. Muslim League as a political movement had a strong presence in Tamil Nadu and simultaneously it also equally claimed Tamil linguistic identity. Evident to that is 'Tamil Muslim literature which reflects the life of Tamil Muslims from at least the sixteenth century and treats all Muslims and Tamil Muslims on an equal footing'.[3] Dravidian identity politics emerged to bring all the backward and oppressed Dalits under non-Brahmin social mobilization after 1922 within the inclusive framework of Tamil cultural nationalism, which included Muslims as 'Tamils' because of their nativity, cultural assimilation, and contribution to Tamil language and literature. It is emphasized that the Tamil identity can be preserved only by ameliorating its language and traditions mentioned in the literature against the Hindi imposition from the north. As regionalism continues to play a crucial role, it tends to split the Muslims on a regional basis in a parliamentary democracy. Since 1967, the DMK's triumph, 'a trend in India towards

---

[1] See Iqbal S. Hasnain, 'North Is North and South Is South: The Great Indian Muslim Divide', *The American Bazaar*, 29 October 2019.

[2] Ibid.

[3] See J. B. P. More, *Muslim Identity, Print Culture and the Dravidian Factor in Tamil Nadu* (New Delhi: Orient Longman, 2004), 22.

the politics of regionalism has been evident'[4] in Tamil Nadu. Muslim identity politics in Tamil Nadu operates within the framework of Dravidian parties and their alliance factors. But the spatial and temporal identity of Muslim politics has been an inevitable exercise in the parliamentary democratic system where representation in legislative bodies plays a crucial role in legitimizing their existence in the society and polity. In the process of political formation, Muslims as a religious minority base their politics which is protecting their cultural rights as the foremost priority associated with social emancipation. In a broader perspective, political representation as a recognition allows them to raise the voice for their sociopolitical, economic and cultural assertion. In this regard, Muslim identity politics and representation have undergone different phases since the colonial and post-colonial periods.

Muslim identity in Tamil Nadu has also seen shifts over a period of time from Dravidian ethnic–linguistic to exclusive religious politics. The epicentre for this shift has been perceived as two different kinds: One is overwhelming political consolidation of dominant backward castes backed by Dravidian political parties and, in the process, the isolation and exclusion of the socially and economically vulnerable to establish their hegemony. Irrespective of caste and religion, this itself becomes the causal effect for their assertion. Particularly in the case of Muslims in Tamil Nadu, they have contributed towards national freedom struggle and emergence of the Dravidian movement, and more prominently their identity is deep rooted in Tamil language and literature. Muslim identity politics has religious traces since colonial period, but it adopted norms much closer to the Tamil identity rather than the religious. The colonial construct of Dravidian identity as primarily based on ethnicity and language and then against the Brahminical hegemony over the backward castes and Dalits has drawn the attention of the nationalist politics of the country. And with regard to locating Muslims in the larger Dravidian political discourse, their space has been

---

[4] See Lewis P. Fickett Jr, 'The Politics of Regionalism in India', *Pacific Affairs* 44, no. 2 (Summer, 1971): 193–210, cited from Iqbal Narain, 'Democratic Politics and Political Development in India', *Asian Survey* (February 1970): 90; Iqbal Narain, 'Revolt of the Region', *Eastern Economist* (22 February 1969).

delimited as Tamil and Urdu Muslims in the 1980s; it is further limited to the response of the emergence of Hindutva politics as an effect across the country, having the same but much lesser degree in Tamil Nadu. When the Scheduled Castes (SCs) opted to embrace Islam in Meenakshipuram in 1981, the Muslim identity politics resurfaced with Dalit identity, which problematized the Dravidian political discourse.

The 1990s have seen an upsurge in identity politics amalgamated with caste and religion. The caste identity politics was left with the rise of Other Backward Classes (OBCs) through the agitations of the implementation of the Mandal Commission report and the emergence of Dalit identity politics across the country. The religious identity politics explicitly came into existence through the Ram Janmabhoomi movement in North India. The same kind of political polarization had an impact among Dravidian politics of Tamil Nadu. On religious question, the AIADMK was in support of religious identity politics aligning with the BJP, and the DMK was in support of caste identity politics by heading the National Front.[5] The caste conflicts in the 1990s had deeper political impacts among OBCs and Dalits in Tamil Nadu, which altered the political landscape. The shadow of the caste clashes paved way for caste assertion. The caste assertion also had religious dynamics against minority identity as an impact of national politics. The coexistence of caste clashes and Babri Masjid demolition posed serious challenge for the Dravidian parties, which had never encountered the religious identity politics as it is in North India. Since the 1990s, the religious politics has started playing a minimal role in the state that the caste identity politics has been so vibrant; as a result of this, most of the dominant backward castes have started emerging with their own political parties such as Pattali Makkal Katchi of Vanniyars, Kongu Vellala Goundergal Peravai of Gounders, Forward Bloc of Thevars and then the political outfits for Dalits—Puthiya

---

[5] The grand alliance primarily comprised the Janata Dal, BJP, Left parties, regional forces like DMK, Telugu Desam Party under the leadership of N. T. Rama Rao and Asom Gana Parishad led by Prafulla Kumar Mahanta formed against the dominance of the Congress under the leadership of Rajiv Gandhi and in support of OBC reservation by implementation of Mandal Commission recommendations.

Tamilagam in southern districts and Dalit Panthers of India in northern districts. It was in response to the dominant castes' emergence that a shift in Dravidian identity politics occurred—from a movement inclusive of all oppressed OBCs and Dalits against the Brahminical social order to the exclusive political formations of the same oppressed OBCs and Dalits that participated in electoral politics. The two principal Dravidian parties had to deal with these splinter groups along with their own party cadres of the respective castes. Simultaneously, the Muslim identity politics also emerged after the demolition of Babri Masjid, other subsequent riots and Islamic fundamentalism in the 1990s, in response to the Hindutva politics at the national level which had its presence felt in Tamil Nadu. Since caste has been the driving factor, the religious identity found less significance among the OBCs, but it was a complex issue for the Muslims' identity, because the identity politics is so far rooted through ethno-linguistic identities at par with Islamic principles.

The New Economic Policy at the national level was proposed and implemented in the era of political instability. Although it was initiated by the Congress headed by P. V. Narasimha Rao as a structural adjustment programme, the beneficiaries were mostly the upper-caste Baniya Hindus, who were already controlling the economy in the private sector. As the patterns of economy and employment are decided by the private enterprises, the role of state as an interventionist was reduced to that of a facilitator. This factor of economy and market competition naturally had social bias, exclusion and discrimination in the private sector. The penetration of religious identity politics was driven from within and outside the state in relation to the New Economic Policy, where privatization, liberalization and globalization operated in support of the dominants and excluded the disadvantaged groups of distinct social and religious identity. The Muslims in Tamil Nadu had organic relationships with the West Asian and Southeast Asian countries which were involved in maritime trade for the past centuries. Also, Muslims have been working in Gulf and Southeast Asian countries as migrant labourers for more than four decades and their socio-economic status has undergone significant changes.

In the wake of privatization through the New Economic Policy, religious politics took such a different turn that Muslims increasingly started depending on the Gulf and Southeast Asian countries for employment and livelihood. However, they were largely brought under the Backward Castes from 1971 onwards in Tamil Nadu, but they were not given due representation in government jobs through the reservation policy. The dominant castes in the lists of Backward Castes which had the political patronage have garnered the fruits of reservations. Although Muslims come under the lists of Backward Castes, their political affiliation with the Dravidian parties did not favour them at large after the 1980s, before the religious polarization took place in Tamil Nadu politics. The combination of economic liberalization and religious identity politics affected their representation in education and employment in the public and private sectors. As Deepak Nayyar viewed it, the people who are excluded from the markets are included by the politics of democracy[6]; probably, this could have been one of the additional reasons that accelerated the exclusive identity politics among Muslims in Tamil Nadu. Liberalization was helpful for 'asset owners, profit earners, rentiers, the educated, the mobile—those with professional, managerial or technical skills are the winners, whereas asset-less, wage-earners, debtors, the uneducated, the immobile and the semi-skilled or the unskilled are the losers.'[7] As the reservation policy in Tamil Nadu has been relatively effective, the beneficiaries are mostly the dominant castes and the spillover effect had little impact among the marginalized OBCs including Muslims. In the larger discourse on neoliberal economy and religious fundamentalism, the reservation issues had been sidelined categorically, in which many backward communities including Muslims were affected the most, particularly in terms of private sector jobs. Due to these kinds of economic consequences with political polarization, there was a widespread realization that Muslims were far away from the mainstream of social justice, and thereby the Muslim community started to organize by bringing all the social groups under one single fold towards the demand of separate reservations.

---

[6] Deepak Nayyar, 'Economic Development and Political Democracy: Interaction of Economics and Politics in Independent India', *Economic & Political Weekly* 33, no. 49 (5–11 December 1998): 3129.
[7] Ibid.

## ETHNIC-LINGUISTIC IDENTITY OF MUSLIMS

The Dravidian political discourse was started as a rallying point for representation for socially backward castes on the basis of numerical strength and inequality in distribution of resources. This paved the way for identity politics in Tamil Nadu. The Brahminical construction of Hindu religion as an institution was questioned in terms of its everyday functioning and was demystified by the Self-Respect Movement headed by Periyar E. V. Ramasamy. The identity politics of Muslims was solely on cultural and religious grounds. When the Justice Party was voted to power in 1920, Muslims and the untouchables were soon disenchanted with its policies. In the 1930s, the party lost popular Muslim support. During this period, there developed cordial ties between Muslims and the avowedly atheist non-Brahmin movement.[8] The gravity of Hindu religious politics was set aside by various counter-discourses through the ethos of rationalism, Tamil nationalism, Self-Respect Movement and finally non-Brahmin movement by consolidating OBCs and Dalits under one ideology, which is still finding relevance in the contemporary politics. Periyar and his question on representation hold contemporary relevance whenever a debate resurfaces on reservation and representation. The concepts of reservation and representation are two sides of the same coin of the social emancipatory arrangement. However, reservation as a concept and in practice is guaranteed by the constitutional provisions rather than by asserting political representation, which is to be tested as per democratic methods by participating in electoral politics.

Muslims in Tamil Nadu share most of the identities with any other fellow Tamil community over linguistic, regional and ethnicity issues. The historical evolution of Tamil Muslims always had a linguistic dimension. Tamil Muslim literature from the 14th century onwards is a living proof of this dimension. It became more prominent under the influence of Self-Respectors.[9] Islam as a religion has strong cultural

---

[8] See S. M. Mohamed Koya, 'Muslim Politics in Madras in 1930s and 1940s: The Rise of Muslim League and Related Developments', *Proceedings of the Indian History Congress* 63 (2002): 757.
[9] Ibid., 758.

and linguistic roots in Tamil literature, social history, maritime trade, economy and educational institutions for many centuries. There were some tussles over the adherence to the Dravidian movement among Muslims who supported the Muslim League during the colonial struggle, because they did not want to engage their religious identity with race. On the one hand, the Muslim League did not show any support to the demand of Dravida Nadu; on the other hand, Muslims in Tamil Nadu could not get away with their linguistic identity. The paradigm shift that had taken place over the Dravidian–Islam identity after the independence, parliamentary democracy, was set in motion to operate electoral politics based on caste and religious identity in Indian politics. The Dravidian politics kept the Hindu religion as an institution controlled by Brahmins categorically away, as it was contested by Periyar very seriously, and their humiliating practices meted out to common public in the early centuries but not the rituals of temples, mosques and churches. In the process of inclusive secular politics, Dravidian parties mobilized and strengthened their social base through participation in rituals to insulate their Tamil cultural nationalism against the Hindu nationalism.

Muslim and Dravidian identity politics have coexisted since the 1920s. But the difference between them was that Muslim politics was nationalistic in consonance with the Congress and Dravidian identity politics was about social reforms. Muslim politics of Madras Presidency had become significant after the formation of All-India Muslim League (AIML) in 1906 in Dacca. The Prince of Arcot, Ghulam Muhammad Ali, served as its president from 1908 to 1917. At this time, the Tamil or Malayalam language's role in the foundation of the League was insignificant. Muslim politics in the presidency was virtually under the control of the aristocratic merchant elite. The elite was a by-product of the British takeover of political power in South India at the expense of the Nawab of Arcot.[10] Dravidian politics accommodated, within its broader framework, Muslims as a religious minority whose identity primarily based on Tamil, also recognizing their unswerving contributions in various important spheres of Tamil identity such as literature,

---

[10] Ibid., 759.

economy, education and assimilation of Tamil culture. However, it was realized by the Muslim leaders and Dravidian movement to be subsumed by 'Tamil identity' politics under Dravidian parties' rule. Its ideology of secularism towards Muslims had undergone series of changes and paradigm shifts from the 1980s onwards prior to the popular Hindutva politics at the national level. It was untenable of course, as Dravidian political ideology proposed by Periyar E. V. Ramasamy challenged the Hindu religion as a root cause for the existing caste system and the way it distorted the belief system of God and faith towards the priests, which led to alterations in its spiritual character to superstitious beliefs and practices controlled by Brahminism. So, to justify and support Islam within the Dravidian political discourse, it was emphasized that Islam by its very nature follows equality before God and place of worship, and more profoundly it had not practised untouchability as still alive in Hindu religion as an open oppressive practice. He characterized the Brahmins as Aryans, and the non-Brahmins including the Tamil Muslims as Dravidians.[11] To bolster the fraternity among Dravidians, Periyar's inclusive approach towards social reform crossed religious limits. Tamil Muslims were allowed to express their views on Islam and Dravidian linguistic–cultural relationship in these journals[12] which are *Kudiarasu* and *Viduthalai*, and he was against not only the caste system in the Hindu religion and Christianity but also the irrationality and un-Islamic habits infecting Islam. This naturally seems to have drawn the Muslims of Tamil Nadu towards him.[13]

There had been two different schools of thought among Muslims in Tamil Nadu—one was in support of nationalists and other was in support of the Dravidian movement. This had led the Muslims to have alternatives in the political sphere; the Muslim League primarily had differences with the Congress, which chose to get along with the Dravidian movement led by Periyar and Self-Respect Movement. But the linguistic divide had been central among Muslims; Khalilullah, the Tamil Muslim leader from Tiruchirappalli spearheaded the agitation from the Tamil Muslim side. In fact, Khalilullah by allying himself with

---

[11] See More, *Muslim Identity*, 141.
[12] Ibid., 142.
[13] Ibid., 142.

the Self-Respect Movement brought about the affirmation of Tamil Muslim identity in South India on a linguistic basis. This linguistic dimension became more pronounced after 1947.[14]

The contemporary Muslim identity formation was largely the result of representation and self-respect during India's independence movement if one looks at the point of Dravidian ideology. The Muslim League was formed in 1903, and it emerged as a major platform to address the concerns of Muslims, which led the movement for partition of the country. However, a vast majority of Muslims in Tamil Nadu did not accept the ideology behind the partition and chose to live in India, appreciating and adopting a multicultural, secular democracy since their sociocultural linguistic roots were very strong within the Tamil society. Now Muslims in Tamil Nadu constitute 5.86 per cent of total Tamil population (according to 2011 Census). Muslims in Tamil Nadu belong to two distinct groups. They are broadly categorized as Tamil- and Urdu-speaking Muslims. The contemporary political icon for Muslims in Tamil Nadu was 'Quaid-e-Millat' Muhammad Ismail, who was the all-India convener of the Muslim League in independent India. His association with the Dravidian movement intertwined the sociocultural and political formation, and the Dravidian movement had an advantage of appropriating the Tamil-speaking community irrespective of religion. This move turned out as a successful political formation and helped to build a strong political alliance against the Congress in Tamil Nadu. When the subject of partition arose among the Muslims of Tamil Nadu, most of them rallied behind the nationalist movement and opposed the partition on the basis of religion. The major reason and pragmatic approach towards the partition that could be attributed is that it was viewed as an integral part of the unique identity of ethnicity, which is of primary importance along with their religion.

Since independence, Tamil Nadu has seen very scant political developments based on the religious identities. The major advent was the emergence of the Dravidian movement and redefining the nationalist discourse in Tamil Nadu. The Dravidian movement brought about a

---

[14] See Koya, 'Muslim Politics in Madras', 761.

major change in the sociopolitical life of Tamils—to hear the voice from the bottom and to support the backward castes and Dalits who had embraced Islam. It had an inbuilt structure as a secular movement and was found to be suitable to appreciate Islam as a religion for the basic reason that Islam preached and propagated equality among all communities. This approach and principle towards equality brought the Dravidian movement and the Muslims in Tamil Nadu together on many political fronts and drew reciprocation. And in the course of time, the Muslims of Tamil Nadu who always had strong roots in their Tamil ethnicity became a natural ally to the Dravidian movement. This was strongly proved by the active participation of the Muslims in Tamil Nadu in the 1963 anti-Hindi agitations.

The rise of the Dravidian movement and its vertical and horizontal growth among the backward castes and Dalits and its inclusive framework for the Dravidian ethno-cultural identity assimilated the Muslims in Tamil Nadu, and the Muslim League was continued to be the opposition party as there were no political parties to support and ally with the Muslim League until the DMK was formed. After starting in 1949, the DMK led by C. N. Annadurai had political aspirations towards state power and had interest in participating in parliamentary democracy. It started contesting elections 1957 onwards. It simply believed that the social reforms of its parental organization, the DK, could be optimally possible only if there is a political participation—which Periyar seriously opposed as he had strong disbelief in parliamentary democracy. However, the DMK, being an independent political party, based its ideology on the DK. But the DMK had the same secular, multicultural outlook of the DK to expand its pan-Tamil identity across the sections of the Tamil society that included the Muslims of Tamil Nadu in its political processes. Their involvement in literary production, maritime economic contribution and establishing educational institutions for Muslims naturally attracted the DMK. The Muslim communities also appreciated this, and a strong bond was formed. In fact, the bond created a situation which represented a composite political movement where the Muslims' identity was appreciated and amalgamated within the overarching Dravidian political movement. After the partition of India, in 1948, the AIML became the Indian

Union Muslim League (IUML), the name signifying the will to support the formation of the Indian Union.

The IUML in Tamil Nadu was largely a sociocultural organization since Indian independence, addressing their issues and representing the needs and aspirations of the Muslim community. The IUML, though being a national-level independent organization, largely functioned at the regional level, where there was a strong leadership and people participation. In Tamil Nadu, the IUML was indeed strong under the able leadership of 'Quaid-e-Millat' Muhammad Ismail. He was a strong leader at national as well as regional levels, who referred to Tamil as a classical language having all the qualities to be a national language when he spoke in the Constituent Assembly Debates as a member of the Muslim League. This proved that the Muslims in Tamil Nadu regarded Tamil language as equal to their religion. The organic relationship in the political sphere between the DMK and the IUML increasingly became stronger. In the electoral politics, they mostly supported the DMK, being a natural ally. The DMK also supported and raised the problems of the Muslim community in its political programmes. In 1962, the IUML became a political party on its own and started contesting elections. However, this was not a departure from the DMK; in fact, it further reinforced their relationship. The DMK supported the IUML candidates and vice versa from the 1962 assembly elections. In 1967 Tamil Nadu assembly elections, the DMK captured power having alliance with the IUML and the Swatantra Party—a breakaway party of the Congress led by C. Rajagopalachari. Both ideological opponents had become alliance partners to defeat the Congress in Tamil Nadu. This victory of the DMK shaped the party further to continue to uphold the basic ideological position. Since 1967, the political landscape of Tamil Nadu has changed into an unchallengeable subregion controlled by Dravidian parties for the Congress and any other party. The support of the IUML in this election played a vital role to achieve power, but they did not share any power in the government. However, the newly formed ministry had its own fair representation of Muslims who were DMK candidates, allowed to groom at all the levels of the party organization, including the top significant positions like the treasurer of the party. This trend continued up to the death of

Quaid-e-Millat in 1972. Until then, the IUML was one of the strongest political forces that stood with the DMK, and the demands of the Muslim League were accepted by the DMK. This inclusive approach of the DMK towards social recognition and representation helped to avoid the exclusive religious politics in the state. Subsequently, both the DMK and the IUML were split and dissidents formed new political parties. The ADMK was formed under the leadership of M. G. Ramachandran, popularly known as MFR, breaking away from the DMK. The IUML got split into two groups: IUML (Abdul Samad) and IUML (Abdul Latheef). The decline of the IUML started with this split, which led to the shrinking of the space for Muslims in the larger Dravidian identity politics and politically weakened the community over a period of time.

The split in the IUML was largely attributed to the friction between the leading second rank leaders. The IUML (Abdul Samad) supported the DMK, while the IUML (Abdul Latheef) supported the ADMK. In spite of the splits in both the IUML and the DMK, there was no estrangement between the Muslim identities and Dravidian politics. Some of the major issues addressed with regard to the Muslim communities were as follows:

1. State-level minority commission
2. Creation of an Urdu academy
3. Recognition of Urdu as a mother tongue for Deccan Muslims
4. Inclusion of Muslims in the OBC category
5. Birthday of Prophet Muhammad declared as a paid regional government holiday
6. Memorials constructed commemorating Quaid-e-Millat

## DILEMMA AND DICHOTOMY

In recent times, there have been new social organizations emerging out of this discontent as Muslims participate in the political processes, but due representation has been the central question raised in the context of social justice. The IUML is no more the single voice of the Muslims in Tamil Nadu. As it had faced severe split into two major factions under the leadership of A. K. A. Abdul Samad and Abdul Latheef, and partnered the Dravidian parties during every assembly and parliamentary election, it got weakened. Its vibrant participation in Tamil politics became a token representation until the 1990s. The Babri Masjid demolition and subsequent religious conflicts across the country and the world, particularly the wars that had taken place in West Asian countries, forced the Muslims to become an organized political force at the state level in order to respond to the political problems they faced within the local dynamics. On many occasions, the international issues concerning Muslims were directly linked or implicated with the local issues, be it Kashmir, the Gulf crisis or Indo-Pakistan border problems.

A new social organization called Tamil Nadu Muslim Munnetra Kazhagam (TMMK; Tamil Nadu Muslims Progressive Federation) has emerged among Muslims in order to address the serious questions of their overall socio-economic development. They focus on external issues like separate reservations in education and employment. There are similar social organizations such as Tamil Nadu Thowheed Jamath, Jamaat-e-Islami Hind (Girls Islamic Organization) and Anjuman (Women Wing) emerging from the Muslim community, carrying out reforms which are pertinently internal issues such as abolishing the dowry system, equal property rights for Muslim women, a fair practice of divorce and maintenance, and women's education. There is a religious reform organization like Tabligh, which is streamlining Muslims to live their life within the framework of the Qur'an.

These new social, political and cultural movements have emerged to rescue the Muslims from religious fundamentalism and terrorism to a large extent. The interventions made by the new sociopolitical movements and political parties were incredible, but their efforts could not alter the political discourse against the Muslim minorities across the country. The Tamil Muslims have taken many serious steps to minimize the effects of the provocation towards the Muslims after the Babri Masjid demolition, though Tamil Nadu had limited political impact due to the Babri Masjid issue, as the Dravidian parties did not get involved with it. It is obvious that Tamil Muslims continue to use till today the slogan '*Islam engal vazhi, inba Tamil engal mozhi*'

(Islam is our way of living, lovely Tamil is our language).[15] There were differences of opinion on God, which implies clashes of interest between Muslims and the Dravidian movement. Many Tamil Muslims, though they did not relish Periyar's atheistic propaganda, seem to have preferred to maintain a close relationship with him mainly for political reasons. Opposed to the Congress, E. V. Ramasamy was their most important ally in Tamil Nadu. He contributed to the assertion of their Tamil identity, in the face of domination of Urdu-speaking Muslims in Madras Presidency's public life until the 1930s.[16] Also, there were certain important references for their Tamilness and their contribution to the Tamil language and literature. After independence, Muslims had faced the stigma of partition in Tamil Nadu because they followed the line of Muhammad Ali Jinnah and the Muslim League due to their political position. Although partition was supported by the Dravidian movement, the Muslim League headed by Jinnah was not in support of separate Dravida Nadu, which created confusion among the Muslims in the early post-independence period. In spite of Ramasamy's unreserved support for the demand of Pakistan and the conversion of untouchables to Islam, Jinnah—preoccupied with Muslims—decided to distance himself from the Dravidasthan demand.[17] This caused the Tamil Muslims shift their identity position towards Tamilness for which they had been intertwined with the Tamil Dravidian culture. After independence, the AIML under Muhammad Ismail (Quaid-e-Millat) took a firm stand to stay with India, as it could be sensed that Tamil Muslims found it difficult to disown the identity of land and language. At the same time, they could not get along with the Dravidian movement with full involvement due to its position on religion and God. This dilemma continued until 1962, when the DMK abandoned its separate Dravida Nadu demand. The Dravida Nadu demand from the Dravidian movement and the DMK had been a matter of inconvenience for Muslims who were under serious trouble during and after independence. After taking a firm step

---

[15] See S. M. A. Abdul Khader Fakhri, *Dravidian Shahibs and Brahmin Maulanas: The Politics of the Muslims of Tamil Nadu* (New Delhi: Manohar Publications, 2008), 72.

[16] See More, *Muslim Identity*, 160.

[17] Ibid., 160.

to stay back in India, Muslims understood that extending support to the separate Dravida Nadu would cause further disturbance. It would further raise the question of loyalty to the nation and its citizenship based on ethno-linguistic identity. In order to prove their affinity to Tamil identity and strong faith in Tamil language, National President of the IUML Muhammad Ismail proposed Tamil to be the official language, as it was the classical language in the country, when he was speaking on the language in the Constituent Assembly Debate. This has been clearly spelt out that being a national president of the IUML, Muhammad Ismail strongly raised voice for Tamil in the Constituent Assembly Debate, which was seen as an additional advantage to claim the identity. Because of the partition syndrome and stigma, the IUML categorically stayed away from the politics of separation and kept equidistance with both the Congress and Dravidian movement till the early 1960s. Since the IUML was concerned with the preservation of cultural rights of Muslims, by preventing the government's interference in the sharia, its electoral choice was in dilemma. The strife between C. Rajagopalachari's and M. Kamaraj's positions on language in the state Congress was one of the major factors which drove the Dravidian politics successfully in Tamil Nadu. It further carried the Congress in a new direction towards the dominance and appropriation of non-Brahmin leadership. The Gudiyatham bye-election in 1954 proved to be the litmus test for Kamaraj to become a member of the state legislature after assuming power as the chief minister. He tried to separate the IUML from partition, and the Muslim League offered unconditional[18] support to Kamaraj due to his approach, which was a politically strategic move to play a vital role in electoral politics and to prove the mass base of the Muslim League vis-à-vis the Congress. In 1957 general election, the Congress offered 10 seats to the Muslim League to contest in legislature and 3 or 4 in the Parliament.[19] Even though the strategy was well-crafted, its national manifestation was not so warm. Ismail nevertheless rejected Kamaraj's offer to adopt Muslim

---

[18] Theodore P. Wright Jr, 'The Muslim League in South India since Independence: A Stud in Minority Group Political Strategy', *The American Political Science Review* 60, no. 3 (September 1966): 583.

[19] Ibid., 583.

League candidates as Congress candidates for the forthcoming 1957 general election.[20] But Muhammad Ismail was quite sceptical about the offer from the Congress, as the League's candidates contesting for the Congress would have further complicated the Muslim representation question, and so he demanded that the League be recognized as the sole representative of Muslims; leadership selects 'all' Muslim candidates; and these nominees run on a Muslim League ticket which the Congress would then support.[21] The Kamaraj's proposal as patronage of the Congress to the Muslim League candidates was regarded by Ismail as 'tantamount to the dissolution of his party'.[22] Muslim League's demands of these kinds still continued to be part of the agenda for bargaining politics in the state. But due to the changing political climate and the softening of the ideological positions happening across the political system itself, the Muslim League could not sustain the strategic position. It is important to mention that the DMK in Tamil Nadu came forward to have alliance with the Muslim League from 1962 onwards by accepting many of their demands within the Dravidian political framework. In 1967, the DMK came to power under the leadership of C. N. Annadurai by allying with all important political constituents against the Congress at the state and national levels such as the Swatantra Party headed by C. Rajagopalachari and the IUML headed by Muhammad Ismail. Later, the IUML continued to be the natural ally of the DMK. The contribution of the IUML was highly regarded by the DMK and vice versa. This alliance politics continued until the death of Muhammad Ismail.

## Muslim Representation in Dravidian Parties

Since the relationship between the IUML and Dravidian parties was on and off, there was a loss in the traditional camaraderie. In 1977 assembly elections in which the AIADMK captured power in the state, there were 234 assembly constituencies. Seventeen constituencies had Muslim candidates from mainstream parties such as the Congress, DMK

---

[20] Ibid., 584.
[21] Ibid.
[22] Ibid.

and AIADMK. The political rise of Muslims could be seen in 1977, as there were seven Muslim candidates who contested as independents and secured the second place, while the AIADMK had fielded six and the DMK had fielded four. This could have been seen as a threat for the AIADMK, which had newly emerged in the state, to curtail their further growth, and so they resorted to oppressing the converted Dalits. M. G. Ramachandran as a popular leader decided to move antithetically to DMK's political position, whatsoever the issue may be, as the successful formula for winning the elections and keeping the party alive. Meanwhile, there were large changes at both national and state levels. The Hindu outfits like Hindu Munnani headed by Ramagopalan started emerging in the state. They vehemently criticized Periyar in public meetings, and it was left unchallenged. The space was given to the Hindutva forces in such a way that the AIADMK got benefitted, as along with dominant backward castes the Brahmin votes were playing a major role in deciding the electoral fortunes. There had been a latent disagreement among the dominant backward castes with the Dravidian movement's ideology of social reform and against DMK's dominance in politics by implementing social policies and welfare programmes. These mobilized large parts of the weaker sections and were set to bring about a substantial change in the social structure. This disturbed the hierarchical order of backward castes, and M. Karunanidhi's open attack on Brahmins also fuelled the disagreement. This disagreement over Karunanidhi and the DMK resulted in the corruption charges against him on all the fronts during his second term from 1971 to 1976; also, he spearheaded the opposition to the proclamation of Emergency in 1975. All these became factors in the defeat of the DMK in the 1977 assembly elections.

The emergence of the AIADMK and MGR as a political cult had structurally altered the very base of Dravidian political discourse, and the movement started moving away from social justice. These collective disagreements among the dominant backward castes found their voice in the AIADMK and its openness to non-ideological politics. This helped the AIADMK to survive in power for 13 years consecutively. All through the years, the ideological politics and discourse got changed so drastically that populism overshadowed the social reforms, on the one hand, and vote bank politics was controlled by the populist measures as a key to succeed in electoral politics. The end of the Dravidian era started in 1977 through alignments between a large section of dominant backward castes and Brahmins against the social reform politics.

## Politicizing the Dalits' Conversion to Islam

The Dalit Hindus' conversion to Islam is a landmark protest incident against oppressive caste system in the recent past of Tamil political history. The conversion is perceived as a solace from the oppression of caste Hindus. In 1981, there was a mass conversion of Hindu Dalits in the Meenakshipuram village of Tirunelveli district, protesting against the so-called upper-caste oppressive Hindus of that region. The conversions outlined the fact that all was not well with the Dravidian political leadership whose ideology was premised on social equality. In 1977, the AIADMK came to power and ruled the state for the next 13 years. This conversion had drawn attention at the national level, and it had an adverse impact on the rule of the AIADMK. For the first time in Tamil Nadu, there was political estrangement between the AIADMK and Muslims. There were communal conflicts in the region between the caste Hindus and Dalits and subsequently with Muslims. Chief Minister M. G. Ramachandran conspicuously allied with the caste Hindus, and the Muslim community, who were all along ardent supports of other Dravidian outfits and parties, stood with the conversion and justified it saying that it was the last resort to come out of caste humiliation. But the AIADMK government ruling in the state never had such apprehensions, since it routed the DMK, got elected with strong mandate and handled the situation outside the framework of secularism and social cohesion. The government had an anxiety that its claim towards 'a party of the vulnerable masses' may affect their prospects in the electoral politics and governance in the state. Then it mediated and allowed the Hindutva leaders such as A. B. Vajpayee, L. K. Advani, VHP leader Ashok Singhal and Shankaracharya of Kanchi Mutt, who engaged at their individual level and organizations to have dialogue with Dalits. As the entire state machinery supported the arrival of Hindutva leaders of national stature to a small Dalit hamlet, this could be inferred as silently weakening the Dravidian movement ideologically and structurally. As the AIADMK had no faith in social reform in its policies and governance, it started fading away from the educated middle class of backward caste groups and Dalits, which had attained social status through social justice and found that the AIADMK was distorting the ideology of social reform. Thus, it started projecting Dalits as assertive opposition to the backward castes and their hegemony in politics and economy at the grass-roots level. The AIADMK party and its leader M. G. Ramachandran weakened the Dravidian ideology and contained it to continue in power and isolate the DMK in the state politics. The DMK had initiated the social justice policies and social reform programmes to realize the benefits of the Justice Party and Dravidian movement. The AIADMK reversed the entire political discourse of the Dravidian movement that had been against the Brahmins, as the Brahmins were the root cause for the hierarchical, graded inequality of the caste system, for its political gains, and mobilized the Mukkulathor caste group as its strong, unchallengeable social base in the southern parts of Tamil Nadu. This government was supported by the IUML (Abdul Latheef) at that time.

As a result, this conversion brought about many changes in the sociopolitical climate of Tamil Nadu. The Dravidian parties, which were symbolically dead against the caste Hindu culture, lost their steam with the ascendance of the AIADMK in power. M. G. Ramachandran, even though he came from the DMK, did not have core ideological commitment and was hesitant to carry out the Dravidian ideals as part of his political career. He himself relied on popularity of his own, being a leading cinema actor in the past. This ideological shift led to the arrival of Hindutva forces, mostly headed by Brahmins and upper-caste leaders. For the first time, the RSS, Kanchi Mutt and Hindu Munnani (Hindu Front) had an opportunity of interfering in the political turmoil overtly. This event exposed the Dravidian political parties, particularly the AIADMK, on religious issues on the one hand and created scope for Hindutva forces to enter Tamil Nadu politics through the cultural sphere, on the other hand, instead of addressing the caste oppression. These involvements had a lasting influence on the IUML; it resulted in a unified party, which was earlier split since Quaid-e-Millat's death. The unified IUML started reinstating their unique Muslim identity, deviating from the earlier composite Tamil cultural identity. And this transformation and estrangement were both at political levels. However, the party in opposition, the DMK, was continuing its support to the Muslim community. This conversion became a sensitive issue in the politics of representation in allotting seats for the Muslim community where they were the deciding factor in the elections. The AIADMK government headed by M. G. Ramachandran carefully aligned with the caste Hindus and Hindutva forces to have a safe passage in the electoral politics. This was reflected in the seat allotment and fielding of the candidates in the popularly known Muslim constituencies in Chennai, Tiruchirappalli, Ramanathapuram and Tirunelveli districts, by deliberately fielding caste Hindus against Muslim candidates in many constituencies. This opened the space for religious communal polarization along with caste polarization. As a follow-up to the conversion in Meenakshipuram, the southern districts—which were sensitive towards caste issues—had once again become vulnerable to the caste and religious clashes. It added another challenge to the Dravidian movement to strike a balance, since the dominant caste groups had again started engaging with the religious sentiments and valuing the rituals of the Brahmins. This should be carefully analysed. In response to the conversion, the AIADMK did not prefer to field a Muslim candidate from the Kadayanallur legislative constituency and instead fielded a Hindu from a dominant backward caste.

The political climate in India throughout the 1980s was very heated because of the Punjab Khalistan issue followed by riots, military actions and the assassination of Prime Minister Indira Gandhi, which largely occupied the national politics. Subsequently, the Sri Lankan Tamils' issue, prolonged illness of M. G. Ramachandran, leadership crisis of the AIADMK, and problems of governance in its ruling and within the party surrounded the state politics of Tamil Nadu. During this crisis juncture, many of the social issues such as caste clashes, government employees' strike, agrarian unrest, labour protest and religious conversion were looming large but still not given due attention, as these could be settled only with social equality. In order to suppress the agitational politics, the ruling AIADMK resorted to the populist policies which were the driving force since then and strongly paved the way for vote bank politics. It is to be noted that the decline of Muslim representation started right after the 1981 Meenakshipuram Dalit conversion to Islam. The earlier caste clashes and the prolonged animosities gave an advantage to the dominant caste to further politicize itself using a religious identity. The AIADMK perceived the conversion as exposing its failure in the governance part and eroding its social base, which it did not want to lose any further. Ambrose Pinto has rightly observed,

> During the era of M.G. Ramachandran and Jayalalitha, Hinduism received further legitimacy. In fact, MGR had no Dravida agenda at all. He was a populist and spent resources on the mid-day meal scheme, dhoti–saree scheme for agricultural labourers, pension scheme for the aged, rehabilitation scheme for widows and other welfare schemes.[23]

The much-popularized Noon Meal Scheme and freebies were justified as social relevance in the context of poverty, which diverted all the ground realities away from the politics. The AIADMK swept the 1984 assembly elections with a thumping majority in alliance with the Congress.

It could be well asserted that DMK's proximity with Muslims and vice versa had a steady representation within the party structure as well as in the assembly seats allocations, at par with their population percentage and recognizing their involvement in the struggles and agitations that were organized by the party. In the 1989 assembly elections, the DMK came to power in the state after 13 years of long stint in opposition. In the assembly, the Muslims had in total 12 MLAs; among these, the DMK had 10 MLAs apart from the Congress and CPM having each one. So fair political representation played a significant role in bringing about social equilibrium in the context of parliamentary democracy. The DMK government was short-lived for two years and was dissolved in 1991. The coincidence of the DMK government dissolution, the rise of Hindutva politics headed by the BJP at the national level and the assassination of Rajiv Gandhi had a combo effect in Tamil Nadu, so that in the 1991 assembly elections, the AIADMK led by J. Jayalalitha in alliance with the Congress swept the DMK alliance away and there

---

[23] See Ambrose Pinto, 'End of Dravidian Era in Tamil Nadu', *Economic & Political Weekly* 34, no. 24 (12–18 June 1999): 1483–1485, 1487–1488.

was no credible opposition to control the hegemonic attitude of Chief Minister J. Jayalalitha, which resulted in overdominance of backward castes. Dalit and minority issues were seen as unnecessary. During the 1991–1996 term, the southern districts' caste clashes had the roots in the past, where M. G. Ramachandran's rule in the early 1980s allowed the emergence of the dominant backward castes as majoritarian and Dalits and minorities as vulnerable segments to achieve electoral gains. There have been Dalit-dominant backward-caste clashes continuously taking place since the 1980s in Madurai, Tirunelveli, Virudhunagar and Tuticorin districts. Then, it turned out to be 'the Thevar–Dalit conflict and conflicts between different sub-caste groups have increased the conflict between "us" and "them"'[24]. Also, rifts between minorities and dominant backward caste were also on the rise in Tirunelveli and Kanyakumari districts. These caste conflicts had their own reflections in the elections to a large extent. The marginalization of the socially vulnerable and the pampering of the dominant backward castes have become parts of electoral strategy to gain the power at the grass-roots level. The same tactics were used by J. Jayalalithaa in a much more rigorous and effective manner to challenge the DMK on the social and political grounds. In the 1991 assembly elections, the AIADMK had alliance with Congress, which secured only 5 MLAs belonging to Muslim minority as a first-time low in the 234-member legislature. With the emergence of BJP–Hindutva politics at the national level and J. Jayalalithaa in the state, though it was a coincidence, the BJP's politics influenced the AIADMK more than the Congress—as the Congress had been consistently losing ground in the state as well as the Centre. Jayalalitha foresaw that after Rajiv Gandhi's assassination, the Congress party was decaying in national politics. She started to shift her political alliance towards the emerging national party, which was the BJP, and the Congress saw many troubles and completed its term as a minority government under P. V. Narasimha Rao. Her political alignment was very clear and followed her predecessor MGR, who aligned with the Janata Party in 1977 and later switched over to the Congress as it had a chance of coming back to power after Emergency. 'After MGR, Jayalalitha put on the mantle of MGR. Being a Brahmin,

---

[24] Ibid.

she was not at all ideologically tuned to the Dravidian ideology. In fact, she was responsible for the appointment of Brahmin archakas and promoting the cause of Brahmins as Chief Minister.'[25] It could be understood that J. Jayalalithaa as the chief minister went all the way out of Dravidian principles of keeping religion away from politics. She sent a contingent of her party cadres with bricks to construct the Ram Temple. Therefore, Jayalalitha, who came to power with the help of the Congress and shifted loyalty towards the BJP, set the ground for the BJP and Hindutva politics, whose existence was at the cost of minorities in the nation.

## MUSLIMS GAINING LOST GROUND WITH LIMITATIONS

The Hindutva forces started emerging into a major political force, which was reinforced after the Babri Masjid demolition. The BJP, which spearheaded the Hindutva political movement, captured power in the Centre on 19 March 1998. The later part of the decade of the 1990s became very important for the Dravidian movement politics, when it was forced to travel dead against its founding principles. The BJP had become an unavoidable political force opposed by the Congress, socialists and the Left at the national level. Its influence at the regional level had started making inroads, in response to religious fundamentalism and terrorism as a cause of concern, to engage in anti-Muslim politics. The coalition government and share of power at the Centre changed the whole discourse of ideology and hardcore principles of the non-Brahmin movement. It was the AIADMK which, though being a Dravidian party, had alliance with the BJP and helped it open its account in Tamil Nadu. After the fall of I. K. Gujral-headed coalition (United Front), in which DMK and Tamil Maanila Congress (TMC) had fair representation and important portfolios, the alliance broke down in Tamil Nadu due to the Jain Commission report, which pointed out that the DMK was in touch with the LTTE. There was a demand from the Congress, which supported I. K. Gujral, from outside the Parliament to drop the DMK from the cabinet and coalition. The DMK strongly denied the findings of the Jain Commission report.

---

[25] Ibid.

This crisis loomed large and strained its alliance with the TMC, a breakaway party of the Congress. The AIADMK was beleaguered in 1996 and wiped out from the assembly, with Jayalalitha herself—facing many corruption charges including disproportionate assets case—in deep crisis and desperate to have support of an emerging national party like the BJP. Then, in the 1998 general election, the AIADMK forged its alliance with the BJP, also including in its alliance the smaller parties which were aspiring for power in the state, such as the MDMK and PMK. The Atal Bihari Vajpayee-led BJP did not encourage many of her demands and so faced downfall within a year. Jayalalitha threw a tea party in New Delhi, masterly organized by Subramanian Swamy, who had in fact filed the first case against Jayalalitha on disproportionate wealth. The AIADMK broke the alliance with the BJP in 1999. Meanwhile, the DMK, which had an anxiety of 'dissolution of state government' for political reasons, allied with the BJP by replacing the AIADMK, and the other smaller regional parties continued in the alliance from 1999 to 2003. Within a short span of time, both the Dravidian parties, the DMK and AIADMK, compromised ideologically against each other and there was a shift of loyalty towards central powers by these parties. Meanwhile, in the run-up to the 1998 Lok Sabha elections, there was a major speculation of an assassination bid on L. K. Advani at a Coimbatore election campaign public meeting. This assassination attempt was found to be the handiwork of some Muslim extremists. The attempt was followed by major Hindu–Muslim riots in the city of Coimbatore. Moreover, the subsequent elections tipped the scales in favour of the Hindutva forces. Along with these factors, the alliances with the Dravidian parties had a lasting impact on the Muslim community. M. S. S. Pandian observed correctly that 'There are other reasons as well which make Tamil an easy prey for the saffronite agenda. The upper crust of the backward castes, a product of the reservation politics of the Dravidian movement, no longer needs Tamil language to pursue their claim.'[26] During the period until 2001, Muslim interests and questions were not raised as it was done earlier by the DMK. The DMK's alliance with the BJP demoralized the minorities; moreover, it lost faith in the secular behaviour of the Dravidian

---

[26] M. S. S. Pandian, 'Tamil-Friendly Hindutva', *Economic & Political Weekly* 35, no. 21/22 (27 May–2 June 2000): 1805–1806.

parties. The 2001 assembly election defeat of the DMK and victory of the AIADMK made the parties reconsider their political significance and paying attention to their issues.

Probably these events in the history of Tamil Nadu will be a watershed in the identity politics of the Muslim community in Tamil Nadu. The Muslim community was mobilized at various fronts in order to protect and affirm their identity. There were criticisms within the community for the emergence of extremist forces among the Muslims in Tamil Nadu since the demolition of Babri Majid. Their relations and equations since the Coimbatore riots have considerably altered with the majority Tamil Hindu community. The new phase of Muslims identity politics has been multitasking in Tamil Nadu, where they have to prove the solidarity with the Tamil society and maintain the religious order among them. Apart from that, Muslims have to respond to Hindutva politics at state and national levels. At the political level, the IUML became the unitary voice of the Muslims, in spite of the discontent of the Muslim community against the IUML for not addressing their interest and problems adequately. The IUML was criticized for being subservient to the whims of the Dravidian parties. Moreover, there was an effort to rebuild the party to effectively address the aspirations of the community. This process represents the major political currents among the Muslims of Tamil Nadu.

## NEOLIBERAL ECONOMY AND MUSLIMS

As the 1990s are considered as an era of religious fundamentalism, terrorism coinciding with Mandal–Masjid–Mandir politics, when the political instability at the Centre and its new economic policies and structural readjustment started affecting governance, the political representation of Muslims and other minorities had been abysmal during those years. The sociocultural and political spheres were largely filled with the discourse and counter-discourse on terrorism and liberalization, privatization and globalization. The Muslims in Tamil Nadu have been engaged in the maritime trade with the West Asian and Southeast Asian countries for many centuries, and migration to these countries has resulted in immense social transformation in their life. Tamil Muslim migrants to Southeast Asia found several different means such as mosques, associations, publishing houses, bookshops and periodicals through which they could express their being and become a collective.[27] The neoliberal economy came into existence in the 1990s, just after the Gulf War of 1989. Many hundreds of Muslim men in Tamil Nadu preferred to work in the West Asian and Southeast Asian countries due to the employment opportunities and remuneration which had been an attractive factor for the lower-level employment seekers. The neoliberal economy also has created a huge gap between the rich and the poor in general and the private players have become the sources of employment. Religious fundamentalism and terrorism in relation to the neoliberal economic policy have been linked with Muslims in many parts of India, affecting their employment prospects. The factors which have pushed the Tamil Muslims in large numbers to find jobs in the West Asian and Southeast Asian countries were highlighted by Mohammad Shafi Qureshi by compiling findings from the Justice Rajinder Sachar Committee and Ranganath Misra Commission reports, which observed that 'The participation of Muslims in salaried jobs, both in the public and the private sectors, is quite low; in regular jobs in urban areas is quite limited.'[28] When it compared to the SCs/Scheduled Tribes (STs), 'a significantly larger proportion of Muslims are engaging in small proprietary enterprises and their participation in formal sector employment is considerably less than the national average'.[29] Moreover, Muslim women 'doing work within their own homes is much larger (70%) than for all workers (51%)'.[30] The reflections of social exclusion attributed by the Muslims to the neoliberal economic policy had significant outcomes in terms of employment, as employers were perceived to be excluding the Muslims from the private sector due to low preferences.

---

[27] Refer to S. M. A. K. Fakhri, 'Print Culture amongst Tamils and Tamil Muslims in South East Asia, c.1860–1960' (working paper no. 167, Madras Institute of Development Studies, Chennai, 2002).

[28] Mohammed Shafi Qureshi, 'Compilation of Justice Rajinder Sachar Committee and Ranganath Mishra Commission Reports' (July 2010). Available at: http://14.139.60.153/bitstream/123456789/317/1/Doc-COMPILATION%20OF%20MAIN%20OBSERVATIONS%20AND%20RECOMMENDATIONS%20MADE%20BY%20JUSTICE%20SACHAR%20COMMITTEE%20AND%20JUSTICE%20RANGANATH%20MISHRA%20COMMISSION.pdf

[29] Ibid.

[30] Ibid.

The Coimbatore serial bomb blasts in 1998 altered the perception of Muslim identity politics within and outside. It had also posed a serious challenge for the Dravidian politics, as both the principal Dravidian parties, the DMK and AIADMK, had to resort to pre-electoral alliance with the BJP in 1998 and 1999. This caused the representation of Muslims to rise in all other parties in Tamil Nadu. This crucial juncture helped the Muslims in Tamil Nadu to introspect and ascertain the fallacies in their own politics. Then the shift took place from representation to reservation. It was understood that because of the changing political climate against the minorities, particularly Muslims, focusing too much on communal issues would derail the social emancipatory politics and cause further political setbacks for them. The new sociopolitical movements had therefore raised the voice for representation in the constitutional bodies and social justice through reservations in employment and education. TMMK took up this issue of separate reservations for Muslims as a single-point agenda, organized hundreds of public meetings, conferences and agitations across the state, and mobilized the Muslims in general and the youth in particular on this issue.

## CONCLUSION: FROM REPRESENTATION TO RESERVATION

There are many intricacies in dealing with representation in legislature and Parliament, which is primarily based on electoral prospects of the political parties with whom the Muslims are allying. The popular views on Muslims becoming critical, and the natural challenge posed to the majority and minority questions, have caused shifts in the secular ideology of the major political parties. Since the caste-based parties are on the rise in Tamil Nadu, the emergence of Muslim identity-based parties is indispensable. The Muslim political parties had to participate in negotiations with the principal Dravidian and national parties. Sometimes the electoral prospects of the major parties could affect their chances and vice versa. Taking all these into consideration, the TMMK chose to fight for the reservations for Muslims in the state.

As social justice had been the core ideology of the Dravidian movement, the DMK restructured the reservation policy time and again in favour of the backward castes. In the 1970s, the DMK government under the chief ministership of M. Karunanidhi appointed the Sattanathan Commission to look into the possibilities to include some of the marginalized communities in backward castes itself. Then Muslims were brought under the Backward Castes category. This was the first step towards the social inclusion policy to place them in the state institutions. Also, there were initiatives during the Mandal Commission implementation days at the national level, which pushed the agenda for separate reservations for Muslims. There were efforts to raise the demand for reservation for Muslims by the political class (Syed Shahabuddin and Ebrahim Sulaiman Sait, MPs of the Janata Dal and Muslim League), academic scholars (Saiyid Hamid, Former Vice-Chancellor of Aligarh Muslim University) and personalities of civil society organizations like Maulana Mohammad Shafi Moonis (Vice-President of the All India Muslim Majlis-e-Mushawarat), who have founded an Association for Promoting Education and Employment of Muslims. The association organized a convention to discuss and explore the possibilities of reservation for Muslims in New Delhi on 9 October 1994. It can be interpreted that after Mandal agitations and its verdict, the Congress government at the Centre headed by P. V. Narasimha Rao revived its stand on 'reservation for OBCs', but due to economic and political instability during his period the social policies were not given importance. Sitaram Kesri, a senior leader who belonged to an OBC caste in the Congress party and Minister for Social Welfare in the Union Cabinet, 'stated the case for Muslim reservations before the convention, with the tacit consent of the Rao government, on grounds of economic, social and educational backwardness'.[31]

As the Mandal Commission was completely about the OBCs and their politics of reservations led to a new OBC uprise, particularly in the northern states, it did not listen to the voices of Muslims when considering the reservations for Muslims. Because of the Mandal Commission recommendations, the debate on social justice, economic inequality and social backwardness resurfaced. From 1996, there was political instability at the Centre as the BJP led the coalition government with the AIADMK alliance in 1998 and with the DMK during 1999–2004. During this period, the debates over the minorities led to many political and social insights for the opposition parties such as the

---

[31] Refer to Theodore P. Wright Jr, 'A New Demand for Muslim Reservation in India', *Asian Survey* 37, no. 9 (September 1997): 853.

Congress, the Left parties and the DMK. The initiative taken first by the erstwhile Andhra Pradesh state government to reserve 5 per cent jobs for the Backward Muslims renewed the debate on reservations. All those who stand for reservation for Dalits, tribes and backward classes have supported this measure. Ram Vilas Paswan has always supported reservation for Dalits in private industries. Lalu Prasad Yadav too extended his support along with Karunanidhi of Tamil Nadu. Even BJP ally and former Chief Minister of Andhra Pradesh, N. Chandrababu Naidu, has endorsed the reservation. The TDP itself had promised 3 per cent reservation for Muslims in its manifesto for Lok Sabha elections in which the BJP had not objected to it at all.[32] Then the 2004 general elections resulted in a new scope for understanding the issues of Muslims through the appointment of the Justice Sachar Committee to look into the socio-economic status of Muslims. The Sachar Committee hailed the Tamil Nadu model[33] for the inclusion of 95 per cent Muslims into Backward Castes. The Justice Ranganath Misra Commission's recommendations for 10 per cent reservation for Muslims gave a clear picture on how Muslims were excluded on various socio-economic fronts, and it gave the blueprint to frame policies towards their inclusion in all arenas. These two committees' recommendations have played a crucial role in the efforts by the Muslim leaders and parties in the state to negotiate with the major political parties. As in Tamil Nadu, the demand for separate reservations had been there for almost two decades, raised by the TMMK, which mobilized the Muslim youth, women and poor. It organized more than 20 rallies across the state and convened more than 10 state-level conferences to sensitize their cadre and community as a whole. Later, all other prominent political outfits such as the IUML and Tamil Nadu Thowheed Jamath started taking up this demand for reservations to discussions in public and in the political arena. The Sachar Committee had provided valuable data to justify their demand. The TMMK took up this issue for strengthening their electoral prospects by allying with the AIADMK in 2001 and the DMK in 2006. The TMMK made the AIADMK constitute a

---

[32] Refer to Asghar Ali Engineer, 'Reservation for Muslims', *Economic & Political Weekly* 39, no. 36 (4–10 September 2004): 3984–3985.

[33] Refer to Sachar Commission Report, *Social, Economic and Educational Status of Muslim Communities in India*, Prime Minister High Level Committee (New Delhi: Government of India, 2006), 218.

body to look into their demand in 2003, which was considered as half success with Jayalalithaa who had never shown any interest in terms of reservations. The bargaining politics worked out very well when there was a relevance to consider the demand from Muslims. In 2006, the DMK came to power with the alliance of the Congress, PMK, CPI(M) and CPI. The 2006–2011 term of the DMK could be interpreted as the 'renewal of social justice' in principle, headed by M. Karunanidhi, who had been consistently restructuring the reservations time and again within the framework of social justice ideology. During his tenure, he appointed Justice M. S. Janarthanam to look into the demand for separate reservations for Muslims and also Arunthathiyars, a socially and economically weaker section and third largest sub-caste among Dalits in Tamil Nadu. The Reservation Act is based on the recommendations of the State Backward Classes Commission headed by Justice M. S. Janarthanam.[34] The quest for separate reservations attained reality in 2007 by implementing it in its proper spirit. About 90 per cent of Muslims and 75 per cent of Christians in the state already figured in the Backward Castes list.[35] While explaining the relevance and justifying the procedures followed on the basis of political consensus, Chief Minister M. Karunanidhi hailed the move 'on this revolutionary day in the history of social justice'.[36] There were consistent representation from the minority communities for reservation within the Backward Castes for long time prior to Mandal Commission recommendations. Even after most of the Muslims and Christians had been brought under the Backward Castes list, it could not percolate further beyond the dominant backward castes. So it had been decided for providing separate reservations for them in admissions to educational institutions and appointment to government service 'as they could not compete with other communities' in the Backward Castes list 'to their legitimate share'.[37] A precarious condition that has been existing in Tamil Nadu is that about 69 per cent of the reservation faced obstacles while being categorized under social and educational backwardness groups so as to

---

[34] See S. Viswanathan, 'A Step Forward', *Frontline* 24, no. 22 (3–17 November). Available at: https://frontline.thehindu.com/other/article30193437.ece (accessed on 25 August 2020).
[35] Ibid.
[36] Ibid.
[37] Ibid.

expand the benefits of the reservation further. But the DMK which approached the reservation within the framework of social justice in its entire political carrier, as a founding principle of the party, 'making the 3.5 percent share a sub-quota in the reservation for Backward Classes is to ensure that the overall reservations do not exceed the existing 69 percent'.[38] The DMK categorically made it clear to avoid the religious question on its principle of social justice that 'this model of "reservations within reservations" is not based on religion but on the educational and economic backwardness of the minority communities.'[39]

The government passed the order for the implementation of the reservation on 15 September 2007 in *The Gazette*.[40] So the Muslim identity politics balanced the question of representation, which is political, and determined by the electoral prospects and simultaneously as a long-term strategy to raise the standard of living of Muslims and their participation in the state education and employment avenues made their demand for reservations successfully achieved social justice as a constitutional remedy (Figures 1 and 2).

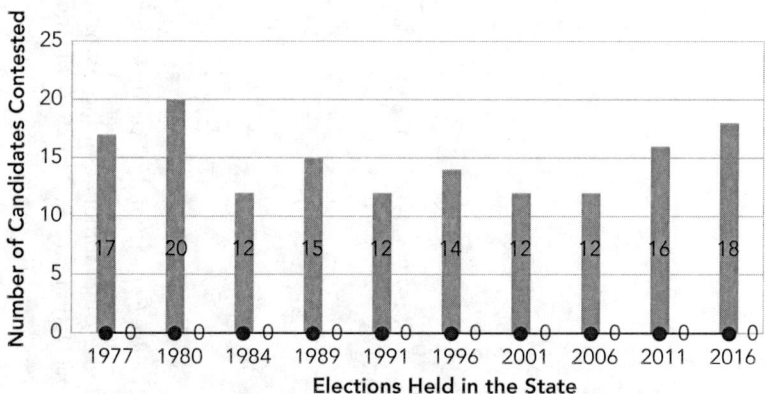

**Figure 9.1** *Muslims in Tamil Nadu's Electoral Politics*

*Source:* Compiled by the author referring Statistical Reports of General Elections and the Legislative Assembly of Tamil Nadu from 1977 to 2016. Election Commission of India, New Delhi. www.eci.gov.in

---

[38] Ibid.
[39] Ibid.
[40] Tamil Nadu Government Gazette Extraordinary, Chennai, Saturday, 15 September 2007, 129–133.

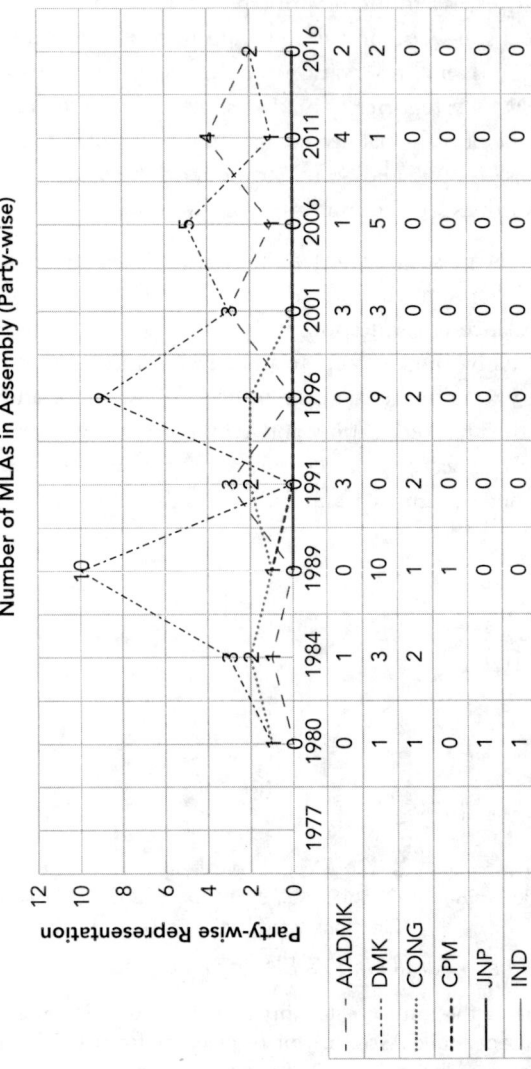

**Figure 9.2** *Party-wise Representation of Muslims in Tamil Nadu Legislative Assembly (Declining Trend)*

*Source:* Compiled by the author referring Statistical Reports of General Elections and the Legislative Assembly of Tamil Nadu from 1977 to 2016. Election Commission of India, New Delhi. www.eci.gov.in

# BIBLIOGRAPHY

Ahmad, Imtiaz. 'Muslim Educational Backwardness: An Inferential Analysis'. *Economic & Political Weekly* 16, no. 36 (5 September 1981).

———. 'Threats and Responses: Conversions in Tamil Nadu'. *Economic & Political Weekly* 17, no. 43 (23 October 1982): 1737–1739.

Ali, Syed. 'Collective and Elective Ethnicity: Caste among Urban Muslims in India'. *Sociological Forum* 17, no. 4 (December 2002): 593–620.

Ansari, Iqbal A. *Political Representation of Muslims in India 1952–2004* (New Delhi: Manak Publications, 2006).

Copland, Ian. 'The Princely States, the Muslim League and the Partition of India in 1947'. *The International History Review* 13, no. 1 (February 1991): 38–69.

Engineer, Asghar Ali. 'Muslims, BJP and Lok Sabha Elections'. *Economic & Political Weekly* 33, no. 6 (7–13 February 1998).

Hasan, Zoya. 'Reservation for Muslims'. *Seminar* 549 (2005).

———. *Politics of Inclusion: Castes, Minorities and Affirmative Action* (New Delhi: Oxford University Press, 2011).

Jaffrelot, Christophe. *Religion, Caste and Politics in India* (New Delhi: Primus Books, 2017).

Judge, Paramjit S., ed. *Mapping Social Exclusion in India: Caste, Religion and Borderlands* (New Delhi: Cambridge University Press, 2014).

Krishnan, P. S. 'Understanding the Backward Classes of Muslim Society'. *Economic & Political Weekly* 45, no. 34 (21–27 August 2010).

Mathew, George. 'Politicisation of Religion: Conversion to Islam in Tamil Nadu'. *Economic & Political Weekly* 17, no. 25 (19 June 1982): 1027–1034.

Pandian, M. S. S. *Brahmin and Non-Brahmin: Genealogies of the Tamil Political Present* (New Delhi: Permanent Black, 2007).

Robinson, Francis. 'The British Empire and Muslim Identity in South Asia'. *Transactions of the Royal Historical Society* 8 (1998): 271–289.

Shah, Ghanshyam. 'The Conditions of Muslims'. *Economic & Political Weekly* 42, no.10 (10–16 March 2007).

Subramanian, T. S. 'Behind the Coimbatore Tragedy'. *Frontline* 15 (5 March 1998). Available at: https://frontline.thehindu.com/cover-story/article30160948.ece (accessed on 25 August 2020).

———. 'New Alignments in Tamil Nadu'. *Frontline* 16, no. 13 (19 June–2 July 1999).

Wells, Ian Byrant. *Jinnah's Early Politics: Ambassador of Hindu–Muslim Unity* (New Delhi: Permanent Black, 2005).

Wright, Theodore P., Jr. 'Muslims and the 1977 Indian Election: A Watershed?' *Asian Survey* 17, no. 12 (December 1977).

# Chapter 10

# Caste, Ideology and Hegemony in Indian Media
## A Critical Inquiry

### Manoj Kumar Jena

### INTRODUCTION

Media as a part of our culture and consciousness has played an important role in our social life; it can be seen as important to our communicative process, which is a large part of our social structure. It has a substantial demonstrative power, which can be exerted and exercised through control of communicative message and meaning. Those who control media hyperbolize and also use the power to subjugate the people who are powerless. It is a well-accepted fact that communication is the foundation of our societal structure; not a single social system will survive without a communicative process, and hence it is an embedded aspect of our social milieu. Seth Siegelaub argues,

> Communication = exchange. Its development, the multiplication of its forms is the foundation and signs, products and producers, of both collective and individual development. The increase in the quantity and especially, the quality, of these exchanges is at the heart of the

advancement of society, one of the principal marks of social progress, the basis of true liberation, whether national, regional, local or individual.[1]

Precisely, many commentators argue that the media does play a dominant role in the society. As a matter of fact, media is central to our everyday life activities; whether we accept it or reject it, we cannot ignore it. This can be viewed as an effect, and the impact of media is multifaceted and complex on individual, community and society at large. In India, the media activities are associated with various complex factors and varying social forces. In order to understand the media and its functional and structural dynamics in India, it is essential to study caste ideology and its relationship with media system/structure. It is argued that the caste ideology, that is, the representation of a particular caste in media, does influence the production and distribution of the message. Indeed it is the upper-caste/class ideas and ideology that get substantially disseminated through existing mainstream media. In a critical sense, the dominant media system reproduces social relations of domination, subordination and exploitation and further deliberates exclusion in the society at large. It further shapes a hegemonic system in the meaning-making structure.

In this chapter, an attempt is made to unravel the critical aspect of media systems in India and its relationship with caste ideology and hegemony in terms of production, control and dissemination of message and meaning. The Indian media system has always been dominated by upper-caste/class ideologies. These ideologies are consistently celebrated and cultivated in news media, television (TV), soap opera, cinema and visual and print news media. Media commemorates upper-caste/class cultural life and denigrates the lower-caste/class cultural essence. This is an undeniable fact that media does play an ideological role in terms of production of content and message. Furthermore, the acceptance and rejection of content can be understood from the production, reproduction and

---

[1] Armand Mattelart and Seth Siegelaub, eds., *Communication and Class Struggle: Liberation, Socialism* (New York, NY: International General, 1980).

dissemination of message among the audiences, whether the audience is a passive receiver or an active receiver. This chapter argues that there is a direct link between caste structure and political economy of production of media content. Moreover, it is also essential to understand how the relations of power and domination are encoded and operated in Indian media. This chapter also tries to unwind the critical aspect of Indian media and its relationship with caste ideology, primarily hegemony of upper castes, where the media production, control and content are largely regulated by upper-caste/class ideologies.

The chapter is divided into three segments. The first segment focuses on the issue of intricacy of media and discusses the historical genesis of media industry and its complexities. The second segment is centred around the theoretical analysis of the question of caste ideology and reproduction of content. The third and last segment discusses the question of caste hegemony and lack of representation of lower caste in the media industry. The chapter is based on the analysis of secondary literature and theoretical insights.

## INTRICACY OF MEDIA

The intricacy of media can be understood by studying the emergence of media as a complex as well as dominant system in our social world. Media encompasses all forms of medium including print, cinema, electronic media as well as digital platforms. Owing to the proliferation of various kinds of technologies, from simple to complex networks, the media indeed has become more diverse and complex. Historically, the emergence of media as an important dominant system is very complex and it is connected with various events and occurrences of innovations. The discovery of paper and invention of printing press led to the growth of media in a more organized form, which later positioned itself as a consequential institution in the society. Print technology was introduced in the mid-15th century, which had replaced handwriting to production of text through machine and initiated a stride towards the emergence of a media institution.[2] Suddenly, there was a substantial

---

[2] Danis Macquil, *Mass Communication Theory*, 4th ed. (London: SAGE Publications: 2000).

transformation, which happened in terms of printing and publishing. Over a period of time, print had become a new craft and crucial part of commerce.[3]

The initial phase of commodification of printing material took place in Europe, America and the rest of the world. Because of systematic development of technologies in the 19th century, cinema emerged as an important medium of communication and business. Similarly, TV evolved as a new form of communication system, and massification of media content became popular among the larger public from the early 20th century onwards, where media was considered a vital force for social transformation. Modern communication in India evolved early with printing of newspapers in different languages. Over a period of time, initially print, then cinema and later on TV took shape in popular sociocultural imagination. It is an undeniable fact that the Industrial Revolution as well as modern technological innovation contributed immensely to the growth of the modern mass communication system. Media has become a more and more integral part of our all-organizational activities. Media including print, film and TV became associated with our culture, and it became a part and parcel of our social structure. It is not only associated with political, economic, educational and religious organizations, but it also directly and indirectly influences the way in which we imagine and perceive our social world. George Gerbner argues, 'Mass production and distribution of message systems transforms selected private perspectives into broad public perspectives and brings mass publics into existence.'[4] At the same time, media significantly influences our behavioural pattern and plays a consequential role in individual mind, body and soul. Simultaneously, cinema and TV have significant impacts on our cognitive level. The image and content of cinema have strong intrinsic effects on us. As Gilles Deleuze argues, 'The cinema does not just present images, it surround them with world.'[5]

---

[3] Febverse L. Martin, *Coming of the Book* (London: Verso, 1984).

[4] George Gerbner, 'Mass Media Discourse: Message System Analysis as a component of Cultural Indicator', in *Discourse and Communication*, ed. Teun A. van Dijk (Berlin: Walter de Guyter & Co., 1985).

[5] Gilles Deleuz, *Cinema 2: The Time-Image* (Minneapolis, MN: University of Minnesota Press, 1989).

Likewise, Roger Silverstone argues, 'We need to think about television as a psychological, social and cultural form, as well as an economic and political one. We need to think about the medium as more than just a source of influence, neither simply benign nor malignant. We need to think about television as embedded in the multiple discourses of everyday life'.[6] Raymond Williams also illustrates,

> Television was invented as a result of scientific and technical research. Its power as a medium of news and entertainment was then so great that it altered all preceding media of news and entertainment. It altered many of our institutions and forms of social relationships.[7]

Cinema and TV may propagate a particular ideological message and significantly influence the audience's choice and preferences, comprehension and thinking.

As a matter of fact, in contemporary scenario, it would be difficult to nullify the very essence of the critical social function of media system in our everyday life. In present-day world order, it is a well-established fact that media is an important institution in our society; it is part of the fundamental social functions comprising transmission of cultural values and socializing individuals, and it helps community members to maintain an integrative cooperation within the society. According to P. F. Lazarsfeld and R. K. Merton,

> The mass media confers status on public issues, persons, organisations and social movements. The mass media bestows prestige and enhances the authority of individuals and groups by legitimising their status. This status-conferral function thus enters organised social action by legitimising selected policies, persons and groups which receive the support of mass media.[8]

---

[6] Roger Silverstone, *Television and Everyday Life* (New York, NY: Routledge, 1994).

[7] Williams, Raymond. *Television Technology and Cultural Form* (New York, NY: Routledge, 2003).

[8] Lazarsfeld P. F. and R. K. Merton R. K., 'Mass Communication, Popular Taste and Organized Social Action', in *Mass Culture: Popular Arts in America*, eds. B. Rosenberg and D. M. White (New York, NY: The Free Press, 1948).

Media has a profound effect on our societal structure and function; hence, it is vital to comprehend the ideological operation of media which cannot be negated. In the background of this ideology, John Storey argues,

> First, ideology can refer to a systematic body of ideas articulated by a particular group of people. Secondly, Ideology is used here to indicate how some texts and practices present distorted images of reality. Thirdly Ideology uses the term refer to 'ideological form'. This usage is intended to draw attention to the way in which texts always present a particular image of the world. This definition depends on a notion of society as conflictual rather than consensual, structured around inequality, exploitation and oppression.[9]

Media has more or less manifested its actions through economic structure, ideological power, selection/deletion of contents, etc. The media system can be viewed as a liberating force from subjugation, but from alternative lenses one can view it as an exploitative force because of its dominant form, which is linked with various exploitative processes. To understand this nitty-gritty, we will now analyse the role of relationship among ideology, caste and media.

## IDEOLOGY, CASTE AND MEDIA

This chapter uses caste as an ideological apparatus, which is borrowed from the idea of ideological state apparatus of Althusser. This segment argues on how the caste ideology and media are interlinked with each other and form a dominant ideological apparatus.

> An Ideological State Apparatus is a system of defined institutions, organizations, and the corresponding practices. The Ideological State Apparatuses function primarily on ideology.... The object of the politics of the class in power and of the State Ideology (dominant ideology = ideology of the dominant class) is to guarantee the conditions for the

---

[9] John Storey, *Cultural Theory and Popular Culture: An Introduction* (Oxon: Routledge, 2018).

exploitation of the exploited classes by the dominant classes, above all the reproduction of the relations of production in which this exploitation takes place, since these relations of production are the relations of exploitation of the class social formation under consideration.[10]

The ideological power of the upper castes in the media can be seen as part of the exclusionary and repressive apparatus for socio-economic weaker sections such as the Other Backward Castes, Scheduled Castes and Scheduled Tribes. In the Marxian sense,

> The class which has the means of material production at its disposal has control at the same time over the means of mental production, so that thereby, generally speaking, the ideas of those who lack the means of mental production are subject to it.[11]

Many a time the upper caste controls both material production and mental production systems in India. In fact, the domination of upper castes in media activities signifies their supremacy over the larger public culture, which itself determines and functions in a particular way to commence a sort of hegemony in the public sphere. In a sense, it can be viewed as legitimization of upper caste norms and values in the operation of public culture. In this context, it is essential to apprehend how the caste-centric socio-economic conditions are associated with the production of meaning. According to the Marxian point of view, 'Ideology of dominant system serves to reproduce social relations of domination, subordination and further exclusion.' Gramsci is also critical about the bourgeois newspaper and argues how the bourgeois newspaper is serving dominant-class ideas and negating the working class.

> The worker must resolutely reject any solidarity with a bourgeois newspaper and so everything that is published is influenced by one idea: that of serving the dominant class. Every day this same worker is able to

---

[10] Louis Althusser, *On The Reproduction Of Capitalism: Ideology And Ideological State Apparatuses* (New York, NY: Verso, 2014).

[11] Marx, K. and Engles, G., *The German Ideology*, (New Delhi: The Peoples Publishing House(P)Ltd, 2010), 67.

personally see that the bourgeois newspapers tell even the simplest of facts in a way that favours the bourgeois class and damns the working class and its politics.[12]

Chomsky also argues, 'The propaganda model shows how the media serve the interests of state and corporate power, which are closely interlinked, framing their reporting and analysis in a manner supportive of established privilege and limiting debate and discussion accordingly.'[13] It is evident that there is a substantial control of dominant caste/class in media industry and content.

In this context, it is further necessary to understand the relationship among production, control and dissemination of message among larger audiences. Stuart Hall argues, 'Of course, the production process is framed throughout by meanings and ideas: knowledge in-use concerning the routines of production, technical skills, professional ideologies, institutional knowledge, definitions and assumptions, assumptions about audience, etc. frame the passage of the program through this production structure.'[14]

The content and message are produced with a hegemonic caste ideology. The lower caste is a passive receiver of the massage which is produced by the upper castes and is antithetical to their social reality. The primacy of upper-caste/class domination and the monopoly and control of editorial content reproduce the dominant culture, which negates the alternative culture of meanings. The socially and economically weaker sections of the society, essentially lower castes including Schedule Castes and Other Backward Castes, lack the representation of production of content; hence, they are subject to consumption of

---

[12] https://www.marxists.org/archive/gramsci/1916/12/newspaperchapters.htm (accessed on 11 November 19).

[13] See N. Ram, *The Changing Role of the News Media in Contemporary India*, Indian History Congress, 72nd Session. Available at: https://www.thehindu.com/multimedia/archive/00863/Contemporary_India__863821a.pdf (accessed on 25 August 2020).

[14] Stuart Hall, 'Encoding and Decoding in the Television Discourse' (CCCS Stencilled paper no. 7, Centre for Cultural Studies, University of Birmingham, Birmingham, 1973).

false content and message. Media has always propagated the upper-caste/class ideology and value, which disregard and ignore alternative diversity and commemorate upper-caste value and norms. On the whole, the media system operates with a particular interest which controls the entire symbolic system, message and meaning to propagate a particular worldview. What Herbert Marcuse argues as emergence of 'one-dimensional thought' is as follows:

> The irresistible output of the entertainment and information industry carry with them prescribed attitudes and habits, certain intellectual and emotional reactions which bind the consumers more or less pleasantly to the producers and, through the latter, to the whole. The products indoctrinate and manipulate; they promote a false consciousness, which is immune against its falsehood. And as these beneficial products become available to more individuals in more social classes, the indoctrination they carry ceases to be publicity; it becomes a way of life. Thus emerges a pattern of one-dimensional thought and behaviour in which ideas, aspirations, and objectives that, by their content, transcend the established universe of discourse and action are either repelled or reduced to terms of this universe.[15]

The dominance of the upper caste or class in the media industry is a well-accepted phenomenon in India. Primarily, the upper castes have monopolized the control and production of editorial content. For instance, a study conducted by Oxfam India, entitled 'Who Tells Our Stories Matter: Representation of Marginalised Caste Groups in Indian Newsrooms', in August 2019 reveals how the Indian media is predominantly represented by the upper castes, that is, Brahmins, Kshatriyas and Vaishyas.[16] This is a significant study because it selected six English and seven Hindi newspapers based on their ranking in the Indian Readership Survey of 2018. Simultaneously, it also included 7 English and as many Hindi TV news channels, 11 digital media outlets

---

[15] H. Marcuse, *One-Dimensional Man*, 2nd ed. (Routledge, 2002).

[16] Oxfam India, 'Who Tells Our Stories Matters: Representation of Marginalised Caste Groups in Indian Newsroom', 2 August 2019. Available at: https://www.oxfamindia.org/press-release/who-tells-our-stories-matters-representation-marginalised-caste-groups-indian-newsrooms (accessed on 25 August 2020).

and 12 magazines covering diverse topics from politics, business, culture and sports.[17]

As per another study conducted by the Media Study Group in collaboration with the Centre for the Study of Developing Societies (CSDS) in 2006, largely 90 per cent upper castes are decision-makers in the English-language print media and 79 per cent in TV channels. The study has tried to find out social backgrounds of 315 key decision-makers in 37 English- and Hindi-language publications and TV channels. It argues that majority of media are represented by upper-caste males. It is a well-accepted fact that lower castes are missing from mainstream English and Hindi media. Now, in this context, it is essential to discuss the question of caste and representation in the Indian media.

## MEDIA, CASTE HEGEMONY AND REPRESENTATION

The idea about hegemony is associated with power, in Gramscian point of view, it can be social power or economic power, and in this context we can see it as media power. Media power can be interlinked with caste ideology and become ideological power to exercise and promote particular caste-vested interest to subjugate others. It can further be seen as a cultural power to control the unconscious and conscious mind.

Ideological hegemony can be seen as an instrument through which a particular caste fulfils its predominant needs to exercise control and command. In a real sense, when the upper caste controls the media industry on the basis of their representable numbers, in such case they do control the cultural meaning produced by the media content. In such a situation, embedded ideological flavour of their upper-caste dominance designs false equilibrium in the social structure, which is antithetical to liberation from sufferings of the lower caste.

Hence, the questions of ideology, hegemony and representation are interconnected with each other. Therefore, it is essential to discuss the question of representation of lower castes in the Indian media. Representation is always concerned with how identities are constructed,

---

[17] Ibid.

and the construction of identities has an impact on the cognitive development of the audience. In fact, the question of representation in media can be deciphered from the absence and presence of caste or class ideology. Stuart Hall argues, 'Representation is a very different notion from that of reflection. It implies the active work of selecting, and presenting, of structuring and shaping: not merely the transmitting of already existing meaning, but the more active labour of making things mean.'[18]

B. R. Ambedkar was always concerned about the representation of the backward community in the media. He also recognized the critical nature of the media for political goals:

> There is the ignorance of our own people, who do not know the critical nature of the times we are living in and who do not know the value of organisation for achieving our political objects. There is a lamentable lack of resources at our command. We have no money. We have no press. The cruelest of tyrannies and oppressions, to which our people are subjected, day in and day out all over India, are never reported by the Press. Even our views on social and political questions are systematically suppressed by an organised conspiracy on the part of the Press.[19]

Ambedkar further went on to question the representation of the Scheduled Castes in the press. He argued,

> The Untouchables have no Press. The Congress Press is closed to them and is determined not to give them the slightest publicity. They cannot have their own Press and for obvious reasons. No paper can survive without advertisement revenue. Advertisement revenue can come only from business and in India all business, both high and small, is attached to the Congress and will not favour any Non-Congress organisation. The staff of the Associated Press in India, which is the main news distributing agency in India, is entirely drawn from the Madras Brahmins—indeed the whole of the Press in India is in their

---

[18] S. Hall, 'The Question of Cultural Identity', in *Modernity and Its Futures*, eds. S. Hall, D. Held, and T. McGrew (Cambridge: Polity Press, in association with the Open University, 1992).

[19] Vasant Moon, *Dr. Babasaheb Ambedkar Writings and Speeches,* vol. 9 (New Delhi: Dr. Ambedkar Foundation, 2014), 440.

hands and they, for well-known reasons, are entirely pro-Congress and will not allow any news hostile to the Congress to get publicity. These are reasons beyond the control of the Untouchables.[20]

Similarly, Kanshi Ram was also critical about the media and declared the media as Manuwadi for not carrying news items related to the achievements of Dalits and Dalit movements.[21] He was convinced about the power of media for the development of the Bahujan movement and therefore launched *Bahujan Nayak* and *Bahujan Sangathak* weekly papers in Marathi and Hindi.[22] The question of representation in media has always bothered many media practitioners as well as scholars. In Kenneth J. Cooper's article 'India's Majority Lower Castes Are Minor Voice in Newspapers' published in *The Washington Post* on 5 September 1996, he asserts, 'India's 4,000 daily newspapers publish in nearly 100 languages, but one voice is largely absent in the press of the world's largest democracy: that of the lower castes, which account for more than 70 percent of the country's 934 million people.'[23] Similarly, B. N. Uniyal highlighted this gap in the article titled 'In Search of a Dalit Journalist', published in *The Pioneer* newspaper on 16 November 1996. In his narrative of the missing Dalit journalist, he says,

> Suddenly, I realized that in all the 30 years I had worked as a journalist I had never met a fellow journalist who was a Dalit; no, not one. And worse still was the thought that … it had never occurred to me that there was something so seriously amiss in the profession….'[24]

The Media Study Group in collaboration with the CSDS survey notes that Dalits and Adivasis 'are conspicuous by their absence among

---

[20] Ibid., 440.
[21] Vivek Kumar, 'Locating Dalit Women in the Indian Caste System, Media and Women's Movement', *Social Change* 39, no. 1 (March 2009): 64–84.
[22] Vivek Kumar, 'Indian Media and Its Role in the Empowerment of Dalits', *Communicator* 12 (January–March 2006).
[23] https://www.washingtonpost.com/archive/politics/1996/09/05/indias-majority-lower-castes-are-minor-voice-in-newschapters/4acb79e3-13d6-4084-b1d9-b09c6ed4f963/ (accessed on 15 December 2019).
[24] B. N. Uniyal, 'In Search of a Dalit Journalist', *The Pioneer*, 16 November 1996, 0.

the decision-makers. Not even one of the 315 key decision-makers belonged to the Scheduled Castes or Scheduled Tribes'.[25]

From Robin Jeffrey's point of view, Indian-language dailies have failed to report various aspects of Dalit life, which is evident from the fact that not a single Dalit (including men and women) is in an editorial position.[26] It is also true that the critical aspect of Dalit lives is not represented adequately, which is problematic for the larger Indian democratic structure.

In the context of recruitment in media houses, Balasubramaniam narrates his own experience of an interview in a media organization. He tells the story of discrimination in media houses; he tells how a person belonging to a Scheduled Caste is treated differently in media agencies. He further argues,

> [The] informal factors like journalist networks may influence the recruitment process. The reality of Dalit absence in Indian media shows the inattention of managements in the media to the social diversity of the editorial desk. It has been reproducing the social prejudice in the content of the media for the last 60 years.[27]

Balasubramaniam's story depicts how the media industry practises the notion of discrimination in terms of caste. This is indeed a visible instance of caste hegemony in media houses. Eighty-nine per cent of the leadership positions across seven English TV news channels including the leading channels were held by upper-caste journalists and none by the members of the Scheduled Castes, Scheduled Tribes or Other Backward Castes.[28]

In fact, in the context of caste domination, Sudipto Mondal, an investigative journalist, asserted, 'Indian media wants Dalit news but

---

[25] *The Hindu*, 'Upper Castes Dominate National Media, Says Survey in Delhi', 5 June 2006.

[26] Robin Jeffrey, *India's Newspaper Revolution: Capitalism, Politics and the Indian-language Press* (New Delhi: Oxford University Press, 2003).

[27] J. Balasubramaniam, 'Dalits and a Lack of Diversity in the Newsroom', *Economic & Political Weekly* 46, no. 11 (12–18 March 2011).

[28] See Oxfam India, 'Who Tells Our Stories Matters'.

not Dalit reporters. Caste privilege and domination in newsrooms must end.'[29] Chaturvedi argues,

> Print capitalism serves the interest of the modern urban individuals who despite their claims for objectivity, secularism and egalitarianism can still maintain a caste identity for personal and political ends, without explicitly participating in caste practices, but by merely subscribing to a print commodity. The caste subcultures have amply used print culture to mobilise shared identities for their end.[30]

Similar instances are observable in the entertainment industry; private entertainment TV channels are predominately promoting upper-caste ideas and values, in terms of its content and production design, which is supplementing with upper-caste/class notion. Nearly very few channels are trying to challenge the caste hegemony and representing the essence of the weaker sections of the society.

Many a time it has been observed that traditional caste practices are reinforced in TV serials and Hindi movies, including portraying upper-caste cultural essence and caste stereotypes. In a certain sense, satellite TV and production houses and private channels tend to encourage upper-caste/class cultural content. The imagination of the content writer is shaped in a particular manner where they are pushing the idea of upper-caste language in cinematic and soap-opera expressions. In the context of the Indian cinema, Suraj Yengde argues,

> Mainstream Indian cinema is notoriously escapist, and many audiences attend it as a heavily invested time-pass activity in order to pass the time, while the darkness in the theatre offers a form of hiding from the pain of reality. Films tend to portray a dominant caste, offering subaltern subjects only a limited form of escapism; through cinema, Brahmans and allied castes have actively imposed their hegemony on the medium of mainstream cultural expression.[31]

---

[29] https://www.aljazeera.com/indepth/opinion/2017/05/indian-media-dalit-news-dalit-reporters-170523194045529.html (accessed on 14 December 2019).

[30] Sumit Chaturvedi, 'Caste Publications: The Space for Upper Case Subculture Politics', *Economic & Political Weekly* 49, no. 17 (26 April 2014): 33–37.

[31] Suraj Yengde, 'Dalit Cinema, South Asia', *Journal of South Asian Studies* 41, no. 3 (2018): 503–518.

Yengde further argues, 'Indian cinema is trapped in the modelling of caste-ego on screen by misdirecting reality into myth.'[32] Therefore, a prominent question which arises is: Who controls the production system?

The question of ownership consistently bothers us to know who owns the lion share of media in India.

As per the registrations of newspapers of India, the total number of registered publications, as on 31 March 2018 was 118,239, out of which 17,573 were newspapers and 100,666 were periodicals.[33] Although the numbers are rapidly increasing, the largest mainstream media industry is controlled by not many. In a sense, the production of media content and its distribution are becoming increasingly combined and, again, concentrated in the hands of a few.[34] There are also similar emerging tendencies of control and regulation in the case of FM radio stations and satellite TV channels including news websites.[35] The ownership model in the media industry may be viewed as a nexus between caste and capital; in fact, the caste and capital relationship has become blurred in terms of operational activities. The ownership of media has larger implication on audience; the ownership control of media can be viewed with caste and capital relationship. As we have discussed earlier, predominately Indian media is owned and controlled by the upper castes. Graham Murdock rightly argues that the increasing reach and power of the large communication corporations give a new urgency to the long-standing arguments about who controls them and whose interests they serve.[36] An imbalance in media ownership among India's castes leads to a narrow definition of the Indian culture, reinforcement

---

[32] Ibid.

[33] http://rni.nic.in/all_page/press_india.aspx (accessed on 28 May 2020).

[34] https://rsf.org/en/news/media-ownership-monitor-who-owns-media-india (accessed on 27 April 2020). For more details, please visit https://www.mom-rsf.org/

[35] Ibid.

[36] G. Murdock, 'Large Corporations and the Control of the Communications Industries', in *Culture, Society and the Media*, eds. M. Gurevitch, T. Bennett, J. Curran, and J. Woollacott (London: Routledge, 1982).

of negative stereotypes and perceptions of superiority and inferiority among different members of the society.[37]

From the above analysis, it becomes evident that the Indian media has failed to provide equal representation to the weaker sections of the society. The lack of representation is a major issue, which needs to be addressed properly.

## CONCLUSION

The media structure in India is much more upper-caste-centric in a sense that the lower castes are marginalized in the Indian media. On the basis of available literature, it is evident that the media industry fails to provide representation to socio-economically weaker sections of the society. The upper-caste hegemony is visible in every sphere of the Indian media industry. It is observed that since the very beginning of the media industry, the upper castes have occupied a dominant position of production of content, control of medium and dissemination of message in India. This is a well-accepted fact that Indian media is unable to provide equal opportunities to backward communities in content production activities. To a great extent, media houses are primarily fulfilling upper-caste/class essence and negating the existence of the weaker sections of the society. Further, the Indian media industry has somehow failed to encourage plurality and diversity in the newsroom. It is also evident that the media institutions in India are controlled and regulated by handful of individuals, and there is a nexus of caste and capital in the media industry. The command of a particular caste group can be seen as an ideological group controlling both cultural production and the public sphere. The caste ideology is further perpetuated and communicated through media to the larger audience. Also, it has been observed that contemporary media often negates the articulation of alternative messages, which challenges hierarchy, domination and subordination and rejects the fundamental principles of the caste system.

---

[37] https://mediaschool.indiana.edu/news-events/news/item.html?n=rao-discusses-indias-caste-system-and-its-influence-on-media (accessed on 27 April 2020).

The author of this chapter would like to thank Mr Sinthanaichelvan, Mr Eelavalavan, and Mr Arutchelvan for their interviews and for sharing the copies of documents relevant to the issues analyzed in this chapter.

## BIBLIOGRAPHY

Chomsky, Noam. *Necessary Illusions: Thought Control in Democratic Societies*. London: Pluto Press, 1989.

Gramsci, Antonio. Avanti! (Piedmont Edition; December 22, 1916); Available at: https://www.marxists.org/archive/gramsci/1916/12/newspapers.htm (accessed on 11 November 19).

Moon, Vasant, ed. *Dr. Babasaheb Ambedkar Writings and Speeches*. Vol. 1. New Delhi: Dr. Ambedkar Foundation, 2014.

# About the Editor and Contributors

### EDITOR

**R. Thirunavukkarasu** is currently Assistant Professor at the Department of Sociology, University of Hyderabad. He held brief teaching assignments at the Department of Sociology, Jamia Millia Islamia, New Delhi, and later at the Department of Sociology, Loyola College, Chennai. He also had short research assignments with the Centre for Culture, Media and Governance, Jamia Millia Islamia and later at the Lokniti Programme at the Centre for the Study of Developing Societies (CSDS), New Delhi. Before joining the University of Hyderabad, he was Associate Director, Institute of Human Rights Education, Madurai, Tamil Nadu. His doctoral research focused on the ideological conflicts within Tamil nationalism during the late colonial Madras Presidency. His current research focuses on the cultural economy of caste in contemporary Tamil Nadu.

### CONTRIBUTORS

**Shaileshkumar Darokar** is Associate Professor at the Centre for Study of Social Exclusion and Inclusive Policies, Tata Institute of Social Sciences, Mumbai.

**Amiya Kumar Das** is currently Associate Professor at the Department of Sociology, Tezpur University, Assam. He has co-edited *Investigating Developmentalism: Notions of Development in the Social Sphere* (2019) and *Neighbourhoods in Urban India: In Between Home and the City* (2021). His research interests include the areas of sociology of governance, development sociology, and sociology of health and illness. He also works as a coordinator of the Centre for Public Policy and Governance, Tezpur University, and is involved in organic farming.

**Tanweer Fazal** is currently Professor at the Department of Sociology, University of Hyderabad, Hyderabad. He previously taught at Jamia Millia Islamia, New Delhi, and Jawaharlal Nehru University, New Delhi. He is the author of *'Nation-State' and Minority Rights in India: Comparative Perspectives on Muslim and Sikh Identities* (2015), and the editor of *Minority Nationalisms in South Asia* (2012) and *The Minority Conundrum: Living in Majoritarian Times* (2019).

**Manoj Kumar Jena** is Associate Professor at the Centre for the Study of Social Systems, School of Social Sciences, Jawaharlal Nehru University, New Delhi. Previously, he taught at the Department of Sociology, Jamia Millia Islamia, New Delhi. His works broadly focus on sociology of media and industry.

**Karthick Ram Manoharan** was Assistant Professor of political science at the Centre for Studies in Social Sciences Calcutta (CSSSC) till July 2020. Since October 2020, he has been with the University of Wolverhampton as a Marie Skłodowska-Curie Actions Fellow. He is the author of *Frantz Fanon: Identity and Resistance (Literary/Cultural Theory)* (2019) and co-editor of *Rethinking Social Justice* (2020). He is currently researching on the political thought of Periyar E. V. Ramasamy.

**T. K. Oommen** is Professor Emeritus at the Centre for the Study of Social Systems, Jawaharlal Nehru University, New Delhi. He was awarded Padma Bhushan, the third highest Indian civilian award, by the President of India in 2008 for his services in the fields of education and literature. He was the 12th President of International Sociological Association (1990–1994).

**P. Ramajayam** is Assistant Professor, Centre for Study of Social Exclusion and Inclusive Policy, Bharathidasan University, Tiruchirappalli, Tamil Nadu. Currently, he is Principal (In-Charge), Bharathidasan University Constituent Arts and Science College, Nannilam, Tamil Nadu. He is also the State Coordinator of Lokniti-CSDS, New Delhi, to conduct surveys on elections and many other issues on farmers and state of democracy in South Asia in Tamil Nadu. He has contributed articles to *The Hindu* (Tamil and English), *The Indian Express* and peer-reviewed journals like *Economic & Political*

*Weekly* and chapters in books. Formerly, he was Sub-Editor in *India Today* (Tamil) magazine.

**C. Jerome Samraj** completed his PhD from Madras Institute of Development Studies, with the study entitled 'The Question of Land to the Dalits: A Historical Perspective', in which he has examined how caste as a social system has determined people's right to land during the pre-colonial, colonial and post-colonial periods. After his PhD, he worked as a Research Associate with the Institute for Financial and Management Research, where he was involved in several projects simultaneously and had done extensive fieldwork in the districts of Thanjavur, Thiruvarur, Madurai, Sivaganga, Virudhunagar, Tirunelveli and Thoothukudi. Since 2011, he has been Assistant Professor at the Department of Economics, Pondicherry University.

**Archana Singh** is Assistant Professor at G. B. Pant Social Science Institute, Allahabad. After completing her PhD in Philosophy, she conducted research on her postdoctoral project entitled 'Eco-feminism: A War Against Survival of the Fittest' under the aegis of the Indian Council of Philosophical Research, New Delhi. Her areas of interest are caste studies, gender studies and cultural studies. Currently, she is working on contemporary caste/gender issues among Dalits, tribes and minorities, especially the method that these women are using to resist subjection hidden in caste–class–gender dynamics. She is a gender trainer. She is also the coordinator of the Museum of Ethnography, Kumbh Study Centre and Dalit Resource Centre (DRC) at G. B. Pant Social Science Institute.

# Index

aboriginal inhabitants, 141
*A Brief History of Neoliberalism*, 73
Acchutanand, Swami
   Adi-Hindu Movement, 197
acute poverty, 3
Adi-Dharmi Mandal, 142
Adi-Dharmi movement, 143
Adi-Hindu Movement of Swami Acchutanand, 197
Advani, L. K.
   march to Ayodhya, 18
advent of modern state, 210–213
AIADMK, 252, 255
   alliance with the BJP in 1999, 258
   government, 252
Aiyar
   emphasis on DICCI, 65
All India Achutuddhar Committee, 141
all-India convener of the Muslim League, 243
All-India Muslim League in 1906 in Dacca, 241
Ambedkar, B. R.
   *Annihilation of Caste*, 71
   arguments
      sociocultural–political category, 14
   broken men theory, 144
   caste and capital, 72–78
   Rao's explanation of Ambedkar's relation to Marxism, 73
Anjuman, 247
anti-caste movements
   Buddhism and Jainism, 11
anti-Dalit violence, 176

anti-Jewish riots broke, 36
Arunthathiyar grievances, 175
Arya Samajis, 142
   strategy and power play, 143
aswachha safai kamgars/scavengers, 150

Baba Saheb
   message, 198
Babri Masjid demolition, 234, 237, 247
backward castes, 239
Balmiki
   community, 143
Balmiki Sabha (Chuhras), 142
Barve, V. N.
   Committee (1949), 162
   Conditions Enquiry Committee (1949), 162
Bhangi, 137, 140
Bhanu Prasad Pandya Committee (1966), 162
Bharatiya Janata Party (BJP), 190
Bihari migrants, 86
   Census data, 2001, 86
   choice of Delhi, 88
   post-independence, 87
   well-heeled middle class, 91
BJP–Hindutva politics, 256
Black capitalism, 58
   Du Bois's position by Haynes, 74
Brahmin archakas, 257
Brahminization of caste ideology, 7
British colonial powers, 213
broken men theory, 144
BSP movement, 203

Index | 289

capitalism, 63, 78
  defined by Yengde, S., 75
  future of Dalits, 69–72
capitalist mode of production, 4
case studies
  Dalits' claim
    Mandagapadi Abishegam rites at Palangkallimedu Sri Bathrakaliamman Temple, 219–223
    right to take out procession of their deity, 216, 218–219
    denial of respectful funeral for Dalit elderly in Thirunelkondacheri, 223–225
    Mohammad Naeem and Waseem, 100
    Palangkallimedu and Vazhuvur, 228
    Paramakudi police firing, 112–115
    Prasad, S., 96
    Prasad, V., 97
    Sekaran, I. Mr, 115
    Sharma, K., 97
caste, 210–213
  assertion, 237
  capitalism
    Prakash's view, 67
    relationship between, 33
  clashes, 256
  conflicts, 237
  Hindu Religious and Charitable Endowments, 226
  multilayered inequalities, 207–210
  violence, 173
caste-afflicted India, 136
caste system, 60
  logic of capital accumulation, 71
  challenges from
    Tamil society, 34
  Natrajan, B., review by, 62
  Samraj, J., 34
  views from Natrajan demonstrates, 62
Census of India, 153

Chamars, 139, 142, 198
Chandals and Paulkas, 137
Charles, T.
  arguments, 187
Charlie Hebdo, 189
Chuhra, 139, 142
citizenization of outsiders, 50
citizenship rights, 49
civil and political rights, 44, 51
civil rights, 47
classical Marxian framework, 26
Coimbatore riots, 259
Coimbatore serial bomb blasts in 1998, 261
colonial regime in India, 12
colonial state, 211
common homeland, 108
Comptroller and Auditor General of India (CAG), 163
Constituent Assembly Debate, 245, 249
constructive social service approach, 161
contemporary capitalism, 27
contemporary neoliberalism, 25
counter-publics, 193
cultural homogenization, 53
Curtis, H., Jr
  Du Bois's position on Black capitalism, 74

Dalit, 78, 141, 216
  assertions, 132, 193
  cultural assertion in North India, 198
  dominant backward-caste clashes, 256
  emancipatory politics, 61
  entrepreneurs, 65
    problem faced, 79
  Herculean task, 231
  mobility, 62–69
  movements, 194, 206
  Non-Brahmin social mobilization after 1922, 235
  politics, 57
  politics in Tamil Nadu, 175

Puthiya Tamilagam, 238
women, 199
women community leaders, 205
women, emergence, 195
women in India, 195
women in villages, 204
women leaders, 202
Dalit capitalism (DC), 58, 78
　arguing for, 61
　capital and entrepreneurship, 78
　contention, 59–62
　Debord's framework, 67
　education and affirmative, 62
　emergence, 61
　Prakash's proposal, 67
　questions on objectives by Mannathukaren, 66
　viewpoint of Anand Teltumbde, 70
Dalit Hindus
　conversion into Islam, 252
Dalit Indian Chamber of Commerce and Industry (DICCI), 59
　Aiyar's view, 65
　foundation, 61
　Kamble, M., 63
Dalit Marxist activist
　Anand Teltumbde, 175
*Dalit Millionaires*, 66, 69
Dalit Panthers of India, 190, 238
Das, B.
　seminal work, 145
Dayanand Saraswati, 141
Debord's framework, 67
democratic
　economic inequality, 38
　emancipatory politics, 189
Denotified Tribes (DNTs), 149
*Discipline and Punish*, 133
dissenting language, 200–202
Dravida Munnetra Kazhagam (DMK), 190
　government, 255
Dravidian
　ethnic–linguistic, 236

identity politics, 235
　parties, 239
　political parties, 236
　politics, 241
Dravidian–Islam identity, 241
Dravidian movement, 34, 236, 241–243, 248, 253, 258
　critics, 174
　guilty of resentment, 187
　politics, 257
　rise, 244
　Tamil Nadu, 174
Dravidian parties, 238
　Muslim representation, 250–252

economic census data, 70
economic entitlement, 45
economic inequality, 38
economic liberalization and social conservatism
　hegemony reinvigorated, 34
eeconomic rights, 44, 52
Employment of Manual Scavengers and Construction of Dry Latrines (Prohibition) Act, 1993, 152, 162
Enlightenment Idea of inequality, 36
enquiry commission, 117–118
　police, 120–125
　recommendations, 127–130
　victims, 126–127
　viewpoint of incident, 118–120
Enthoven, R. E., 137
　arguments, 140
equality, 35
　civil and political rights, 44
　economic entitlement, 45
　economic rights, 44
　idea linked to civil rights, 43
　opportunity, 51
equality of opportunity, 51
Eraiyur Church
　conflict, 230
ethno-linguistic cultural identity politics, 234

Feminist movements of the 1970s, 193
folk legal system (FLS; caste and tribal), 42
Frantz, F., 186–187
   caste identity, 187
   European humanism, 186
free market
   Black capitalism, 66

gender inequality, 38
   *Human Development Report*, 39
General category, 150
Gramsci, A.
   concept of hegemony, 13
Gudiyatham bye-election in 1954, 249
Guru
   analysis of DC, 67
   Debord's framework, 67

Harrison, S., 1
Heim, 94
hereditary occupation, 160
Hindu Dalits
   Meenakshipuram village of Tirunelveli district, 252
Hindu–Muslim riots, 258
Hindu religion
   Brahminical construction, 240
   politics gravity, 240
Hindu society, 137
Hindutva
   forces, 253, 257
   leaders, 252
   politics, 237–238
homogenous civil legal system, 42
housing projects, 62
hybrid identities, 45

India
   anti-British struggle, 12
   crisis of 1990 and redefining hegemony, 18–23
   heterogeneous 'society', 39
   inequality, 36
   nationalism, 13
   religious minorities, 40
*Indian Antiquary*, 60
Indian media system, 269
Indian Union Muslim League in Tamil Nadu (IUML), 245
individual and collective rights
   structural distinction, 44
individual rights, 207
inequality, 35
   Bauman's view, 35
   complexity social structure, 37
   democracy, 38
   Enlightenment Idea, 36
   heterogeneity of the Indian society, 39–40
   Hindu samaj, 41
   insider–outsider dichotomy, 41
   intersectionality between plurality and hierarchy, 42
   issues concerning unit of analysis, 37
   legal pluralism, 42–43
   minority groups, 40
   ratio between the incomes, 38
   religious communities, 39–40
   salience of class, 38
   state–society disjunction, 42
   structural adjustment programme, 37
   worst case of institutionalized, 49
International Monetary Fund (IMF), 111
interstate migration
   Census data, 2001, 86
intervention
   manual scavengers in rural Maharashtra, identification of families, 159
   rehabilitation in alternative livelihood avenues, challenges, 155–160
   rehabilitation of scavengers, 159
Iyothee Thass (Aloysius 2015), 174

Jain Commission report, 257
Jamaat-e-Islami Hind, 247

Jodhka, S.
    study on self-employed Dalits, 68
Johan Galtung
    essay on violence, 176
Judith, H.
    thesis, 80
Justice Sampath Commission
    deciphering the political meaning, 130–134

*Kaadhal* movie by Balaji Sakthivel's (2004)
    theme of caste brutality, in inter-caste marriage, 176–182
Kabir Panthis, 139
Kadayanallur legislative constituency
    Muslim candidate, 254
Kamble, M.
    Bhan, C., proponents of DC, 59
    Dalit Indian Chamber of Commerce and Industry (DICCI), 63
Kathiawar, 137
Kazhagam, D., 175
Khandekar, M.
    *Dalit Millionaires*, 66
Khap panchayats, 228
kingly system, 10
Kisan Sabha-led peasant movement, 92
Kizhavenmani massacre of 1968, 173
Konkan region, 149

Laclau, E.
    letter, 185
Lal Beg, 139
Lal, C., 143
law and order, 215
legal system of the majority, 42
local socio-economic structure of caste, 211
lower castes, 212

Macaulay, T.
    intention of proposing education policy, 8

Mahad Satyagraha, 196
Maharashtra Navnirman Sena (MNS), 86
Mahatma Phule Backward Class Development Corporation Ltd (MPBCDC), 145
Makkal Tamil Desam Katchi, 229
Malkani, N. R.
    *Clean People and an Unclean Country*, 140
    Committee (1957), 162
Mandal Commission recommendations, 18
Mandal Commission report, 237
Mandal–Masjid–Mandir politics, 259
manual scavenging, 136
    abolitionist perspective, 144–145
    caste groups and migration patterns in Maharashtra
    demographic profile of, 147–148
    critical analysis of approaches, 160–165
    deconstructing, construct, 137–139
    deconstructing practice dimensions, 152
    Hindu unity, political strategy, 141–142
    Indian subcontinent, categories, 137
    Maharashtra, 145–147
    Mughal and colonial rule, 139–141
    reformist perspective, 142–143
    theoretico-conceptual status quo, 136
    two contradictory perspectives, 142
    zone-wise concentration by caste and category, 148
marginalization, 62–69
Marshall's conceptualization, 45
Marxist theory of state, 232
media
    caste hegemony and representation, 277–283
    ideology, caste, 273–277
    intricacy, 270–273

Meenakshipuram Dalit conversion to
    Islam, 255
*Mehtar*, 138
Mhaskar, S.
    politics and small businesses, 65
    views on economic engagement of
        caste groups, 64
migration
    anthropological accounts, 95
    anthropological engagement, 84
    farm labour from Bihar, 87
    house, home and the idea of
        politics, 93–104
    interview with labours, 104
    Sharma's, K., longer history, 97
    story, beyond tyranny of statistics,
        86–93
Mishra, P.
    crisp analysis by, 20
modern development process, 215
modern nations, 4
Mukkulathor caste group, 253
Mumbai Metropolitan Region
    (MMR), 149
Muslim, 234
    Christians, two religious minority
        groups, 40
    community, 239
    community, issues, 246
    Dravidian identity politics, 241
    ethnic–linguistic identity, 240–246
    gaining lost ground with
        limitations, 257–259
    identity politics in Tamil Nadu,
        235–236, 238
    neoliberal economy, 259–261
    Tamil Nadu, 238, 240, 259
Muslim League, 243, 249
Muthukulathur riots, 115

*Narada Samhita*, 137
Nara-Maveshi Movement, 197
Narasimha Rao, P. V.
    structural adjustment programme, 238

nation
    Marx and Engels, view, 4
    social structure, 4
National Commission for Safai
    Karamcharis Act, 1993, 162
National Commission on Labour
    (1966), 162
national formation of Western Europe
    Marx and Engels, 5
nationalism
    definition by Ernest Gellner, 108
    India, 13
    India's anti-colonial struggle, 108
nationalization of outsiders, 50
National Scheme for Liberation and
    Rehabilitation of Manual Scavengers
    and Their Dependents, 152, 163
nations
    common language, 5
    concept, 4
nation state, 46
Natrajan, B.
    reviews literatures on caste-based
        division, 62
Natrajan demonstrates
    views on caste system, 62
neo-liberal policies, 63
New Economic Policy (NEP), 24, 238
New World, 45, 49
Nhavi (barber) caste, 64
Nirmal Bharat Abhiyan (NBA), 153
nomadic and warlike tribes, 144
Nomadic Tribes (NTs), 149
non-Brahmin movement, 257
non-places, 93
Non-resident Indians (NRIs), 37
Norval, A.
    argument, 186

open defecation, 151
Other Backward Castes (OBCs), 149

Pallar houses, 229
pan-Indian national politics, 234

Paramakudi police firing, 112–113, 133–134
    Ramanathapuram district, 112
    Sekaran, I. Mr, 114
partition syndrome, 249
Pathak, B., 137
Patriarchal caste privilege, 205
peace and tranquillity, 215
Treaty of Westphalia, 36
peasantization of economy, 7
Periyar and Brahmins, 182–187
personal violence, 176
Planning Commission
    Committees by Government of India, 162
plural society, 50
political climate in India, 254
politics of identification, 188
post-1991 Indian society, 111–112
post-colonial countries, 27
Prakash, A.
    problems faced by Dalit entrepreneurs, 79
Prakash, Aseem
    proposal on changing Indian market, 67
Prasad, C. B.
    Dalits and liberal markets, 69
Prasad, C. B.,
    democracy and capitalism, 70
Prasad, V., 102
Prashad, V., 139
    old practice, 143
privatization, 238
privileges and restrictions
    socio-economic and cultural, 207
Protection of Civil Rights Act, 1976, 46
Punjab Khalistan issue, 254
Puthiya Tamilagam, 229

Quaid-e-Millat, 243
    1972, 246
    death, 253
quest for equality
    evolution, 210–213

radical approach, 163
radical symbolic expression, 142
Ramachandran, M. G.
    caste Hindus and Hindutva forces, 254
Ramanathapuram district, 112
Ramanathapuram Sethupathi dynasty, 113
Ramaswamy, G., 137, 140
Ramnad riots of 1957, 173, 184
*Ratnakar*, 139
regime of modern law
    right to equality, 213–216
relief approach, 161
religious fundamentalism and terrorism, 260
religious legal system (RLS), 42
right to equality, 228
Rural Dalit women, 195

safai karamcharis, 143
Safai Karmachari Andolan (SKA), 164
salience of class, 38
Scheduled Castes and Scheduled Tribes (Prevention of Atrocities) Act, 1989, 46
Scheduled Castes (SCs), 149
    embrace Islam in Meenakshipuram in 1981, 237
    population, 146
Scheduled Tribes (STs), 149
Secular Progressive Alliance (SPA), 190
Selfa links Black capitalism, 58
self-employed Dalits
    Jodhka, S. study, 68
self-employment, 65
self-esteem, 108
Self-Respect Movement, 184, 240, 242
shariat law, 249
Shraddhananda Dalitudhar Sabha, 141
*shuddhi*, 141
Shudra, 150
social change, 63
socialist one-party systems, 47

Social Justice & Special Assistance Department, Government of Maharashtra on 4 March 2013, 155
sociocultural structure, 214
sociology, 84
Srinivas, M. N.
    Brahmin and caste system, 11
    words about Indian caste system, 9
state legal system (SLS), 42
state–society disjunction, 42
stratified society, 50
structural violence, 176
Swachh Bharat Abhiyan (SBA), 143
Swatantra Party, 245, 250

Tamil Maanila Congress (TMC), 257
Tamil Muslims, 240, 247, 260
    migrants, 260
Tamil Nadu Congress Committee, 228
Tamil Nadu Muslim Munnetra Kazhagam, 247
Task Force (1989), 162
Tata Institute of Social Sciences, 145
Teltumbde
    argument on caste, 70
    source of capital and caste, 71
*The Souls of Black Folk*, 58
Thevar–Dalit conflict, 256
Thevar/Maravar caste group, 112
Thirumavalavan
    victory, 190
Thorat and Sadana
    views on neoliberal India, 64
Thowheed Jamath, 247
*topli sandas*, 151
Total Sanitation Campaign, 152
transition, 4

unemployment, 48
unicultural nation states
    obsolescent notion, 53
United Liberation Front of Assam (ULFA), 86
un-see-able
    castes, 209
UN Special Rapporteur to state, 136
untouchable castes, 208
Untouchablity (Offences) Act, 46
*updeshak* (missionary), 143
upper-caste Baniya Hindus, 238
urban local bodies (ULBs), 151
Urdu-speaking Muslims, 248

*Vajasaneyi Samhita*, 137
Vajpayee, A. B., 258
Valmiki, 138
Valmiki Ambedkar Awas Yojana (VAMBAY), 160
Varma, N. L.
    Arya Samaj follower, 143
vedas, 143
Viduthalai Chiruthaigal Katchi (VCK), 190
Vidyarthee
    counter-attack on government policies, 64
violence
    caste basis, 204

water-borne latrine, 151
women leadership, 198

Yengde, S.
    argument on capitalism, 75